THE BEST OF GARY LAUTENS

Mother's Day May 14/95

To E with Love I

Know You Will Enjoy.

D0888064

THE BEST OF GARY LAUTENS

Introduction by Stephen Lautens
Illustrations by Lynn Johnston

KEY PORTER BOOKS

The publisher gratefully acknowledges the assistance of the Canada Council,
the Ontario Publishing Centre and the Ontario Arts Council.

Canadian Cataloguing in Publication Data

Lautens, Gary
    The best of Gary Lautens

Columns previously published in: Take my family —
please! and No sex please — we're married.
ISBN 1-55013-650-X

1. Lautens — family.   2. Family — Anecdotes
I. Title.

PN6231.F3L38 1995   646.7'8'0207   C95-930376-6

Key Porter Books Limited
70 The Esplanade
Toronto, Ontario
Canada M5E 1R2

Typesetting: MacTrix DTP
Printed and bound in Canada

95 96 97 98 99 5 4 3 2 1

Contents

A Short Note About Dad

When I meet people for the first time, the thing they usually ask me is: "What was it really like growing up in the Lautens family?"

The answer is simple. It was wonderful.

There are two reactions to this answer. Most people are happy to know that what Dad wrote about was more or less the truth, and that the Lautens family they felt part of through the columns really existed. A smaller group almost seems disappointed to hear Dad was indeed a happy man and that no dark secrets lurk beneath the surface of our family life.

A few years ago Dad was asked if he and one of the kids would go on a radio show together. The show was to be about fathers and sons. It sounded like fun and we agreed. A few days later we were contacted again and told the show was going to be about fathers and sons in conflict, so to have our best conflict stories ready. During the pre-show telephone interview I told the very disappointed woman that I couldn't remember being in conflict with Dad. For his part, Dad offered to tell the story about how he caught me snowballing cars from our balcony when I was eleven. Conflict was something we assumed you got from other people, while the family was where you went for comfort and support.

In short, anyone waiting for a Lautens "Daddy Dearest" book will be very disappointed. Dad loved family life, although he swore it hadn't been his idea at all. He maintained that he was only giving Mom a smooth line when he asked her on their second date what she was doing for the rest of her life. Next thing he knew, his MG sports car had been traded for a Buick with lots of room in the back for children to wrestle. I think he believed it was a good deal, although he always kept a toy MG on his dresser.

All this doesn't mean that as a family we didn't have minor disturbances along the way. Every family has its ups and downs, and the Lautens family was no exception. As kids we fought constantly. Mom says that originally there were six Lautens children, but with all the fighting we did, Jane, Richard and I are the only survivors. Even so, as we got older and saw more of the world, we began to realize just how lucky we were to be able to take the relative "normalness" of our lives for granted. I also think that many of Dad's readers looked to his column as an anchor in an increasingly abnormal world.

Telling stories was always an important part of our family life. At the end of the day we would all assemble at the dinner table. It was important to share the day's events—good or bad—to know how everyone was doing. Dad was sort of the recording secretary of our meetings, and we had no veto or prior warning about what would be read by half a million readers the next day. Sometimes though, Jane would preface her stories with: "This is off the record."

Dad certainly took artistic licence from time to time, but reading his columns now it's amazing how little he actually exaggerated. I clearly remember Richard, now an adventurous news photographer with the *Toronto Star*, stuffing his favourite blanket down a vent in the Dominion store at age four. And it doesn't seem that long ago that sister Jane—at present the favourite Lautens kid by virtue of recently giving birth to Madeleine Irene, the first grandchild—was trying to convince Mom to let her look after the class rat for the summer. I'm of course the only family disappointment. After starting out as a bright and cute kid (according to Mom), I made a wrong turn somewhere and became a lawyer.

One of the things many people didn't realize about Dad was that for someone with a very public job, he was an extremely private person. He hated to be recognized, although he always took the time to talk. He especially hated testimonial dinners, tributes and awards.

There were only two real exceptions. On his office wall at the *Toronto Star* hung an ornate scroll, festooned with flags and Gothic lettering behind glass in a heavy gilded wood frame. On a floor filled with MBAs, this magnificent scroll identified Dad as having been awarded his Junior First Grade Honour Diploma from A.M. Cunningham School in 1935.

The other exception still hangs hidden in a quiet corner of Mom's living room — a frame with two Stephen Leacock Awards for Humour — one for *Take My Family . . . Please!* in 1981 and another for *No Sex Please . . . We're Married* in 1984.

Dad had more than his share of journalism awards. Although best remembered for his reports on the comings and goings of the Lautens family, Dad began his career as a crime and sports writer in Hamilton. He won South-Western Ontario Newspaper Awards five years running, from 1959 to 1963, and a National Newspaper Award in 1963. Half a dozen other trophies occupy a dusty shelf along with colourfully unidentifiable things my brother, sister and I made in Grade One art. But the Stephen Leacock Awards for these two books were special to Dad. One reason was that originally no one wanted to publish them. Even after *Take My Family . . . Please!* sold over 50,000 copies and won the Leacock award, his publisher wasn't interested in *No Sex Please . . . We're Married*. He had to go to three other publishers before he found one who would print it. No wonder he referred to these two books as "his orphans."

Part of the problem is, if you'll pardon the expression, no one takes humour seriously. Someone gets a Canada Council grant to publish Louis Riel's laundry lists, sells nine copies, and the next thing you know is up for the Governor General's Award and is hailed on the CBC for giving us new insight into who we are as a nation. Write something funny and you're dismissed as trivial. Dad always said it was easy writing 500 funny words a day. All he had to do was roll a blank sheet of paper into the typewriter and stare at it until beads of blood appeared on his forehead.

Later, whenever Dad wrote political columns, or failed to mention what the Resident Love Goddess or Sarah the Wonderdog had been up to, he invariably got a bag of mail telling him to knock it off and get back to the funny family stuff. But Dad was no idealistic dreamer, and had no illusions about what a crummy place the world could often be. Sometimes his columns had a big message or point in there somewhere, but they usually just came down to the same things — be kind, generous, considerate, and love one another — especially family. No big deal, as he would say.

More than anything, Dad used stories about our family to talk about life and people. Looking back, I think that probably explains his very wide appeal. Dad wasn't just writing about our family, but about every family. Or sometimes the semi-mythical ideal family we would all like to belong to.

And now, after being out of print for almost ten years, we are very happy to present the best of *Take My Family . . . Please!* and *No Sex Please . . . We're Married.* Although it would embarrass Dad no end, we're glad to oblige the many readers who have asked to see them published once more. It's nice to know so many people want to keep his writing and memory alive.

We hope you enjoy this collection as much as we enjoyed living it.

Stephen Lautens
January, 1995

TAKE MY FAMILY
... PLEASE!

1

Introduction

I remember taking out this dishy blonde on a first date — it was October 27, 1956, if you are keen on details — and sometime during the evening, either at Maple Leaf Gardens where we saw a hockey game or on the ride home in my cream MG sports car with wire wheels, I looked longingly into said creature's big blue peepers and murmured, "I'd like you to be the mother of my children." Undoubtedly it was something I had heard in an old George Brent movie and, to this very moment, I'm not sure if I was serious.

Probably not.

After all, Jackie was eighteen, I was only a week from my twenty-eighth birthday, and what I was doing, cackle, cackle, was making a pitch, handing out a line, well, let's be frank, softening her up for a little romance, very little if you've ever been in the front seat of a small British sports car with an emergency brake between you and the love object, not to mention enough winter clothing to supply Siberia in a cold snap.

Details aren't important but six months later I have a vague recollection of kneeling together in front of the altar at church and saying "I do" while my bride kept sliding off the satin cushion and giggling, much to the bewilderment of the minister who was already nervous as it was.

Two and a half years later, just in time for Christmas, 1959, we had our first child, a son we named Stephen. Cross my heart, I only assumed we were starting a family, not a cottage industry. I had no intention of using the baby to support me, pay my rent, provide me with luxuries like food and typewriter ribbons; but that is how it worked out.

Although I was writing a sports column at the time, I occasionally broke out in merry paragraphs over our little dish-breaker's latest antic, the cute way he wiggled in his crib, the clever way he mushed his puréed turnip on the kitchen walls and, well, there's no need to go into all of that, especially at this late date. The point I'm struggling to make is that there was no pre-meditation involved. It just happened.

When Jane came along (June 26, 1962) my news sources doubled and with Richard (October 21, 1964) I had more than enough anecdotes, clever sayings and diaper pail lines to fill a column, so we gave up. A good writer can recognize when he's done enough research.

To bring you up to date, some months ago Jackie decided to go through the 7,000-plus columns I've written over the years, take out the ones about the children, compile a family album for each of them and present them with a chronicle of their growing-up years, whether they wanted it or not. Sometime they might be interested in reading what their father said about them, although to date, they've managed to suppress their curiosity very well. Stephen, Jane and Richard (to answer those who might ask) don't think much of my columns about them for the simple reason they don't read them. They think their father is an arsonist, I suspect, and I see no reason to disappoint them now.

At any rate, having put all the family columns together, we then weeded out all but the ones you see between these covers, thinking that there might be an audience for a book that isn't about dieting, Nazis, a religious cult, how to make a million,

Quebec, or how to improve your golf swing in fifteen easy chapters.

So the rest, Dear Reader, is up to you.

Let me merely add that these pieces have appeared in the *Toronto Daily Star*, the *Panorama* section of the late lamented *Star Weekly*, and the *Toronto Star TV Guide*. The wonderful drawings are by Lynn Johnston who lives with her dentist-husband in northern Ontario and is regarded as the premier female cartoonist in North America because of her daily comic strip, *For Better or For Worse*, and her own best-selling books.

But the leading players in this household drama are Stephen, Jane and Richard Lautens who at 20, 18 and 15 are alive and well in downtown Toronto, and still amusing their father every day. I hope they amuse you, too.

Gary Lautens

August, 1980

Is There Life After Diaper Pails?

What's in a name?

Having a baby isn't all clear sailing. Ultimately you have to sit down and face facts: Pablum-puss will need a name.

It's all right to refer to him (or her, since babies come in two varieties in a democracy) as Precious Secret for a little while. But you should pick something more solid for the future.

It's doubtful if the Ottawa Rough Riders would sign a chap named Precious Secret Jones to a contract. The Argos perhaps — but never the Rough Riders.

So the parents must think to the future. You have to do something for that lovely baby bonus cheque.

My wife and I have been going over names at a furious rate, hoping for an inspiration to hit before the Stork.

"According to a poll in the *San Francisco Chronicle*, four out of seven people like the names they were given," I said the other evening.

"Shhh!" she replied. "I'm looking at the credits for this television show."

Yes, that's what she is doing these nights—looking at screen credits in hopes of discovering a name we both like. She also reads birth announcements, bread wrappers and police court news.

"How would you like to give the baby a set of initials and no name—you know, J.J. Lautens?" she asked.

Apparently there is an assistant casting director named J.J. Finque, or some such, in Hollywood and my wife was prepared to name the baby after him.

"No," I replied. "I don't know this Finque. Besides, the Fitz-simons have already used initials. We can't copy them."

"I had forgotten," she admitted.

It's one of the rules of baby-naming that you don't copy anybody else in the entire world. The second rule is that the name must be familiar.

"If it's a girl, how about Lilo?" I suggested.

"Lilo? That's a silly name."

"I like Lilo."

"Is that the name of one of your old girl friends? I bet that's it. Who's this Lilo?"

"But . . ."

"How can you bring up an old girl friend's name when I'm in such a, a, a, delicate condition," she whimpered, throwing a pillow at my head and kicking me in the shins.

I got the impression my wife wasn't in favour of Lilo. She didn't like Casey, Liz, Zizi, Zoe or Rebecca either.

"I like Sarah," she announced.

"Where did you get that name?"

"Never mind. It's simple, homespun, down-to-earth . . ."

It turned out that a lady named Sarah Something-or-other had broken off relations with her breadman in Cape Town, with an axe, according to a news item.

"Sarah is definitely out," I announced. "Besides, the only Sarah I ever knew had thick ankles. I don't want a daughter with thick ankles."

"I like Richard for a boy," my wife continued. "Or Mark."

"We could call him Archbishop—Archbishop Lautens. It

would get him a good table at any night club in the country when he grows up," I pointed out.

I could tell by the way my wife dug her fist into my ribs that she didn't like the idea.

"Let's call it off," my wife finally suggested.

"The Baby?"

"No, this discussion about names."

But tomorrow it will start all over again. Have you read any good panel trucks lately?

Pickles and ketchup

The doctor had said my wife was going to have a baby toward the end of September but thirty days later, and still no baby, we were beginning to get suspicious.

"Maybe he's just kidding us," I said at the breakfast table.

"Pass the pickles," my wife replied.

"How can you eat pickles at a time like this?" I exploded. "Are you sure he said you were pregnant? I just hope this isn't some kind of practical joke."

"Ketchup."

"Ketchup?"

"Yes, ketchup."

"For your pickles?"

"Don't be silly. For my eggs. Who ever heard of putting ketchup on pickles for breakfast?"

"Be serious," I complained. "Maybe it's just your imagination."

"Would you slip on my shoes?" she asked. "I can't bend over my imagination."

"Don't be smart. Why do you want your shoes anyway?"

"Because I think we'll be going to the hospital around noon."

"You mean . . . ?"

"Yes."

Fortunately, we give our baby business to a hospital that is way behind the times.

You don't have to sit around the delivery room holding your wife's hand, sharing the rich experience of labour, witnessing the actual birth of a baby.

No. My doctor tells the father-to-be to get lost. He fails to see what good my fainting on the tile floor would be to my wife.

I suppose the nurses could say, "Look at the Jolly Green Giant!" and other amusing things, but he feels that is the wrong kind of encouragement for the mother.

So I always tell them to call me after everything is over. A chap who has to close his eyes when he takes an Alka Seltzer just can't afford to take risks.

But I am very good after the baby is born when everybody is scrubbed and shining. Fairweather friends don't come any more loyal than me.

The test which separates the novices from the seasoned pros (like me) is the nursery room window. That's where you need that extra touch of class.

"Isn't he beautiful?" my wife said as I got my first glimpse of our new son.

"Yes," I replied. "Is the nurse holding him right side up?"

"Of course," she stated.

"I think he looks like your side of the family," I suggested. "Especially when he drools."

However, after studying the other babies in the nursery, I can honestly say we got the pick of the litter. It's remarkable how quality stands out even in one so young.

"Mine's the big fellow over there — the one with the smile and the intelligent look," I mentioned to another father standing by the nursery window.

"Nice," he said, fighting to hide his jealousy. "That's our little guy in the next crib."

"The one with the wrinkled face and all that black hair?"

"He's laughing," he tried to alibi.

"Sure," I agreed.

"How come your boy has waxy hands?" he asked. "Not that I have anything against waxy hands. Some waxy hands are very attractive, especially with that colour of skin."

"I can see that waxy hands wouldn't look good with the colour of skin your baby has," I admitted. "What colour would you call that?"

"What do you mean?"

"Nothing. It's just that it's so mottled. But I'm sure those blotches will go away in time."

"Your son should have very good hearing," he replied. "My! What nice generous ears. Or maybe they just look big because his eyes are so tiny."

"I see they've let your son have a rattle. Oh, I'm sorry. That's his nose, isn't it?" I countered.

"Yours would be quite tall — if he didn't have such bowed legs," my new friend suggested.

And so we bantered back and forth for almost twenty minutes, smiling at each other, he trying desperately to ignore what is as plain as the nose on his child's face — the clear superiority of my son.

I'll be back at the nursery window today, challenging all comers, ready to put our reputation on the line.

Having a perfect baby is quite a responsibility. This is our third. I think a string of successes like that would turn an average man's head. Fortunately, I'm as modest as ever.

Nothing but the tooth

We had the baby christened Sunday at Olivet Methodist-Presbyterian-Anglican-Congregationalist-Wesleyan-United Church of Canada and things went pretty well. Which means the baby didn't throw up all over my good blue suit during the service. Nor did the church steeple fall down, a fear the minister had when he spotted my father-in-law in attendance.

The closest we came to an incident was when the minister asked the baby's name. Officially, he's Richard but that's not what we call him around the house.

Our little girl calls him Mr. Nuffin', my other son prefers Porkchops and my wife and I alternate between Peter Perfect and Rotten Kid, depending on the relative humidity of his diapers.

So when the minister asked for a name, I had to do a little thinking and it isn't easy when you're also worrying about a blue suit.

But I came up with it and didn't even break a smile, not even when our baby flashed this big tooth of his to show up the other babies in the church.

I don't like to rub it in when somebody else's kid only has gums. So I felt just awful when the fathers (the ones with the plain children) heard me whisper, "Tell the usher to close the window. The baby's tooth is chattering."

Naturally I apologized and said I could bite my tongue for letting it out and bet our baby felt the same way.

It was cruel the way the church lights just caught his tooth and sort of reflected back on the other parents. I tried to stop him but he put my finger in his mouth and, as I told the other parents, I was surprised he didn't draw blood.

He really crunched. Later, in the church parlour, I pointed out that having a baby with a tooth isn't without its drawbacks, hoping that the others might find some consolation in that.

The other fathers tried to pretend they didn't notice the tooth. One combed his little girl's curl; another tickled his baby's foot to show how he could laugh; two others made a big fuss out of the fact their children were sound asleep and practically toilet-trained.

Some people will do anything to hide a broken heart.

On the way home from church I asked my wife's folks how they liked the service. My father-in-law said it was all right although he didn't recognize the hymns. Any time he's been there in the past, he explained, they always played *Silent Night* or *O Come All Ye Faithful* and *O Little Town of Bethlehem* and he couldn't understand why the minister had got rid of them.

Jackie's mother was too busy to comment. She always is when she's with my children. You see, she has this full-time job of stuffing candies into their mouths.

Apparently she saved all the sweets she wouldn't give Jackie

when she was young and now is forced to feed them to her grand-children so that they won't go to waste.

I would never have found out except that one of my kids begged me not to kill "Granny."

"Why would I kill Granny?" I asked.

He explained that whenever Granny gives him a candy, she warns: "Don't tell your father where you got it. He'll kill me." The rum-and-butter runner is pretty slick.

"What were you thinking about during the service?" I asked my wife who, like me, is very sentimental about such things.

She shifted the baby, a portable crib and the baby linen she was carrying and replied:

"Me? I was thinking—*Stephen! Stop zinging your sister. I was—Jane! Don't eat that candy after it's been on the ground. Or at least brush it off.* It seems that—*Stephen! Didn't I tell you to stop zinging your sister? Now quit it.*"

The baby had a little accident—a moist burp—and my wife had to clean that up before she could finish.

Then the baby pulled off her hat. He would have got her earring, too, but it's the kind that goes right through the ear lobe so he couldn't get it loose no matter how hard he yanked.

"I was just thinking," my wife finally continued, "about how, when we met, you looked at the office where I worked and promised to take me away from all that."

"And I'm as good as my word," I beamed.

"Yes," she said, tears of gratitude and formula running down her cheeks, dress and shoes.

The rotten kid

Remember when you were young and had just busted something, like your brother, and your mother would look at you and say, "I hope when you grow up you have a child just like you. It will serve you right."

I guess it's the most famous of curses.

Well, it's happened to me. His name is The Rotten Kid. Outsiders call him Richard but we always say, "Where's The Rotten Kid?"

His sister Jane, who is three, just calls him "Rotten" for short but you know who she means.

The Rotten Kid just turned one and is the reason I look like this a lot of mornings. Last night, for example, we caught him eating the dog's dinner.

Now that may not seem unusual but the dog weighs 195 pounds and The Rotten Kid weighs twenty-three pounds, soaking wet, of course.

Most people are a little timid about taking food from the mouth of a cranky, 195-pound dog but The Rotten Kid isn't impressed by long teeth and bad breath. He wades in anyway, figuring the dog should learn to share.

The other day we left him alone for about eleven seconds, came back into the kitchen and found him standing on top of a glass table, gnawing on a candle.

I know. The child psychologists will say The Rotten Kid needs more love, that he really feels hungry for affection and is eating my candles as a substitute.

I would give him all sorts of love and affection. I swear I would. But The Rotten Kid never stays in one spot long enough for me to deliver.

The other kids were normal enough about walking. Stephen walked at his first birthday, Jane at thirteen months. But The Rotten Kid was walking at ten months.

He had learned to fall down the front porch steps by eleven months, a clear edge of eight months over his brother and sister.

And he was just as precocious on the cellar stairs although he hasn't quite learned how to make a non-stop fall since the side-door landing still interrupts his trip.

My father had a birthday recently and everybody said how young he looked. They especially admired his colour, the glow of his cheeks.

Actually, he can thank The Rotten Kid.

Whenever my father comes for a visit, The Rotten Kid rushes to the door and spends the next hour swinging from the end of his grandfather's tie.

He likes that almost as much as stuffing towels down the toilet.

In any case my father has come to be known as a man with rosy cheeks and long ties.

We have to close off the rooms in the house because The Rotten Kid can get into trouble wherever he is. For example, he likes to go through his mother's things and trail them through the house.

You can't very well entertain and keep your composure when a little kid walks through the living room, swinging a brassiere over his head, my wife has discovered.

We lose more tradesmen that way.

No, The Rotten Kid is an absolute terror. He eats crayons, knocks over tables, flips his cereal on the walls, bites anyone he can reach on the nose, hollers unless you share your dinner with him, climbs up the furniture so he can swing on lamps, pictures and drapes.

13

And when he goes to bed at night he has enough energy left for one last kick, surrendering to his sleepers only after a final, monumental battle.

Then he gives you a big smile, tucks the corner of his blue blanket in his mouth and falls asleep.

In his crib he looks like a tiny angel. And, between you and me, that's what I think he is.

The Terrible Two's . . . and Three's . . . and Four's . . .

Don't blame me

For years the experts have told us that behind every rotten kid there is a rotten mother. And, like everybody else I accepted that.

However, a new school of thought is developing which suggests that maybe fathers have something to do with the behaviour of youngsters, too.

Obviously I can't let a charge like that go unanswered. I'd like to say a few words in my defence.

For example, when the television repairman was at our house the other day, up to his shoulders in tubes, transistors and trouble, I did not instruct my five-year-old son to say, "Do you know what you're doing, mister?"

That was his own idea. Or, perhaps, his mother's. But not mine. I never talk that way until after the bill is made out.

And then there was the incident at the restaurant when I had the family out *en masse*, scrubbed, polished and on their best behaviour.

We were all seated at the table except for my oldest child (who was in the washroom), when a radio executive came over to meet my wife.

It was very pleasant and proper until he asked my three-year-old daughter, "And who's missing from the table, honey?"

"My brother, the skunk," she said.

I think you know me well enough to realize I don't teach children to talk like that. I don't teach them to fight either but that's what they do constantly.

Just last evening they were at it again, grabbing, poking, pinching.

Apparently their fists got tired because Jane, who is three, finally suggested, "Let's not fight any more. Let's play house."

Stephen thought about it and then replied, "Okay. And, Jane, let's pretend we like each other."

I don't see how the experts can blame me for that.

The next thing you know they'll be saying it's all my fault that Stephen gave his mother a big hug, patted her blouse and said, "Gee, you're lumpy, Mom."

Nor have I encouraged the baby to retrieve diapers from the pail and drag them across the living room floor as a present for our company.

And the way he screws up his nose when he hands over the gift is his idea, too.

Consider their eating habits.

They don't have any because they never eat, not the two oldest ones.

In fact, when I gloated the other day that neither of them has had a cavity yet, my wife replied, "Why should they? They never use their teeth — except to bite each other."

Certainly that's not my fault. I eat until I see the little bear's face at the bottom of my dish and it's been years since I bit anything that might bite back.

No, the experts are wrong. This father is clean.

I don't throw lamb dinner on the walls. I don't bounce on chesterfields. I don't sneak into the cupboards and throw pots and pans all over the floor. I don't try to catch the goldfish in my hand. I don't suck marking pencils. I don't walk around trying to stick my finger in my brother's nose.

(And on the way to nursery school I don't try to wind up the car window with somebody's head sticking outside.)

Those are things they picked up on their own or, possibly, from their mother while I've been at work. I would never treat me the way they do.

Hanging around

It's getting more and more fashionable to hang objets d'art in your home. And no wonder.

A beautiful painting brings an enrichment to the soul. A lovely sculpture communicates great feeling without a word. Art stirs the emotions and gives expression to the torment and joy of the human spirit.

It also bugs the neighbours.

Most collectors specialize in a particular period or school or style. However, I prefer to concentrate on a particular colour — green.

It should be on the face of your best friend when he spots your latest acquisition if you are to feel the kind of satisfaction that real art can bring.

Unfortunately, art collecting is an expensive hobby, and, if you are like me (cheap), you try to find a loophole.

We had a bare spot on a front room wall which just cried out for a bit of colour—you could hear the sobs on a still night halfway to the corner—but, after looking at prices, I decided it would be better to have a broken-hearted wall than a broken-hearted me.

That's when I came up with a brilliant idea.

I dug out a self-portrait my son did when he was four, a wild thing executed by the artist with several well-placed thrusts of his pointed brush into the vital organs of some yellow construction paper.

It consists of black circles, maroon blobs and patches of blue and red paint.

I can still hear the artist when he presented it to me and I stood, mouth agape, spellbound by its beauty.

"You're holding it upside-down, Daddy," he complained.

Anyway, I purchased an expensive wooden frame, making certain the artist's signature—a simple but sincere "S"—was clearly visible, and hung the painting in plain view.

Frankly, it's worked like a charm.

People who visit are immediately attracted to it and feel obliged to make some comment, usually generous, often extravagant.

"I do like the brushwork," one neighbour admitted. "Imaginative, full of excitement and probably awfully expensive."

I just smiled, delighted that I had finally evened the score for that swimming pool she put in her backyard last summer.

"Who is the artist?" she asked, levelling a cold stare at her husband and his cheque book.

"That's my secret," I said. "Once the word gets out I'm afraid his prices will skyrocket. So I'm keeping him to myself a little while longer."

"A hint wouldn't hurt surely."

"Let me just say he's young, Canadian and very promising. I like to think I ruined her day. It was marvellous.

When the family doctor stopped in after making his rounds (in the low eighties, he said), even he was impressed. "Now that's what I call a painting," he admitted.

Others have called it "bold" and "primitive" and "daring in concept." The "freedom of expression" was commented upon six times and two men took me aside and asked: "How do you get away with it? My wife would never let me put anything as risqué as that on the walls. Wowee!"

The closest we got to criticism was when the milkman stopped by for his money and said he wasn't sure if he liked modern art. "But that one kinda grows on you, doesn't it?" he qualified.

However, I made one mistake. I invited my neighbour to make a comment.

"It looks like something a kid would do," he stated simply.

Can you imagine that? I have a notion not to invite him back next week when we have an unveiling of the artist's latest self-portrait, done in his mother's lipstick and mascara.

Dig those bones

The other morning my son announced that he would like to go to the museum and see dinosaur bones and some of the other items which his kindergarten teacher told him were on display.

"Why don't you turn on the television and watch cartoons," I suggested. "Popeye's Playhouse is on now."

"I don't like Popeye," he whined. "I want to go to the museum."

"It's too cold," I said, rattling my newspaper and sinking a little deeper into my easy chair.

"I'll wear my pyjamas under my pants," he offered.

"They don't have a TV at the museum," I warned.

"I don't like TV," he stated sullenly.

"You can even watch one of those shows which gives you nightmares," I bargained, figuring he could never resist that bit of cheese.

"I want to go to the museum," he replied.

"Why don't you wrestle your sister or crayon on the walls like any normal five-year-old kid?" I wanted to know.

"I'm going to tell my teacher you wouldn't take me to the museum," he threatened.

That was the clincher. On a Saturday morning when it's cold and windy the last thing I need is a museum. But I'm not going to take the chance of getting a bad reputation with any kindergarten teacher.

"Let's stop for something to warm us up," I suggested as we walked into the museum. "They have a swell coffee shop in the basement. You can have . . ."

"I want to see all the guns and swords," he reported, heading straight ahead.

I trailed along as he marched from one exhibit to another.

"This one has eight barrels," he would say. Or, "Did they use swords when you were young, Daddy?"

"These exhibits are all pretty much the same," I pointed out. "I think we can skip the rest of . . ."

"No. I want to see them all," he insisted.

So we trooped from one aisle to another until I suggested that, perhaps, I could wait for him at the door.

"I need you to read to me," he stated, scuttling that plan.

"Don't you have to go to the bathroom?" I asked after we had knocked off a couple of rooms and about ten million exhibits.

"No," he said. "What's up the stairs?"

I told him it was mostly a storage area and not worth looking at. However, he wanted to see for himself.

"You're wrong, Daddy," he said joyfully as he hit the second floor and spotted some dinosaur bones fastened together with wire.

"They must have changed things," I grumbled.

We walked through that wing of the building and saw some stuffed animals and paraded past an array of fish and snakes and then paused at the stairway where I had to hold him out over the railing so he could see the top and bottom of the totem pole.

"I'll bet you could use a nice, cold drink and a piece of chocolate cake," I tempted.

"Let's go up to the next floor," he answered.

So we saw Chinese exhibits, Greek exhibits, Egyptian exhibits and young school children giggling at the statues.

The best thing I saw was the elevator which, however, we didn't use.

"We had better sit down," I said. "I don't want to tire you out. Your mother might get mad at me."

"I'm not tired," he unfortunately revealed.

However, I finally convinced him he should stop for something to eat so that he wouldn't wind up looking like that mummy he stared at so intently in the wooden box.

"Let's take the stairs down to the cafeteria," he suggested. "We can race."

During lunch he said he would like to hurry because there was plenty of museum we hadn't seen yet—like the Indian stuff in the basement.

That's when I put my foot down.

"We're going to go to the show this afternoon and see a Disney movie whether you like it or not. And we're going to sit through the whole thing," I instructed.

So that explains why that little boy I was pulling by the hand out of the museum was crying. I just hope he doesn't blab to his kindergarten teacher.

One Christmas card coming up

Every year in December we go through what is known as picture time at our house. It's sort of like World War Three but without rules.

The tradition started years ago when my wife and I thought it would be a good idea to have a Christmas card featuring our children and dog. It would be folksy, we agreed. And, since we didn't intend to be explicit about the children's faith, nobody could take religious offence.

However, there was one problem: we didn't have any children or dog.

I was all for renting but my wife figured it would be cheaper in the long run to have our own.

So I wound up having these three kids and a St. Bernard dog (my wife can do anything if she puts her mind to it) on my hands.

For 364 days in the year they cost me money but on the 365th they have their one duty to perform: they pose for our Christmas card.

Well, yesterday was it.

For some unknown reason we never get the same photographer twice. In fact, last year the one we had never even came back for his hat.

All we want is a simple picture of three sweet kids and a lovable 195-pound dog smiling in the Christmas spirit.

I can't think of anything easier than that.

But it never quite works out that way.

I assembled the cast and converged on the rec room only to find the floor littered with laundry.

"What are the sheets doing all over the bar stools?" I asked.

"They're supposed to be there," my wife replied.

"Why?"

"To look like snow," my wife explained. "Could you tell they're barstools covered with sheets?"

"Never in a million years," I said. "It looks exactly like snow."

"Should we put the children on a toboggan and have it pulled by the dog?" my wife asked. "I could bend a coat-hanger and make it look like a pair of antlers."

"Sounds swell," I encouraged.

"You don't think it looks a little phony, do you?" she wanted to know.

"Don't be silly. I would never guess that it's a dog pulling a toboggan across a rec room floor past some bar stools covered with white sheets," I said. "If I didn't know better, I'd swear I was looking in on a scene in the Laurentians."

My wife seemed pleased with that.

"Stephen!" she ordered. "Stop crossing your eyes." And then she added to me, "Do you think we should dress them like elves?"

I said it was fine by me. "Everything's fine, just as long as we hurry."

The photographer, meanwhile, was setting up his lights and trying to keep out of reach of the dog who was going around smelling everybody's breath to see what they had enjoyed for dinner.

"Didn't you give the dog a tranquillizer?" I asked.

"No, I thought you had," my wife said.

"He's just a little excited," I explained to the photographer who was trying to get his camera bag out of the dog's mouth without much success. "C'mon, boy. Give us the bag."

"Jane! Stop punching your brother," my wife interrupted. "You'll make him blink for the picture."

We finally got the camera bag and the kids took their place and our "reindeer" gave a big yawn.

"Smile!" the photographer pleaded.

I made faces.

My wife waved toys.

It was swell except that nothing happened. One of the elves had pulled the floodlight cord out of the wall socket and was trying to screw it into his sister's ear.

There's no point going into all of the details. Within ninety minutes or so, we had our picture and the photographer gratefully retrieved his camera bag and left. Next year I think I'll handle it differently.

I'll mail out the kids and the dog directly and not bother with a photograph.

Grime and punishment

I am afraid I haven't kept up with the eating habits of children and am a poorer father as a result.

Let me explain.

The other day I got home from work to be greeted by my wife at the front door. She was mad. I could tell by the way she tapped her fingers nervously on the baseball bat in her hand.

"Well, do something," she said. "They're your children."

"Hi, there," I replied.

"Which one do you want to punish first?"

"Nice day," I persisted. And then I grabbed her hand and kissed it, right smack on top of her white knuckles.

Well, charm didn't work; obviously I was going to be required to listen to the whole sordid story.

It seems that my young son, Stephen, had spent most of the day picking flowers, lovely tulips, to be specific.

"That's nice," I said.

"They were in someone else's garden," my wife added. "He had picked twenty-eight of them before he was caught."

I made a note of that on the dossier.

"And your daughter! Well, I've never been so embarrassed in my life."

Let me quickly sketch in the details.

The assistant minister of the church, a kindly old gentleman, dropped by the house to see if we've changed much since Christmas. I think our smiling envelope has been missed.

Before leaving, he said he would like to give a little prayer. Heads were bowed and it was appropriately silent — until the little girl shouted out the only word she knows to indicate a visit to the bathroom would be in order.

And she persisted. So did he.

I think it was about the time he was blessing the people who held the church mortgage that my wife peeked.

Jane was standing in the middle of the living room with her leotards at her ankles. It sort of broke up the meeting.

I summoned the culprits.

"Okay, just for that, no candy tonight," I decreed.

"Hurrah," said the children.

"Didn't you hear me? No candy, I said."

They clapped their hands and came over and gave me a hug.

"We hate candy," Stephen said.

My wife kicked my ankle and said I had played right into their hands. "The candy drops are really vitamins," she whispered. "I make them take them every night before they go to bed."

Obviously I had to try something else and was pretty baffled until it struck me that, as a boy, the worst punishment of all was to be sent to bed with only porridge for supper.

"And for supper tonight you can only have cereal," I stated firmly.

"What a good daddy!" Stephen exclaimed, hopping up on my knee and giving me a kiss.

Jane jumped up and down to show her happy reaction to the sentence.

My wife cleared her throat and I knew right away I was in trouble.

"I want that new cereal with the marshmallow bits in it," Stephen suggested. "Or else the fruit flakes."

"But . . ."

The female convict had fled to the kitchen meanwhile and come back with caramel-flavoured puffs which, so I learned later, are made especially for little girls.

By then Stephen had second thoughts. He liked the raisins (although not the bran) in one variety and said there was much to commend the cereal which has been "shot, through and through" with sugar.

They both liked another type, the one that comes with peanuts, but finally decided on something that tastes exactly like a malted milkshake, "only crunchy."

I think that was the one with the storybook package. Or did it have punch-out pictures of the farm animals on the back? It doesn't matter.

"I only give them cereal as a reward," my wife said without moving her lips.

But by now the children had the cocoa flakes and were out on the front lawn, showing the other kids, who were filled with envy and begging for a taste.

"And we don't have to eat any candy," I heard Stephen shout to his host of friends.

I think they were all heading up the street to pick tulips when I saw them last.

Getting the bird

The turkey was in the middle of the dinner table, stuffed, steaming and roasted to a beer brown.

"Boy oh boy!" I said. "Hand me the knife. I'll carve."

"What is it?" my son Stephen, who is six, asked.

"A turkey."

"I don't want any," he said.

"Sure you do. It's good. Try some white meat."

DAD... HOW DID THE TURKEY DIE?

"No. I don't want any turkey."

"Aren't you feeling well?"

"I feel fine but I don't want any turkey."

"Okay," I said, cutting off some slices for other members the family, saving the hip for myself, of course.

"Dad?" said Stephen as I reached inside for a spoonful of dressing.

"Yes."

"That turkey was alive, wasn't it?"

"Why, I guess so," I answered.

"How did it die?"

"I don't know," I admitted.

"Did somebody kill it?"

"If you don't want to eat, leave the table," his mother said. And then she added, "I don't think I'll have any dressing tonight."

"But Dad, why did they kill the turkey?" Stephen insisted.

27

"Maybe it just dropped dead," I said.

"Dad, the turkey didn't drop dead, did it? Somebody killed it."

"Maybe," I replied.

"How did they kill it?"

"Let's talk about it later," I suggested, trying to think of some way I could get around that child psychology book which claims you should always be honest with children.

"Dad, isn't it cruel to kill things, especially animals?"

I just smiled, putting some of the turkey and dressing back on the platter. "I'm not as hungry as I thought," I explained.

And then, with great dramatic flair, Stephen proceeded to explain his version of how the turkey was rubbed out.

"The farmer took off his feathers and chopped off his head with an axe," Stephen stated.

His three-year-old sister, Jane, loved the story.

"Why didn't you tell him that turkeys grow on trees, like apples?" my wife complained.

"It wouldn't be honest," I said. "At six he's just sensitive about these things."

My wife and I decided to skip the turkey and go right to dessert. Nobody had much appetite anyway, except Jane.

"What's for dessert?" Stephen asked.

"Rice pudding," my wife said.

"I don't want any."

"What's wrong with rice?" I asked "It isn't an animal. Nobody killed the rice or chopped off its head."

"I know," Stephen said. "But I had a sandwich over at Greg's before dinner and I'm not hungry."

And then he left the table.

Show and Tell

I hate to be the one to squeal but school has turned my son into a liar.

It's true.

For seven years Stephen was a regular little George Washington. Sodium Pentothal ran in his veins.

We didn't have to worry about a credibility gap.

Stephen would always come clean.

Now that's all changed.

Stephen has discovered that truth doesn't pay — not at Show and Tell Time in Grade Two.

The trouble started a few weeks ago because I appeared on a television show.

Stephen felt he should release the news to his classmates at Show and Tell.

However, I could tell by his face when he got home at four o'clock that it had been a flop.

"They wouldn't believe me," he said simply.

And he went into his room and played quietly until supper.

He didn't even have the heart to wrestle his brother or choke his sister that night. He was deeply hurt.

A couple of days later Stephen decided to make a comeback at Show and Tell.

"I'm going to tell the kids about Geordie," he announced at breakfast. "I bet nobody else has a dog that weighs 200 pounds."

He went off to school, skipping and whistling.

Well, you've guessed it.

Stephen told the kids about his dog; he explained how his dog sleeps outside even when it's ten degrees below zero. And he concluded by saying his dog is practically big enough to ride.

The kids just hooted.

They accused Stephen of making up the entire story and nothing he could say would change their minds.

"Could I take Geordie to school and show them?" he begged that night. "Then they'd have to believe me."

We told him he couldn't.

About that same time Stephen brought home a report card and it commented on his "wonderful imagination."

Then came the final, crashing blow.

A friend of ours is an amateur taxidermist and he brought out his latest specimen to show us — a tropical fish that must be five feet long.

Stephen couldn't wait to tell the kids at Show and Tell.

I didn't even ask Stephen about their reaction that evening. One look was enough to tell me it was a disaster.

Yesterday was Show and Tell Time again and Stephen was trying to determine what to use as his contribution.

"Why don't you tell them about my cousin, Morris, and how he's a fur trader up north with the Eskimos?" I suggested.

Stephen shook his head.

"I think I'll tell them I had a nosebleed," Stephen said.

"But you haven't had a nosebleed," I said.

"I know," Stephen replied. "But I think they'd believe that."

Fly now — zip later

We have wall-to-wall kids at our place. Ours and somebody else's. I'm either living in a nursery or in a home for midget wrestlers. But I wouldn't have it any other way.

It's not exactly that I'm a Father Goose who enjoys being accosted by tiny sheriffs popping up from behind the chesterfield and announcing, "Bang! I gotcha!"

But where else can you get so many laughs for a peanut butter sandwich and bathroom privileges?

Take my six-year-old son Stephen's crowd.

First of all there's Donald. Now Donald looks as if he should be a butcher when he grows up. He's plump, rosy-cheeked, never without a smile.

And he's never zipped up.

I have seen him perhaps a thousand times and I have never yet seen him with his trousers done up.

When you greet Donald, you say: "Hello, Donald. Zip up."

He says, "Oops. Hello, Mr. Lautens."

The other day he knocked on our door, calling for Stephen.

There he stood, plump, rosy-cheeked, smiling and unzipped. The only difference was he had a paper mask over his eyes.

"Hello, Donald," I said. "Zip up."

"How did you know it was me?" he asked, genuinely shocked. "I'm wearing my Batman mask."

"It was just a guess," I suggested.

Not long ago Donald asked me if I ever saw his mother in church.

"No," I admitted. "I don't."

"I didn't think you would," he answered. "She goes to the Catholic church."

In the same crowd is another grade-one student named Art. A few days ago his mother was going to the store and wanted Art to come along.

"I don't want to," he complained. "And I don't want you to go either."

His mother argued for a few minutes and then decided that Art could stay in the apartment while she and Art's small sister walked over to the store.

Simple, right? That's what Art's mother thought.

She got back about twenty minutes later, opened the apartment door and was confronted by a burly policeman.

Art's mother was slightly shaken. Was there a fire? An accident? Had something gone wrong?

"The boy telephoned the police station," the officer explained, "and told us his mother had run away and left him."

The look was pretty accusing.

Art's mother tried to explain, finally satisfied the constable — and all the time Art stood there, smiling innocently.

My own children (The Rotten Kid and his older brother and sister who are sometimes referred to as Frank and Jesse) got up before we did the other Sunday morning.

When we arrived in the kitchen there was an empty cake box on the table.

"We took a vote and decided to have cake for breakfast," Stephen announced. From what I could gather, the vote was 3-0 although it's difficult to get anything out of The Rotten Kid who only says, "da-da-dada" and an occasional, "tickle-tickle."

Stephen and his three-year-old sister have bunk beds and were talking and arguing (that's what they do best) when I overheard them a few evenings ago.

"I'm not going to marry you when I grow up," Jane threatened.

"And I'm not going to marry you," Stephen replied. "I'm going to marry my mother."

"You can't," Jane stated.

"Why not?" Stephen asked.

"Because she'll be dead," Jane replied.

I'd tell you more but my group took the snow shovel out before the big blizzard and left it lying somewhere in the back-yard although nobody remembers exactly where.

So I'm still looking.

Have you ever tried to find a shovel buried under a snow drift sixty feet wide, fifty feet long and up to your ascot deep?

Yes, I owe a lot to my kids but, if I wear a hat, it'll never show.

One-up-boy-ship

Doctor, it's those headaches again. They've come back. I can't face people any more and I have this hopeless inferiority complex.

What? Lie down? Of course, Doctor.

Doctor, I've been hypersensitive. I mean, I didn't take it per-sonally when automatic elevators let me off at the wrong floor or when soft drink machines rejected my coin.

But now I know the truth. Doctor, I'm inadequate. I've failed as a parent and everybody knows it.

Max, at the office, tells me his kids are learning Russian and do the crossword puzzles in *The Times* and have been accepted for advanced ballet.

And the oldest is just seven.

Charlie informed me just the other day that his son won three ribbons at the school field day, has just finished building a working model of the Polaris and plays the violin.

I hate to say this, Doctor, but I'm the only man in the world with dumb kids.

My kids speak only one language — and we haven't been able to figure out which one that is because they always have their mouths full.

We're not even sure the youngest can talk because he always goes around the house with a blanket in his mouth.

The only trick he knows is how to put raisins up his nose.

But he can't speed-read, scuba dive, make out an income-tax form or drive the family car.

And he's already past two.

I know, Doctor, you're going to say he'll outgrow it. But his sister is four and all she does is watch television, pinch her brother and steal her mother's perfume.

Oh, I thought I had met somebody with a kid as ordinary as mine. But it was a false alarm.

Bill and I were talking about children and he admitted to me that his kid was "just average."

Naturally, I was delighted. Thank God there's another kid in the world who doesn't understand Einstein's theory or can't quote Ovid in the original Latin or doesn't build hi-fi systems in his spare time, I said to myself.

"Yes, my kid's just average," Bill repeated, "average — among the gifted, of course."

Pow! My bubble burst.

So my oldest kid is seven and all he does is bring home fish in a pail and want to keep them in the bath or put his pyjamas on over his clothes so he doesn't have to dress in the morning.

And what he does in his spare time is throw mudballs at frogs.

He doesn't skip grades, paint in oils, read German science texts, do brain surgery, fix carburetors or captain his Little League baseball team. In fact, he isn't on any team.

What's that, Doctor? You want to show me a photograph of

your son? You say he's only five and Harvard has offered him a scholarship and the Yankees consider him a sure-fire major league pitcher and . . . Help! Help!

Till kids do us part

Our house was filled with murderers again last night. That's the fourth time this month.

We've also had three attacks by savage Indians, an invasion from outer space and twelve curtains that made threatening gestures.

And, if you don't believe me, ask my children.

It was the seven-year-old's turn last night to discover the bloodthirsty plot to wipe out the family.

He woke me up at three a.m. to report, "Somebody's hiding in my closet. Can I sleep with you?"

"There's nobody in your closet," I told him.

"Yes there is. I heard him," he insisted.

"Go back to bed," I reasoned.

"What's wrong?" my wife interrupted.

"Somebody's hiding in my closet," my son explained.

"He's having another one of those dreams," I said.

Well, before I knew what hit me (it was a sharp elbow and a bony knee) there were three of us in bed.

And I was the one on the outside, the one with the bare overhang.

But of course, Dear Parent, you know what I'm talking about.

It's not what you had in mind when you cornered that lovely, shy girl after the basketball game and asked her to be your wife.

You got married so that the two of you could be alone.

Ninny!

Husbands are never alone with their wives. The children won't stand for it.

Have you ever tried to sneak a kiss from your wife before you go to work in the morning? More important, have you ever succeeded?

Of course not.

Just as you go into the embrace, something comes between you — something named Leonard who has a runny nose and wants a drink and steps on your toes.

Surely you don't think that's an accident?

No, it's part of a vast international plot by children to make sure adults are never left alone.

Try to talk to your wife quietly. Make a date to meet her in the basement behind the furnace. Tell her you'll knock on the cold air return three times and that you'll wear a carnation in your buttonhole so she can recognize you.

Schedule your rendezvous for midnight. Schedule it for the Gobi Desert if you want. It doesn't matter.

The children will beat you to the punch.

They will be there first, asking for piggyback rides, wanting you to read them a story, begging for the loan of a kitchen knife so they can carve their initials in the family dog.

They come at you in shifts.

That's why they invented the nightmare (in 1923) — so that they can watch you 'round the clock. Then they came up with the ultimate weapon — the quivering lower lip.

Now, besides never being alone with your wife, you don't get any sleep either.

Why are children doing these things?

Simple. They plan to take over the world. By gradually destroying adults, bit by bit, they feel they can eventually be in charge without firing a shot.

Birthday competition

We've been worrying about my daughter's birthday party for weeks. After all, it isn't every day a girl turns five.

However, as I discovered, a birthday party isn't just a party in the suburbs.

It's a happening. It's an occasion. But, mostly, it's a status symbol.

"I think we should go over the menu for the party," my wife said to me about a month ago.

"What menu?" I replied. "You serve wienies and chocolate milk. Who needs a menu?"

"Do you want us to be the laughing stock of the neighbourhood?" she asked in horror. "You can't serve wienies and chocolate milk at a birthday party."

"The Fitzsimons had a caterer for Carrie's birthday," my wife reminded me. "We can't let them get away with that."

"I was thinking of sirloin roasts, an assortment of salads and an ice cream cake carved into the shape of a little girl — life-sized. We can do it for about ten dollars a guest, counting help. That's about $400."

"Four hundred dollars?"

"Yes. Now for the entertainment. The Johnsons hired a magician for Donald's party. The Turliuks took the kids on a hay ride and the Ruddys had the bowling party, remember?

"I think a theatre party would be nice. You could get thirty-five orchestra tickets — better make that forty just to be sure — and the closer to the stage the better."

"Are you out of your mind?" I asked. "This party will cost $1,000."

"Just $600," my wife answered. "Matinée tickets will be fine."

"Those kids will eat wienies and drink chocolate milk and play pin-the-tail-on-the-donkey," I blurted. "And I'll give you two dollars in dimes to put in the cake. But that's it."

Then my conscience began to work on me. Some time ago we were at a house party and my wife volunteered to be a subject for a minister who dabbled in hypnosis.

To show what the subconscious can recall, he asked my wife various questions, including one about her own fifth birthday.

She began to cry.

Later we learned that my wife had never had a fifth birthday party because it was wartime and her father was away in the Navy.

Naturally, I didn't want that to happen to my daughter.

"Okay," I shouted through the bedroom door. "I'll give you seventy-five bucks to put on the birthday party."

That seemed to soothe my wife some.

However, yesterday I got a call at the office.

"The birthday party's off," my wife said, obviously fighting back the tears.

"Why?" I asked.

"Jane's got chicken pox," she replied.

Debbie, the babysitter

I'd be sunk if anything happened to Debbie.

Debbie is our babysitter and that makes her about the most important person in my life.

I can't make a move without her and she knows it. If I want to go to the show or the ballgame or the ballet or even to a house party, I have to ask Debbie's permission first.

If she agrees, I go. If she says no, I'm as immobile as a statue on a postcard.

Sometimes it's confusing to the people who invite me out.

"Yes, a barbecue sounds like fun," I tell them, "but I'd better check with Debbie to see if we're free that night."

They immediately think I must have a girlfriend because they know my wife's name is Jackie.

But there's no point calling Jackie. I know she'll go anywhere, provided the kids don't come and she doesn't have to do dishes.

The key is Debbie.

Every Monday night my wife telephones Debbie to make our booking and it turns into a three-way conversation.

"Debbie wants to know what night we want her?" my wife asks.

"Saturday," I suggest.

My wife relays the message and then turns to me again.

"Debbie says Saturday is out of the question this week. She's got a date."

"How about Friday?" I ask.

"Debbie says Friday may be all right," my wife reveals, holding her hand over the mouthpiece of the phone. "She wants to know where we're going."

"Just to a movie or something," I answer.

"Debbie wants to know if we'll be late," my wife asks next.

"I don't think so," I tell her.

"Can we be home by midnight?" my wife wants to know.

"Yes."

"Good." Then it's all right with Debbie. She has to get up early Saturday morning and she doesn't want to be late."

Gratefully, we await Debbie's arrival on Friday night.

We put on the TV for her. We tell her there's grape soda (her favourite) in the refrigerator. We show her the new magazines. And we promise to telephone to see if the kids are behaving.

Why not?

She is only fifteen or sixteen, slender as a blade of grass and terrifically shy. But she looks like Sophia Loren, Venus de Milo and Joan of Arc when she comes through the front door.

Sometimes she even lets us out of the house two or three times in the same week. Just last month she gave us permission to stay at a party until almost 1:30.

Alas! Debbie is on holidays right now. She doesn't get home until the 3:09 train Sunday afternoon.

And we can't even get to the corner unless we take all three kids with us, including Richard who is the rotten one.

We're all going nuts — my wife, my kids and me.

It seems as if we've got a terminal case of togetherness. My wife has missed a sale of material. I can't see that movie downtown I've been waiting for. The kids are tired of going to bed without grape soda.

So hurry home, Debbie.

We love you.

Rent-A-Kid

A lot of people are getting married at this time of year — the autumn wedding is lovely with the leaves turning brown and the groom turning green.

And these young couples are usually undecided about one thing: should they have a family right away or should they put it off?

Without any experience in these matters, it's very difficult for them to make a decision.

Therefore, I've decided to start a little business on the side. I'm calling it Rent-A-Kid and the idea is so simple I'm surprised somebody hasn't thought of it before.

I plan to rent out my kids to childless couples so they can see for themselves what being a parent is all about.

For five dollars a day, I'll provide Stephen, seven, who is my oldest.

I guarantee Stephen will bring home snakes, never comb his hair, grind plasticine into your best rug and never hear you when you talk to him.

Yes, all that for just five dollars.

Stephen has two jobs around the house: he gives the dog a drink every morning and he makes his bed.

Since he has conned the kid across the street, a boy named Brian, into watering the dog, we can forget about that.

Now, about the bed.

My wife looked at Stephen's bed the other day and commented on what a bad job he had done of making it.

"It's Richard's fault," he revealed, Richard being his two-year-old brother.

"What has Richard got to do with it?" my wife asked.

"Richard was in the bed when I made it," Stephen said. "And he kept wiggling."

Next I have my daughter, Jane, who is five and available for $3.98 per diem.

Jane is a perfect example of what a couple can expect in a daughter. She collects garbage and hides it in her "corner"; she loves perfume, eye makeup and lace panties; and she wants a brassiere as soon as she can grow some "elbows" which is how she describes a bosom.

Jane gave me this lesson about life the other day.

"If you find a better man, you don't keep the one you've got," she said. "You get a vorce."

"A vorce?" I asked.

"She means divorce," my wife chirped in.

And then my stock includes Richard who is two. I plan to charge at least twenty-five dollars a day for him.

Couples that see him often vow never to even hold hands again the rest of their lives. He is our version of The Pill.

Richard swings from drapes, writes on the dog and tries to put his sister in the dishwasher.

He also falls off walls, jumps into swimming pools (he can't swim) and throws stones at the big hornets' nest in the tree in our front yard.

The other day I caught him stuffing a pencil down the bathroom sink.

"Don't do that!" I said.

"Have to," he answered.

"Why do you have to?" I asked.

"To get my penny," he explained.

You see, he had stuck this penny down the drain and was trying to . . . oh, never mind. I get this awful headache when I even think about it.

So there's my plan.

If you want to rent the entire set, I'll let them go for thirty dollars a day. You can have the three of them for ten dollars if you promise to keep them over a weekend.

And I'll give you fifty dollars if you want them Monday through Friday.

Just call Rent-A-Kid.

A mother is . . .

A mother knows where the other sock is.

A mother blows on your cut after applying iodine.

A mother lets you win.

A mother wants to watch dancing or some other sissy stuff on TV instead of *The Hulk*.

A mother keeps your kindergarten stories in a special envelope in the cedar chest.

A mother can't throw overhand.

A mother can tell what you're doing downstairs even when you try to be quiet.

A mother eats cold toast for breakfast.

A mother has room in her bed at three o'clock in the morning if you've had a nightmare.

A mother puts her hand on your forehead if you say you're not hungry.

A mother can't whistle with her fingers.

A mother doesn't embarrass you in front of friends by kissing you.

A mother sews up the hole in the knee of your new pants before your father sees it.

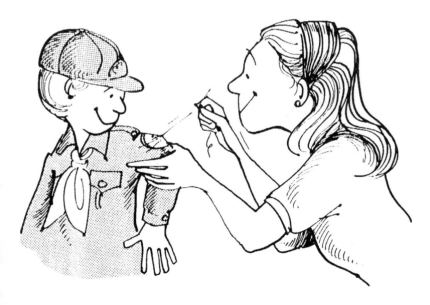

A mother listens to your dinosaur project twenty-seven times, and always seems interested.

A mother never gets the last piece of pie.

A mother sews on Cub badges.

A mother always asks you why your sister is crying.

A mother wants to know what your best friend's mother gave you for lunch, and if you said "Thank you."

A mother doesn't laugh when you cry.

A mother thinks you should wear an undershirt.

A mother, when you say you have nothing to do, always replies, "Why don't you clean up your room?"

A mother can't get the tops off bottles.

A mother feels soft.

A mother always wants to know where you're going.

A mother, when you spill something at the dinner table, always tells your father, "It was just an accident."

A mother doesn't like talking to your friends when she's having a bath.

A mother wishes you'd eat porridge.

A mother dances around the kitchen when she's happy.

A mother sticks your best schoolwork on the refrigerator door.

A mother says you can't have a kitten.

A mother asks now and then for a cuddle.

A mother has to explain to the lady down the street that you didn't start the fight first.

A mother gets a funny look in her eye when somebody says how fast you're growing up.

A mother is good at scratching backs . . .

Want to T-P-Y-R-A-B-S?

My daughter Jane (who is five) was giving the grace before dinner last night and this is what she said:

"God is great. God is good.

Thank you for the lovely men."

What do you think? Can she be helped? Do you think she's seeing too much of her mother?

Then there was the incident the other day when I caught her taking a poke at her little brother.

"Don't punch your brother!" I scolded.

"I didn't punch him," Jane replied.

"Don't lie. I saw you." I told her.

"I didn't punch him," Jane insisted. "I just gave him a pat in the mouth."

What are my chances of surviving a diabolical mind like that?

Jane came home from school and gave me this lesson on living.

"Donna calls everybody 'mental.' That means you don't go in other people's garages," Jane reported.

I haven't told you the whole story. There's another problem. His name is Richard and he just turned three.

We spell a lot when he's around because we don't want him to catch on to what we're saying. But he's turned the tables on us.

Last week Richard came up to me and said: "I want to go out and T-P-Y-R-A-B-S."

"What's 'T-P-Y-R-A-B-S'?" I wanted to know.

"You know—play," he informed me.

He was in an awful state recently and ran up to me in tears, holding up his thumb in obvious distress.

"Did you hurt your thumb?" I asked.

"No," he said. "I want to suck my thumb and I can't find my blanket."

You see, he won't suck his thumb unless . . . do you think a quiet room at the YMCA for a week or so might help?

Richard was telling me the story of *The Three Little Pigs* before bed the other night.

When he came to the part where the pigs set off to build their homes, Richard revealed, "One went down the road to the right and one went down the road to the wrong."

There was a lot of noise downstairs last Saturday and I shouted, "Richard! What are you doing down there?"

There was a silence.

"What are you doing, Richard?" I repeated.

"I'm just looking to see," he finally reported.

And, you haven't suffered until you've had a three-year-old swing by a rope from the hall railing, yelling, "Tar-than!"

My other boy Stephen (who just turned eight) explained it pretty well the other night after we had been out visiting a neighbour for about half-an-hour.

"Any calls?" I asked.

"No," he said. "But lots of close ones."

Hi, California ranch!

Life in the suburbs isn't easy.

For example, I was at a meeting at the school the other evening when a woman gushed up to me and said, "You don't know me but I know you."

My face must have been blank because she didn't even pause.

"I'm the apple green split-level with a ravine lot at the end of the street," she revealed.

"Oh," I replied. "I'm . . ."

"Don't tell me!" she interrupted. "I know. You're the California ranch with the sun deck. I go past you every day on the way to the nursery school."

"I'm sorry," I said. "I didn't quite catch who you were."

"The apple green split-level," she repeated. "Maybe you know my husband. He's the dark green T-bird with white walls and air conditioning."

Finally, I caught on.

People in the suburbs aren't named after grandfathers, Old Testament prophets or even New York Yankee outfielders.

They're named after their possessions.

"So that's your husband," I replied, getting into the swing of the conversation. "I've seen the T-bird a hundred times but I always connected it to the Cape Cod on the corner with the swimming pool."

"No, the Cape Cod is married to the Mercedes," my neighbour corrected.

"Then where does the Starfire convertible live?"

"In the Spanish contemporary with the circular drive, the one with the treed lot and the colour TV antenna," she explained. "Unfortunately, they don't get along."

"I'm sorry to hear that," I said.

"It's just a rumour," she confided, "but I hear he's fooling around with the two-storey colonial on the next street. I'd hate to be there the night the Buick station wagon comes home and catches the Starfire in the driveway."

"It could be nasty," I agreed.

"By the way, have I ever met your wife?" my neighbour asked.

"I don't know," I answered. "She's the white Austin Mini, the one with the dent in the rear fender."

"I can't place her offhand," she said.

"She's at the garage getting new points right now," I added.

"How about children?"

"Three," I said. "A bicycle, a tricycle and a doll buggy."

"I think I've seen the tricycle playing in your driveway when I've gone by," she said. "Why don't you send him down to my place some afternoon? I've got a wagon the same age."

"It sounds wonderful," I replied. "I'll send Richard. I mean, the tricycle."

No cavity turtle

I've always told my son — that's Stephen, who is eight — anyway, I've always told him to make sure he brushes after meals.

This morning I walked into the bathroom and Stephen was brushing — but what he was brushing was his pet turtle.

They were taking turns on the toothbrush.

First Stephen's teeth, then the turtle's shell.

Stephen told me he didn't want his turtle to get cavities either.

Is that why I get these headaches? Yes, they're back again.

They started to kick up last week—right after I had that heart-to-heart talk with Richard.

You know Richard. He's the baby—just turned three.

Anyway, Richard has a slight lisp. For example, we ordered a new pair of Batman slippers for him and every time anybody came to the door, Richard would ask: "Are you the thlipper man?"

It went on for three days.

But that's not the problem. The problem is he's playing too much with his sister. And, because she's older—five—she always wants him to play girls' games.

I didn't worry, until I asked Richard the other day what he wanted to be when he grows up.

"I want to be a printheth," he thaid, I mean said.

He talks funny in other ways, too. I picked him up just yesterday and he commented: "Isn't I'm heavy?"

Is that any way for my son to talk?

We were out for a ride in the car last Sunday and he put his hands over the heater outlet to get them warm.

"Is there a dragon down there?" he wanted to know.

Maybe it's television. We took Stephen to the doctor last week—no, only three or four stitches in his chin. Well, he should know better than to slide on the hardwood floors in his stocking feet.

Anyway, Richard was in the waiting room when the nurse walked past.

"She's got dandruff," he announced in a loud voice, just the way they do in the commercials.

Jane turned to Richard and said, "Stop yelling. I'm not blind."

She worries me. She wants fancy underwear, high heels, lipstick—and that's to go to kindergarten.

All she talks about is getting married. Maybe that's natural. But do most five-year-old girls close their eyes when they kiss their teddy bears goodnight?

"I wish I knew how to make people," Jane grumbled the other day at the dinner table.

"Why?" I asked.

"Then I'd make another beautiful Jane," she replied.

Aquarium in the sky

There was a crisis at the house this week but, fortunately, it worked out all right.

Several months ago my son, Stephen, bought a tiny turtle at the five-and-dime store and immediately named him Captain Cook.

Each day he washed Captain Cook's bowl. He put the captain in the sunshine. And he fed his quarter-sized friend with great devotion.

Needless to say, Captain Cook flourished and each day Stephen told us of the turtle's latest antics — how he had made a particularly amusing dive, how he had looked at him and blinked, how he had enjoyed a run on the bedroom floor.

Yesterday my wife was cleaning out Stephen's room and she noticed Captain Cook flopped over in his bowl and suspiciously still.

He was very, very dead.

Stephen, fortunately, was at school and had no inkling of his personal tragedy.

And a good thing.

He is given to taking wounded birds to the school nurse or bringing home lame frogs for first aid or begging tidbits for passing pussy cats.

My wife realized she would have one very sad son on her hands when he discovered the fate of his Captain Cook.

So she put the remains in her purse and drove to the nearest store with a stock of turtles.

And there she spent the next hour trying to find a turtle that matched Captain Cook.

Some were too big. Others lacked the spots of colour near the ears. Others were the wrong shade of green.

Finally, she came up with one that wasn't exactly a twin but was the best stand-in of the bunch.

The bogus Captain Cook was then rushed home and deposited in the turtle bowl before Stephen came home from school.

Now came the moment of truth.

Stephen was in his room changing into his play clothes when he took the turtle out for his daily cleanout, stroll and feeding.

He gave "Captain Cook" a studied look and then called his mother.

"Captain Cook looks different," he said.

"What do you mean?" his mother asked innocently.

"His tail looks longer," Stephen commented.

"Maybe he's just stretching," was the careful answer.

My wife then came up with a story about applying a coat of paint to the shell to give it extra strength. "His shell underneath looks darker, too."

"Mom," he said, "are you sure this is Captain Cook?"

"Of course," she replied.

Frankly, I don't think he believed her but often in this world what we are looking for is a little lie, not the truth.

"Look, Mom," he said a moment later. "Look at Captain Cook dive! Isn't he neat?"

Comic book Solomon

Children are little hoarders at heart and seldom interested in sharing. They see. They want. They keep.

My five-year-old daughter was listing off her possessions the other day when she brought out her supply of comic books.

"This is mine and this is mine and this is mine and . . ." she droned on picking up each comic book separately.

"Wait a minute," my wife said. "That one isn't yours. That's Richard's."

"No, it isn't. It's mine," Jane insisted.

"It's Richard's. It's got his name written on the top."

"It's mine."

"It isn't yours. Look. It has R-I-C-H-A-R-D written right there."

The evidence wasn't accepted.

"I don't care. It's my pile of comic books and it's mine," Jane persisted.

"You have to give it back to Richard," my wife countered.

"No."

"Wouldn't you be mad if Richard had something of yours and wouldn't give it to you?"

Jane then burst into tears, her answer for practically every argument.

"But it's mine!" she blubbered. "Grandma gave it to me."

"Grandma didn't give it to you. Richard got it at Christmas. I can remember . . . well, I can recognize Santa Claus's printing. He printed each of your names on a comic book for your stocking."

More tears. More yowls. More Bette Davis. And a tighter grasp on Exhibit A.

The prosecution proceeded to clinch its case by calling upon an independent witness (Jane's older brother, Stephen) and asking him to verify the name on the comic book.

"Richard," he swore.

Even Perry Mason couldn't have helped Jane after that damaging testimony.

The verdict.

"You've got to give the comic book back to Richard," my dishpan Hammurabi decreed.

Then followed a long discourse on the rights of others, the many advantages of being honest (especially in the afterlife) and, finally, the promise of a spanking if Jane didn't cough up the comic book.

"Now, for the last time, whose book is that?" my wife asked.

"Richard's," Jane admitted sullenly.

Richard was then summoned from the backyard.

"Go on," my wife encouraged Jane. "You know what you have to do."

"Here's your comic book, Richard," Jane said.

"I don't want it," Richard replied, running off to rejoin his pals.

Next case.

Free enterprise

It's pretty obvious my kids intend to get government jobs when they grow up. In fact, they've already started their training.

Yesterday they decided to set up a stand on the front lawn and sell sweets and strawberry drinks to passersby.

It was a classic government operation.

The first thing the kids did was give themselves fancy titles.

Jane was named Candy Lady; Richard received the appointment of Chief Helper; Stephen was satisfied to take the position of Head Man.

Next they enlisted the services of two ordinary citizens (their mother and me).

All they wanted the volunteers to do was prepare the drinks, make a few dozen cookies, whip up some fudge, find the paper cups, cart some chairs and a table to the front lawn and take care of the expenses.

Head Man, Candy Lady and Chief Helper could handle the rest.

Proceeds, we were informed, would go to a good cause, probably the Junior Red Cross or "to some poor children."

Sales were very brisk, thanks to Chief Helper.

He came into the house several times to ask for money so he could buy fudge from Candy Lady.

And Candy Lady was delighted to learn Head Man would sell her drinks at wholesale prices — three cents a glass instead of the five cents charged the regular public.

Fortunately, Head Man didn't charge when he dipped into the stock himself so we saved that much.

The first non-Lautens customer was Ricky who lives across the street and has a very good appetite.

I was positive Head Man would make a killing.

Instead, Head Man offered Ricky full partnership in the stand and they had a drink and piece of fudge to seal the deal.

Brian suggested that a few games, operated as a sideline, might be a profitable addition to the enterprise so he got the job of Games Boy.

Naturally Brian wanted a break for Alan and Karen because they are his brother and sister and Head Man decided a free drink and two cookies would be fair.

About this time Candy Lady informed her mother that supplies were running short and could she do something about it.

And a few more chairs would be nice, too.

Pretty soon my wife was back at work over the stove, I was lugging furniture around and we had a lawn full of kids having a whale of a time, eating, drinking and playing.

By the end of the afternoon, my wife and I were bushed, we were out of pocket $3.50 and the lawn was a mess.

Total proceeds (according to Head Man) were thirty-seven cents.

And if that doesn't sound like a government operation, I don't know what does.

Sex and dragonflies

I can recall my first man-to-man talk about sex as if it were yesterday.

Actually, it's almost a week now. But I'm still shaky.

"You'd better talk to Stephen about the facts of life," my wife said. "He's been asking questions."

"But why me?" I protested.

"Because you're his father," she explained.

"But . . ."

"I don't want to hear another word," my wife interrupted. "I'll get Stephen."

Stephen came into the room.

My hands began to perspire, I could feel a twitch developing in my left eye and I had to clear my throat several times.

"Mom says you want to see me," Stephen opened.

"Yes," I replied. "Sit down."

"Could you hurry, Dad? Brian's waiting for me."

"This won't take long," I began. "I just thought you and I should have a little talk. I thought maybe you'd like to ask me some, well, questions about things."

"No, I don't," Stephen replied. "Can I go now? Brian and me are . . ."

"Brian and I," I corrected.

"Brian and I are going down to the creek to catch bugs," Stephen told me.

"Bugs! That brings up a very important question, Stephen. Do you know where bugs come from?" I asked.

"From the grass around the creek," he answered.

"I mean, do you know how they're born?"

"Not exactly," he confessed. "Do you?"

"No," I said. "I hoped you might."

"Can you hurry, Dad? Brian's going to go home if I don't come out soon."

Throwing discretion to the wind, I went directly to the point. "Do the boys and girls at school ever discuss, well, boys and girls? You know — sex," I finally blurted.

"Sometimes," Stephen confessed. "I caught a dragonfly yesterday, Dad. Brian and me . . . I mean, Brian and I are keeping him in a jar."

"I don't want you to think that it's dirty or shameful," I said. "It's beautiful. And you should never be ashamed or embarrassed about something that's beautiful."

"What's beautiful, Dad?" Stephen asked.

"It's beautiful," I explained. "What we're talking about."

"You mean dragonflies or sex?" he wanted to know.

"The second one," I answered.

"Oh. Can I go down to the creek now or do you want to talk some more about sex?" Stephen requested.

"Your mother thinks we should talk," I said.

And, for the next ten minutes, that's what we did.

I looked Stephen straight in the shoulder and told him all I knew about, life and kissing and girls and babies. I didn't hold anything back.

When I finally looked up, there was a pained expression on Stephen's face.

"What's the matter?" I asked, fearing I had said too much.

"My foot's asleep," Stephen replied. "Besides, Brian's gone home."

Cleanliness is next to impossible

I have one child who's a dream. Jane picks up. She makes her bed. She's polite. She eats everything on her plate. And she never jumps on my stomach when I'm asleep on the chesterfield.

Jane's only fault is that she's not an only child.

You see, she has two brothers — Richard and Stephen — and they are rotten to the core. They are so rotten that when they pick up a toad, the toad gets warts.

Richard and Stephen fight. They tease. They won't change their socks. They wipe their noses on anything that's handy — tablecloths, shirt-tails, the family dog.

Grubby? My kids are so grubby that the White Knight detours when he comes to our block. Mr. Clean actually had a full head of hair until he tried to get my kids to wash.

When my wife housecleans in their room, she doesn't use a broom; she uses a rake. We've got the only room in the country with wall-to-wall underwear.

Anyway, I came up with a terrific plan to get the two boys in line.

"Starting today, we're going to have a new system around here," I announced at the breakfast table.

Richard (who is three) looked at me and crossed his eyes. Stephen (who is eight) kept reading his comic book. And Jane (who is six) looked up, folded her hands in her lap and paid perfect attention.

"I'm going to award cash prizes to the best children in this family every week," I continued.

At the word "cash" everybody settled down and Richard uncrossed his eyes.

"I'm going to award twenty-five cents to the child who keeps the neatest room and helps most around the house.

"I'm going to award ten cents to the child who eats his meals and shows the best manners at the dinner table.

"And I'm going to give an additional ten cents to the child who cleans his, or her, teeth most regularly," I concluded.

"How much does that come to?" Stephen (who is saving up for some kind of plastic thing-maker) wanted to know.

"If you're best in all three categories, you can get forty-five cents," I explained.

"Goody," he said, rushing off to brush his teeth, giving his brother a perfect elbow in the ear so he could get into the bathroom first.

"Maybe I should have made an award for the boy who throws the fewest elbow smashes, too," I said to my wife.

"Don't overdo it," she whispered. "But I like the idea. I like the idea of appealing to their competitive spirit, or giving them a challenge, of working on their psyches."

"I'm working on their greed and you know it," I corrected. "This is out-and-out bribery but what the hell, nothing else has worked."

My wife put a chart in the kitchen and revealed she would give stars every day (a gold star for three points, a silver for two, etc.) and that Friday would be awards day.

Well, I'd like to report that my plan worked perfectly, but it wasn't quite that way.

Stephen made a great start. He cleaned up his room, made his bed and even picked up the eighty-six sets of underwear scattered on the floor.

But then he didn't want to use his bed the rest of the week.

"It'll get messed again if I sleep in it," he complained. "Why can't I just sleep on the chesterfield in the front room?"

We told him he was missing the entire spirit of the contest and ordered him to sleep in his own bed.

By the middle of the week, Stephen's room was back to normal — rumpled bed, his entire wardrobe laid out on the floor, bits and pieces of a chemistry set everywhere.

"Your room's a mess," I mentioned. "You won't win that way."

"Jane's so far ahead I can't catch up," Stephen replied. "So might as well save myself for next week. I think I'll go out and play."

Richard? He never even got that far. He threw in the towel, or the underwear, if you prefer, the very first day.

So there you have it.

Stephen and Richard still live in disaster areas. They brush when they remember. They eat if they feel like it.

Meanwhile, Jane's room is still neat as a pin. She still eats everything on her plate. She still brushes after meals — and sits with her hands folded in her lap when I talk to her.

Only now it costs me forty-five cents every week.

Leaving home — sort of

We had another crisis this week.

Jane left home.

She put on her best dress; she packed her bags and she struck out on her own.

A six-year-old girl doesn't have to put up with spankings and baby brothers and a lot of other indignities.

So there!

But let me go back to the beginning.

My wife caught Jane throwing some nifty punches at her brother Richard (who has just turned four) down in the playroom.

Jane claimed Richard had slugged her first. Richard said she was nuts. Anyway, Jane had been making faces at him. Jane said she wouldn't make faces if Richard would stop calling her teacher "Miss Schnook." Her name, Jane pointed out, is "Miss Shook."

My wife settled the case out of court.

Smack! Smack!

And right on the bare legs, too.

Richard took the punishment like a true man. He rushed to his room and stuffed his blue blanket up his nose.

Jane, however, was incensed.

"I'm leaving home," she announced with her hands on her hips.

"Go ahead," my wife bargained.

"And I'm never coming back," Jane vowed.

"Don't forget to write," my wife replied.

"I won't write," Jane guaranteed.

"Suit yourself," my wife shrugged.

Jane then stomped into her room, muttering to herself. She began tossing a few belongings into an overnight bag. Just necessities — underwear, her best doll, a partly-licked grape sucker, a nightie (the one with the lace on it) and her piggy bank.

"Well, I'm going," she repeated when she reached the door, giving us one last chance to reconsider her reckless decision.

"Goodbye," my wife said, hardly looking up.

That was the point of no return. The two of them were committed and nobody was going to give in.

Jane walked to the front door and she was gone.

My wife jumped up and ran into the front room, where she hid behind the curtains.

"Jane's walking down the walk," she whispered. "She's looking back at the house. Keep down! She's crossing to the other side of the street."

My wife lost sight of Jane for a few moments and raced into the bathroom to get a different vantage point.

"Jane's going over to Karen's," my wife continued. "Karen must be out. Her mother's talking to Jane. Oh! Jane is crossing the road again. She's going around the corner . . ."

This play-by-play report went on for about twenty-five minutes.

My wife rushed from one side of the house to another, always keeping one eyeball ahead of Jane.

And then Jane started to walk toward our house again.

"Quick! Pretend you're reading the paper, or something," my wife ordered as she sprinted past me.

That wasn't difficult since I was already reading the paper at the time.

"And don't say a thing," she added.

My wife then rushed into the kitchen, where she turned on some taps, rattled dishes and made herself look very busy.

Jane walked into the house.

Jane walked down to her room.

And Jane didn't say a word. But I could hear her unpacking.

A few minutes later Jane walked into the kitchen.

"I'm back," she revealed.

"That's nice," my wife said.

Pause.

"Do you know why I came back?" Jane finally asked.

"No," my wife admitted.

"Because I love you," Jane said.

"Dinner will be ready in about ten minutes," my wife said, turning away and blowing her nose a couple of times. Hard.

"What's wrong, Mom?" Jane asked.

"I've got something in my eye," my wife explained.

I guess I'll never understand women—not even the six-year-olds.

That Richard

Our four-year-old's name is Richard. But we never call Richard, Richard.

As far as we're concerned his first name is That.

He is That Richard Lautens.

When I come home from work, for example, the first thing my wife always says to me is, "Do you know what That Richard did today?"

Neighbours comment, "That Richard is sure a live wire, isn't he?"

And a thousand times every weekend when I hear a silence in the house, I shout, "Where's That Richard?"

I know he's up to something.

In any case, "That Richard" is his name, regardless of what it says on his birth certificate. And no hyphen, please.

Which may explain what I've got to say.

The news has just been brought to me: That Richard's in trouble again.

"Do you know what That Richard just did?" his brother Stephen asked. "He took my toothbrush, rubbed it in soap and then dunked it in the toilet — twice."

As an afterthought, Stephen suggested: "When I catch That Richard, I'm going to kill him."

But That Richard is nowhere to be found. Undoubtedly he's hiding in some closet or barricaded behind the chesterfield sucking on his blue blanket.

Whenever there's any kind of crisis in his life, which is always, That Richard always resorts to his blue blanket.

He puts his thumb in his mouth, stuffs the corner of his blanket up his nose — and then he's ready to face all comers.

Frankly, we're ashamed of the blanket.

It's been washed, patched and mended. It's been used as a whip, rope, tent, trampoline, Batman's cape and God-only-knows what else.

It's been dragged hundreds of miles. It's been snapped, skipped and soaked.

And it looks it.

The man at the service station uses a better cloth to clean my windshield. If the Board of Health ever spots it, we're all going to be condemned.

We've tried to break That Richard of the habit but our efforts to date have failed.

Take the last time.

Somebody suggested we should cut off a corner of the blanket and give that to you-know-who as a mini-substitute. Then, while he's not looking, gradually cut more and more off until he's left with just a couple of threads.

Presto! No more blanket. Just one normal, well-adjusted, disarmed kid.

Well, it sounded like a sure thing until That Richard was over at the supermarket with his mother and began bawling his head off.

The manager of the store rushed over to see what the trouble was. That Richard explained he has lost his "ko-knee"—which is his baby-talk way of saying "corner," meaning the corner of the blanket.

"Where is your ko-knee, little man?" the manager asked.

That Richard just pointed to the meat counter—about forty feet of gleaming meat counter.

He had stuffed his patch of blanket down one of the little cracks—he wasn't sure which one—and he wasn't going to budge until he got it back.

About forty minutes later the counter was in pieces and so was the manager. Finally he discovered a scrap of cloth big enough to cover a gnat, provided the gnat didn't sleep in a double bed.

"Is this it?" the manager wanted to know.

Without a word, That Richard took the cloth, stuffed it up his nose, and walked away.

Since then we've made sure he carries the entire blanket. At least it won't fit down cracks in the meat counter.

I don't know why the toughest of all our kids should need a blanket. That Richard will take on the entire block in tackle football. He loves to swing on his curtains and make Tarzan yells. He wrestles our 200-pound dog. And wins.

It's very deceiving.

Just the other day my wife was over at the plaza getting a pair of shoes for That Richard, who moves so fast he wears them out from the inside, too.

My wife watched as the clerk tried a pair on That Richard's feet.

"Will these shoes wear well?" she asked.

The shoe salesman looked at That Richard, who was sucking on his blanket and looking like a perfect angel, or sissy.

"Madam," he said. "These shoes are Savage."

"So is he," my wife replied.

Stephen Spendo

One of the great lessons every parent tries to teach his children is the value of money.

You know the pitch.

Daddy works hard for his money. Money doesn't grow on trees. A penny saved is a penny earned. Put your money away for a rainy day.

And a lot of other catchy phrases like that.

Well, with that in mind, we have had the children on the weekly payroll for some time now. Yes, allowances.

Stephen (who is eight) gets twenty-five cents a week; Jane (who is six) gets ten cents; and Richard (who is four) gets five cents.

In addition, as I mentioned before, the kids can earn bonuses for cleaning their teeth, eating their meals, keeping a neat room and not biting each other any place it shows.

The prize money totals forty-five cents — but I throw in an extra five cents if anybody can perform a grand slam and top all divisions of the competition.

Every Saturday morning the kids line up for their loot.

We have no trouble with Jane. She takes her dough and runs into her bedroom, where she counts it and then hides it under a loose floorboard or something.

She, in a word, is a saver.

Richard is different. First of all, he seldom gets any bonus. Unless we give money for fist fighting, there is no way Richard is ever going to get rich.

So he takes his five cents and usually loses it, swallows it or tries to stuff it up his nose.

But Stephen is something else.

Stephen likes to spend. He is drawn to stores like a magnet. He is so good at getting rid of money I'm sure he's going to wind up in government, probably with CBC.

Anyway, we've been working on Stephen, trying to get him to keep his money in a large piggy bank instead of at the plaza.

If I say so myself, we weren't doing too badly.

Stephen must have had five or six dollars in his bank. But, apparently, the strain was too much on him.

"I'd like to take some money out of my bank," Stephen informed his mother when he reached that financial pinnacle.

"Why?" she asked.

"Because there's something I want to buy," he admitted.

"Ste-phen!" my wife began.

She always breaks his name in the middle that way when she's annoyed — and he knows it.

"Ste-phen!" she said. "Why can't you leave your money alone? You're just starting to save nicely and now you want to go out and spend it on something foolish."

"It's not foolish, Mom," he promised.

"Stephen, you always say that," my wife complained. "You can find more ways to spend money than any boy I know. Why does money burn a hole in your pocket? Why can't you save like your sister?"

"I don't know, Mom," he replied. "Can I have my money now?"

"You realize, Stephen, if you spend your money you won't be able to get that microscope you said you wanted to save for?"

"Yes," Stephen said.

"If you saved just a few more weeks you could get a light for your bicycle," she continued.

"I know," Stephen answered. "But there's something I want to get now."

"I give up," my wife surrendered. "Get your bank. Take the money out. But don't come to me when you're broke. You've got to learn the value of money."

Stephen took the rubber plug out of the piggy bank's stomach, emptied it to the last penny, and walked out of the house.

"I don't know what we're going to do about Stephen," my wife muttered. "He just won't save."

"Mmmm," I commented, a comment I find very useful when I don't want to take sides.

"He only thinks of today. For Stephen, there's no tomorrow," she nattered.

"Mmm," I said.

And then my wife went back to the kitchen, still muttering about Stephen the Spendthrift, her wastrel son, the Diamond Jim of the sucker set.

About an hour later Stephen walked into the house with a package in his hand.

"This is for you," he said, handing it to his mother.

"What is it?" she asked.

"Open it," he begged.

Well, she did. And inside a blue box, folded in white tissue paper, was a pair of earrings.

"I saw them in a store yesterday and thought you'd like them," Stephen explained.

Stephen's mother didn't reply. She just gave Stephen a big hug.

The earrings turn my wife's earlobes a little green, but on special occasions, those are the earrings she always wears.

After all, they represent the lifetime savings of a young boy — and his love.

What can be more precious than that?

What are you doing? ... *Nothing!*

Will all the new parents in the audience please raise their hands?

Ah, yes.

Well, this is for you.

Right now you're only worrying about the little tyke throwing up on your new suit or getting that funny look on his face when you've got company and you're passing him (or her) around.

But pretty soon baby will learn to talk and that's when the real fun begins.

You're going to discover that children can talk all right—but what they say has no connection with what they mean.

Let me explain.

Very soon you'll hear a crashing silence downstairs in the rec room (parents quickly recognize silence as a danger signal) and you'll ask:

"What are you doing, Harry?"

I will bet you one million dollars that little Harry will reply, "Nothing!"

That is the standard answer all kids give.

But what exactly does "nothing" mean?

"Nothing" means little Harry is scribbling on the walls with a marker pen, sawing through the legs of your pool table or trying to plug the family cat's tail into a wall socket.

With that explanation, I'm now going to attempt to give you new parents an interpretation of some of the other things you'll hear in the next few years.

Question: Why is Susie crying?
Answer: I don't know.
Translation: Susie is crying because I judo-chopped her in the mouth, ate her candy bar and told her there's a big ghost hiding behind the curtains waiting to swallow her up.

Question: Do you have to go to the bathroom before I do up your snowsuit?
Answer: No.
Translation: Yes.

Question: Who left these wet boots on the hardwood floor I just waxed?
Answer: Susie did.
Translation: Susie did. I left my wet boots on the new broadloom in the front room. The only thing I left on the hardwood floor was a coat, hat and the one mitt I've got left.

Question: Can anyone go to the store for me?
Answer: I'm busy.
Translation: I'm watching Willie Weirdo and the Unimaginables on TV and I've only seen this particular show thirty-four times.

Question: Are you sure the shoes fit?
Answer: They fit.
Translation: They don't fit but I'm not going to complain until tomorrow when they're scuffed up and the store won't take them back.

Question: Did you remember to flush?
Answer: Yes.
Translation: In fact, I flushed seven times. It took that many to flush down my toothbrush, a powder puff, two rolls of tissue and a china figurine that's been in the family seventy-five years.

Question: Has anybody seen the china figurine I had on my dresser?
Answer: No.
Translation: (See above.)

Question: Were you a good boy at Grandma's?
Answer: Grandma says I was a very good boy.
Translation: I raised hell all day but Grandma did say I was a good boy. (Grandmothers always say their grandchildren are good and are completely unreliable as character references.)

Question: What are you doing in the bathroom?
Answer: I'm washing.
Translation: I'm washing — I'm washing the walls, the floor, the medicine cabinet, the door. And I'm using the good towels as a washcloth and the scented soap that's seventy-five cents a cake.

Question: Are you getting into trouble?
Answer: No.
Translation: No. I already am in trouble.

Question: Who broke the lamp?
Answer: I was just playing quietly when Susie and her friends came in and they started to wrestle and fight and call me names and I told them to stop and they wouldn't and they made a face at me and I told them I was going to call my mother but you weren't around so I couldn't call you and I didn't know what to do so I just tried to ignore them but they . . .
Translation: I did.

Anyway, those are a few tips that may come in handy. And, in the difficult days ahead, always remember one thing: your kids probably like you almost as much as they do the dog next door.

Painting the town peanut butter

If you ever walked into our home, you'd probably swear you were at RCMP headquarters.

In fact, we've got more fingerprints on file than the Mounties, the FBI and Scotland Yard combined — and all on the walls.

Our kids can't walk, talk, eat, watch TV or anything without leaving a telltale trail. Every day is Palm Sunday at our place.

Sometimes when I get home and look at the smudges I don't know which to get plastered first, me or the living-room wall.

Take Stephen.

His favourite lunch is a grape jelly sandwich. As a result we have a lovely purple wall in the kitchen behind his place at the table.

Now I have nothing against purple.

But it clashes with the peanut butter splattered on Richard's side of the room.

And trust Jane to love pizza.

Have you ever tried to get curtains that match grape jelly, peanut butter and pizza?

Believe me, it's impossible.

Apparently there's another unwritten law in the Lautens residence: you can't sit on a chair. You have to lie on the floor and put your feet on the walls.

The only time my kids are erect is when they're eating grape jelly sandwiches, peanut butter, etc.

As a result, I have more tracks than CN.

The walls in the dining-room are supposed to be oyster but you couldn't bring that oyster back to life with mouth-to-mouth resuscitation.

Don't think I haven't tried to fight back. I've told the children that the floor is just a horizontal wall in the hope they might try to walk on that for a change.

I've also suggested they wash their hands at least once a week, whether they need it or not, figuring if I'm going to get the digit I might just as well go for a clean one.

It hasn't worked.

Finally, it got so bad I had to call in the painters this past week.

My suggestion was that we paint the entire house in some shade the children couldn't mark.

However, the paint charts don't have a colour that exactly matches the stain left when a sock, worn for a week or so under a rubber boot, hits the wall and sort of slithers to the floor. We settled for cream.

The painter, a nice fellow named Ernie, finished the living-room the first day.

However, by the time he arrived the next morning, there were fingerprints all over the doorway leading to the kitchen.

By checking twirls, swirls and lifelines, we were able to determine it was Richard.

Besides, Richard had one cream hand and an ear to match.

"Kids will be kids," Ernie said, a little weakly, I thought. And he spent most of the morning scrubbing Richard's hand and his ear and repainting the door frame.

That afternoon it was Jane's turn.

She had to get something out of a downstairs closet. Not later. Now!

Anyway, she was searching in the closet when she brushed against the closet door and turned a blue velvet dress into a cream velvet dress.

Ernie got out the turpentine again. He got Jane cleaned up — and then gave the closet door another coat.

"You'll need three gallons for the house and four gallons for the kids at this rate," I joked.

"Ha, ha," Ernie replied without exactly rolling on the floor in amusement.

That night I really chased the kids. Every time they even looked at a wall or a door I yelled at them. I told them Ernie was sore, that I was sore and, that they would be sore, too — on the behind — if they left any more marks.

Ernie was able to finish the painting in a couple of days and we were all just delighted that there was no trouble.

"I guess I was the only one who didn't get in the paint," Stephen gloated as Ernie was packing up to leave.

Unfortunately, Stephen was leaning on a wet wall when he said it.

Ernie unpacked.

4

Three to Get Ready

Kindergarten crisis

This has been cram week at our place.

The Board of Education sent us a letter stating that Richard Gary Lautens, aged four, should know his name and address and telephone number before enrolling in kindergarten.

That's no sweat.

But he's also expected to tie his own shoelaces.

Well, I've got some bad news for the Board of Education.

Richard Gary Lautens can swim, climb fences, open the door, print his name, change the channel on the TV set and do up his pants — but he can't tie his shoelaces.

We have worked with him for nearly ten days. We've shown him how to make loops. We have shown him where the knot goes.

But Richard Gary Lautens still can't figure it out.

If the kindergarten teacher gives the class a test today in shoelace tying, Richard Gary Lautens is going to flunk.

He may be a drop-out even before he's a drop-in.

During the summer he never wore shoes. Before that, he had loafer-style footwear that posed no problem.

So, if the Board of Education is listening, I want them to know he only needs a little experience.

I want them to give Richard Gary Lautens a second chance and not turf him out on the street or recommend that he be transferred to a trade school.

I'm sure he'll get the hang of it if they'll just be patient.

The reason I'm begging is simple: If they reject Richard Gary because he can't tie shoelaces, they'll break somebody's heart — my wife's.

For ten years she's dreamed of this glorious day.

When times were tough and she was up to her ascot in dirty diapers, she'd turn to me and sigh, "Some day these kids will be at school and I'll have some time to myself."

It was all that kept her going.

Well, today's the day.

Stephen is in grade five. Jane is in grade two. I've got a job. And Richard is in kindergarten, if the Board of Education isn't too picky.

That may not seem much to you but, to my wife, that adds up to 150 minutes of free time every day.

From 9 to 11:30, five mornings a week, my wife will have nobody underfoot, or under anything else, either.

That's 750 minutes every week not to make sandwiches, 750 minutes not to tell somebody to keep his hands off the walls, 750 minutes not to ask if they flushed.

My wife has oodles of plans for those 750 minutes, so if the Board of Education doublecrosses her now, I'm not responsible for what she might do.

Personally, I'm sorry to see Richard Gary Lautens leave his babyhood behind.

My wife's more practical, however.

"If his kindergarten teacher didn't start on tranquillizers at least two weeks ago, she'll never catch up," she commented.

Bedroom rules

Jane is the only one at our house who really knows how to handle my wife.

That's because Jane has heart. She also has chin, which she sticks out whenever she gets involved in an argument.

For example, when my wife and I have a fight, I calmly explain my position with cold logic. Next I point out the weakness in what my wife has to say.

And then I apologize.

The boys are the same.

They are feathers off the old chicken.

But not Jane.

She could give a bulldog stubborn lessons. I would match her against Gibraltar any day.

In fact, when Jane and her mother lock eyeballs, the male members of the family hide behind the chesterfield to escape the fallout.

Let me explain just how Jane operates.

A few days ago my wife thought everyone was out of the house when she heard some noises coming from Jane's bedroom.

When she opened the door, she found Jane playing cutouts with a little boy name Hugh.

Hugh is the one who hangs around the house and turns skipping rope for Jane and puts her bike away in the garage if she's busy.

Like Jane, Hugh is only seven—but, as you can tell, he's perfect husband material.

Anyway, Jane was ordering Hugh around as usual, telling him what he could cut, which scissors he could use, and where to put all the scraps of paper that were on the floor. In short, Jane was having a lovely time.

"What are you two doing?" my wife asked.

"Playing," Jane replied.

"That's nice," my wife said.

And then, figuring it's never too early to start breaking in the house rules, my wife added:

"If you're going to play with Hugh in your bedroom, make sure you leave the door open."

Jane was furious.

She couldn't care less about the bedroom door being open or closed.

But the idea of somebody coming into HER bedroom and giving HER orders!

And in front of Hugh!

Well, it was just too much for Jane to take.

Her chin almost bounced off the wall, it stuck out so far.

In any case, my wife thought that was the end of it and went back to the kitchen to her usual chores.

That night Jane was busier than ever in her room and the next morning we found out why.

On her bedroom door was posted this notice:

Please do not disturb.

Knock first.

If nobody answers, no
one is here.

And please do not disturb.

Not only was the message stuck to the door, it was written in black marker pencil on red paper so nobody could miss it.

My wife insisted I talk to Jane.

I took Jane aside and explained that it's polite to leave the bedroom door open when a young lady entertains a young man, especially when they're both seven.

I also assured her that we had only her best interests at heart.

Then I said her ponytail was coming along beautifully — that's always the clincher with Jane.

Anyway, she smiled.

Later that day she slipped a tiny piece of paper in my hand.

It read:

Ticit to Jane's room.

You dirty rat!

My daughter finally asked the question that strikes terror in every father's heart.

Oh, we know it's coming.

We can brace ourselves. We can rehearse our answers. We tell ourselves it isn't the end of the world.

But all that goes out the window when your daughter looks you in the eye and says:

"Can I have a white rat, Daddy?"

It is a matter of record that every child in the entire world wants to own a white rat of his own, a rat he (or she) can hold, play with and feed and stick in the face of grownups. It is just as provable that everybody over the age of twenty-one thinks that white rats are creepy.

But when you're a father, you're supposed to be fearless, brave and strong.

You're definitely not supposed to be afraid of an itty-bitty white rat with beady eyes and a long pink tail that wraps around your arm and is probably a distant relative of something that carried bubonic plague around Europe a couple of centuries ago.

The question is: how do you get out of keeping the rat and still keep your Galahad reputation intact?

Do you pick up the sinister creature when your daughter brings him home and lets him run up your arm and nibble on your nose?

Do you say he's terribly cute (through gritted teeth) and that it would be worth getting the Black Death just to have such a gorgeous pet?

And then do you explain that it would be heartless to take the wee fellow away from his brothers and sisters at the garbage dump?

Why, he'd pine away!

I did none of these things.

A neighbour and former friend named Garside gave our

seven-year-old daughter a white rat and when Jane brought it home she was terribly excited.

"Look what I got!" she said. "It's a white rat and Mrs. Garside said I could have the cage, too, and he's real friendly and he doesn't take up much space and I promise to take care of him myself and he hardly eats at all and can I keep him?"

Alas! I lost my head and resorted to those three words that always get me out of a jam around the house:

"Ask your mother," I said.

Jane took the rat into the kitchen and her mother took care of the situation in twenty seconds flat.

"What's that ugly thing?" she asked.

"A rat," Jane began.

"Take him out of here," came the order.

"But . . ."

"Now!" Jane's mother insisted.

That was the end of the discussion.

"It's easy to be a mother" Jane muttered as she left the house to return the white rat. "All you have to be is crabby."

The fly in the ice cube

If there's one thing a nine-year-old boy can't resist it's a mail-order catalogue, especially one that promises "2,000 novelties PLUS useful and fun articles."

Stephen got his hands on such a booklet and I know exactly what he went through.

When I was a kid, my eyes popped, too, at the pages of neat items just waiting to be mailed out to me upon receipt of a money order and a small sum to cover the cost of handling, no postage stamps, please.

Alas, as every adult knows, a mail-order catalogue from a novelty firm is like a girl with false eyelashes, false hair and a padded bra—it advertises more than it can deliver.

However, nine-year-olds don't understand that fact of life.

Therefore, I couldn't blame Stephen for getting excited about the veritable cornucopia of delights at his fingertips.

"It's fun to get things by mail," the catalogue encouraged on its cover.

Why, you could get an engagement and wedding ring set—"for fun or for real" for a measly one dollar, with "an attractive plastic gift box" as a bonus.

Or, at $4.50, a young boy might purchase a telephone "snooper" and listen in to conversations like a secret agent.

Stephen didn't know what to mark down on his order form first.

Would it be the $2.50 microphone that would permit him to talk over the family radio and "imitate Bob Hope or Bing Crosby" at parties?

Would it be the $13.95 "lie detector machine . . . which registers emotions, feelings and reactions even when people try to conceal them?"

Or, for fifty cents, would he get the booklet on ju-jitsu and learn to "beat the bullies" with a devastating series of "kidney squeezes" and "throat grips," not to mention the "etc., etc." which is included with every lesson?

Obviously, Stephen could have made a decision in seconds if

he possessed one of the company's $5.75 "mechanical brain computers" which are even capable of "playing games."

But all Stephen had to work with was the space between his own ears, and a very limited budget.

He finally decided on four items:

A plastic ice cube "with real bug—a real shocker when discovered in a drink!" Price—twenty-five cents.

Garlic (Awful!) Gum that "ruins the breath for hours." Package of five sticks—twenty cents.

Magnetic lodestone, regarded by many as "a lucky symbol" and often sold "for fabulous amounts!" Yours for fifty cents.

And finally, a "miracle light bulb that lights without wires—amazing, mystifying!" A bargain at twenty-five cents.

Stephen figured all that stuff was probably better than the fake bullet holes or even the bleeding dagger, both of which he considered as possible purchases.

Anyway, he got his money and his order form and his letter—and sent away for the fabulous treasures.

The next few days were hell.

Stephen was certain that delivery—"speedy service!" the company promised—would be practically instantaneous.

A mailman couldn't turn our corner without Stephen's being on him and wanting to check through his pouch.

Finally, the big day arrived.

Stephen opened his package and the first thing he noticed was that his magic light bulb was a little small.

In the catalogue it looked large enough to light downtown Montreal but the cold truth of the matter was that it was only the size of a pea.

The lodestone looked like a very ordinary piece of gravel and, when Stephen rubbed it, no genie appeared out of the thin air. So much for "lucky" symbols.

He put a stick of the garlic gum in his mouth and breathed all over his brother—but his brother said it smelled nice and asked for some too.

However, I was the one who delivered the *coup de grâce*.

That evening at the dinner table I was sipping a cool glass of iced tea. The kids were giggling but I didn't pay any attention.

Anyway, I finished the drink, put the glass down — and looked into a collection of the most disappointed eyes I've ever seen.

Yes, the plastic ice cube "with real bug" was in my glass and I hadn't noticed.

"Things aren't always what people say, are they, Dad?" Stephen commented at bedtime, more as a statement than a question.

I just smiled. Somehow, I think he got his money's worth out of that catalogue don't you?

The tooth fairy
arrives—late

I don't know whether you realize it or not but the tooth fairy has upped her prices.

A few years ago the most you could get for a tooth under your pillow was a nickel — a dime at the outside.

But the going rate these days is a quarter.

I know because I've just had to put my money where Jane's mouth is.

Yes, even without teeth my kids can put the bite on me.

For weeks Jane went around with this loose tooth in the front of her mouth. She wiggled it. She moved it from side to side.

And, whenever we had something for dinner she didn't like, she'd point to it and say she couldn't possibly eat because her mouth was coming apart.

Obviously, she still had plenty of lip.

Jane really played the tooth for all it was worth and her brothers were green with envy, especially Stephen.

"When the tooth comes out, you'll be able to put it under your pillow and get money," he advised his sister, who didn't know about such things until he opened his big mouth.

Stephen is so money-hungry that he'd get his gums removed if he thought there was a buck in it.

Anyway, from then on, Jane knew she was walking around with a potential fortune right under her nose so she gave that tooth some pretty good tugs.

But it didn't budge.

Stephen, who is very brave when it comes to his sister's pain, said Jane should tie a string around the tooth, tie the string to a doorknob and . . .

I vetoed that.

"With my luck, the doorknob would come off," I told him.

So the tooth just dangled, and so did we.

A few days later we were at the breakfast table when Jane ran into the kitchen, sobbing her heart out.

"My tooth's gone," she blubbered, "but the tooth fairy didn't leave me any money."

My wife (who makes a career of telling it like it isn't) was horrified.

"When did the tooth come out?" she asked.

"Last night in bed," Jane sobbed.

"Why didn't you tell me?" my wife demanded.

"Because I wanted to surprise you," Jane explained. "I put my tooth under my pillow but I didn't get anything from the tooth fairy and my tooth's gone!"

Jane was crying her eyes out by now.

That's when my wife pulled the old let-me-take-a-look-to-make-sure-you're-right trick.

The two of them disappeared into Jane's bedroom.

A few minutes later Jane shouted, "I've found a quarter!"

She was ecstatic.

When we got a minute alone, I asked my wife how she had pulled it off.

"Easy," she said, "I palmed a quarter and slipped it into the pillowcase when Jane wasn't looking. Then . . ."

". . . then you suggested she shake the pillowcase," I broke in.

"Right," she admitted. "By the way, I found the tooth in the covers and put it in your dresser drawer. Oh, yes. You owe me a quarter."

Frankly, I was a little annoyed with my wife.

"Jane's seven years old," I complained. "Why weren't you honest with her? Why don't you just say that the tooth fairy doesn't really exist? Why don't you admit that I'm the one who leaves the quarter for teeth?"

"Maybe you're right," she conceded. "Maybe we should be more frank and direct with the children."

The lecture really sank in.

That night at the dinner table Richard was just toying with his vegetables.

"You'd better eat them up," my wife warned. "Otherwise the little bear on the bottom of your dish will beat you to them."

I give up.

Don't drink the water!

When I was a child, one of the big treats after playing hard was to come home and have a glass of water.

Sometimes, if we were good, mother would even put a chip of ice in it.

However, things are different today as I found out when three young members of the Affluent Society stormed in the house and announced they were thirsty.

"Could we have some soda pop?" their spokesman asked.

"There isn't any," I informed them.

"How about some instant milk shakes?"

"Your mother hasn't gone shopping yet but they're on her list. Sorry."

"Okay, we'll have apple juice, orange juice or lemonade."

"We're out of them all," I apologized.

"But we're thirsty," they protested. "What can we drink?"

"You'll have to have water."

"What's water?"

"It's a drink."

"I thought water was something you washed your car in."

"It is, but you can drink it, too."

"Are you sure?" I was asked.

"Try some," I suggested. "You don't have to finish it if you don't like it."

They agreed and I brought in a pitcher of water with some ice.

"Don't you have to mix it with anything?"

"No."

"Does it come in any other colour?"

"Not usually."

"How about flavours?"

"This is it," I had to confess.

"Will it fizz if I shake it?"

"I'm afraid not."

"Is vitamin C added?"

"No."

"Does it come in a tin, a bottle or a paper package?"

"It comes out of a tap," I said.

"Then you don't get any prizes, coupons or baseball pictures for drinking water?"

"No."

"What kind of a drink are you trying to palm off on us?"

"Try a sip before you make any decision," I begged.

They agreed.

The first member of the Affluent Society put his lips to the glass and announced, "It needs a couple of scoops of ice cream, or something."

The next took a sniff and complained, "It's flat. It doesn't have any taste."

And then he spat it out.

The third refused to go even that far. "I may be thirsty but I'm not thirsty enough to drink that icky stuff."

And they walked out.

I don't know why experts worry so much about the world running out of drinking water. Most people under the age of twenty have never tasted it anyway.

Brownie points

Our Jane (who is nine) has just joined the Brownies.

And she's enthusiastic.

She's bought the Brownie handbook; she's learned the Brownie salute; and she's dickering with a friend for a second-hand Brownie uniform.

However, the road to sainthood isn't without pitfalls, as Jane discovered this morning.

Jane's first Brownie meeting is Wednesday.

So today she was in her bedroom reciting aloud the Brownie Motto, the Brownie Promise and sundry other bits of Brownie philosophy.

"*A Smile and a Good Turn,*" she announced.

"*When helping others all the while,*
Brownies always wear a smile;
When things go wrong or they fall down,
Brownies never . . ."

That's as far as she got.

"Mom!" Jane bellowed. "Get Richard out of my room. He's making faces at me."

I could hear Richard (who just turned seven) giggle.

"Richard, leave your sister alone," my wife ordered.

Jane started again.

"... *Brownies never wear a frown;*
Frowns or scowls make ugly things,
Smiling gives them angel wings ..."

There was another break in the recitation.

"Richard, if you don't stop bugging me, I'll kill you," Jane threatened.

A door slammed.

"*While in the home or on the street,*
Brownies watch each one they meet,
Whispering to themselves they say,
Is my good turn for you ..."

The stanza was left hanging there.

"I warned you, Richard," Jane shouted, interrupting herself.

Richard came charging along the hallway and down the stairs with Jane in hot pursuit.

By the time I got to the scene, Richard was on the ground with his sister shaking him by the neck.

"I'm trying to learn my Brownie poem," Jane fumed, "and he keeps opening my door and sticking his tongue out at me."

"Richard will leave you alone," I said. "Won't you, Richard?"

Richard couldn't talk, not with Jane's hands around his throat, but he nodded in agreement.

"If you do it again, I'll pull your tongue out," Jane vowed. Jane then let him up.

Richard decided to go over to Chippy's and play on the swing, which appeared to be a hell of a lot safer than heckling our resident Brownie.

When I left for the office, I could hear Jane in her bedroom. *"Brownies' smiles go all the way,*
And with them a good turn a day."
Her right hook isn't bad either.

Bits and overbites

Everybody has some physical characteristic that's embarrassing.

With my daughter Jane, it's her teeth.

When Jane smiles, she tries not to open her mouth or, if she does, she quickly covers it with her hand to hide the view.

The problem is, Jane's teeth are straight and even.

That's right, Jane doesn't have braces.

Nor does she have much hope of ever wearing braces. The family dentist says her teeth are coming in straight and, sorry, there's nothing he can do about it.

I don't have to tell you how Jane feels.

Most of her friends have enough metal in their mouths to build a Japanese sports car.

When they smile, you don't see pearls; the view is pure Stelco.

So Jane feels left out.

Orthodontia is the adolescent chic of suburbia. It's status and, according to psychologists, proves your parents care.

I've tried to explain to Jane it's nobody's fault her teeth are perfect. We all have crosses to bear and this is something she'll have to accept.

For a time my explanation worked, but now we have a new crisis on our hands.

Jane's brother Stephen has developed a list of dental problems as long as a basketball player's leg.

Stephen has overbite; he's cutting into his soft palate; he's a mouth-breather; there's a space between his front teeth.

What that adds up to is 800 bucks worth of work.

The day Stephen got his braces I could tell from the look on Jane's face we were in for trouble.

"Will Stephen have to wear braces long?" she asked.

"Two years," I admitted.

"Did he get cat whiskers, too?"

I said he did.

Jane stormed out of the room, gnashing her perfect little teeth.

The next day when Jane came home from school I saw something glistening in her mouth.

"What's that?" I asked.

"A paper clip," Jane revealed.

"A paper clip?"

"Yes, a paper clip. I straightened it out and hooked it across my teeth," Jane stated. "I'm not going to be the only one in the entire world without braces on my teeth."

Wheeler dealer

Our Richard (who is seven) said he wanted to talk to me.

"Dad," he began, "would you buy me a bike?"

"You're not old enough," I informed him.

"Murray and Peter and Bruce have bikes," he argued.

"That's their parents' decision, not mine. Besides, the street is too busy for you to be riding a bike."

"I wouldn't ride on the main streets — only the quiet ones,"

Richard bargained. "And I'd be very careful."

"You can't ride a bike," I reminded him. "I don't want you learning . . .

"I can ride a bike," Richard interrupted. "I learned last summer on Donald's."

Realizing I was on the run, I threw a low blow.

"Look, Richard," I said, "any boy who still sucks on his blankie isn't old enough to ride a bicycle out on the street."

Immediately I felt guilty, but triumphant.

Richard is mature, reliable and able to cut his own meat — but he does whip out pieces of an old baby blanket to suck in moments of stress and at bedtime.

In fact, he has about a dozen bits of "blankie" stashed around in case of emergency.

Besides the one by his bed, he has a scrap in the glove compartment of my car, another in the sports jacket he wears to Sunday school, etc., etc.

After my bombshell, Richard looked at me.

"Would you buy me a bike if I gave up my blankie?" he wanted to know.

"Well, I suppose so," I replied.

What else could I say?

"Would you get me a real two-wheeler, with a bell?"

"Yes — if you give up your blankie," I said, emphasizing every syllable so Richard would understand what he was getting into.

"All right, I'll give up my blankie," Richard sighed. "When do I get my bike?"

"In the spring, when the nice weather arrives," I said.

"Can I pick it out myself?"

"Yes," I agreed. "Do you think you can give up your blankie?"

"I think so," Richard answered. "But Dad, would you do me a favour?"

"If I can," I promised.

"Will you hide all my blankies so I can't find them?"

Good deeds

I made a terrible mistake a month ago. I let our Richard join the Cubs.

Believe me, I have nothing against the Cubs. I respect their traditions and buy their apples.

But I have come to learn that no kitchen in the world is big enough to hold a Cub AND a Brownie.

As you may recall, Jane is our resident Brownie and has been since last September.

Naturally, she's come to look upon every dirty dish in the house as her own.

So along comes the upstart Cub who immediately tries to horn in on her good deed racket.

You can imagine the result.

Every night there's a fight after supper between our Cub and our Brownie over the dishes.

Last evening, for example, Richard grabbed a dirty dinner plate from Jane's hands and said, "It's my turn to do the dishes."

"It is not," Jane replied, snatching the plate back. "You set the table for dinner. It's my turn to do a good deed."

"Oh, yeah?" Richard shot back. "You made Mom's bed this morning."

"Yes, but you fed the dog and took her for a walk after school," Jane accused. "You know I'm trying to get my pet badge."

"I only fed the dog because you vacuumed the rug in the living room," Richard answered. "That's my job. Mom said so."

"Can I help it if you were outside helping Dad stack the firewood?" our Brownie sniffed.

"Give me that dirty plate, Jane."

"Try and make me . . ."

At that point my wife interrupted. "Stop fighting or I won't let either of you do the dishes," she warned.

Faced with that ultimatum, they agreed to share the good deed.

"But don't take more than your share of dirty dishes," Jane cautioned, "or I'll tell."

"I get to wipe the table!" Richard shouted triumphantly.

Jane's face dropped a mile.

Fortunately, Stephen (who is twelve) belongs to no group and never bugs us to do a good deed. Thank heaven!

There just isn't enough dust, cutlery, dog and firewood to keep THREE kids in badges.

Jane's ballet recital

Watching your daughter perform in her first dance recital is a moving experience, especially if she has brothers.

It's a recognized fact small boys don't like (1) dancing, (2) sitting still for longer than twelve seconds, and (3) sisters.

So an evening of dance is a challenge.

However, I was insistent.

If Jane (who is nine) could spend every Monday evening for the past two years at ballet, the least her brothers could do was clap.

We took our seats—me on the aisle, then Jane's mother, Richard (who is seven) and Stephen (who is twelve).

The house lights dimmed, the music (taped) began, the group of little girls came on stage and . . .

"How much longer?" Richard asked in a loud whisper.

"Shhh!" I informed him behind his mother's back.

"How much longer did Dad say?" Stephen demanded of Richard.

"Dad said, 'Shhh!'" Richard repeated.

"Shhh!" I said.

"When's Jane coming out?" Richard wanted to know as soon as the first number was almost half over.

"Soon."

"How soon?"

"Pretty soon."

"How soon is 'pretty soon'?"

"About thirty minutes."

"Can we leave as soon as Jane . . .?"

"Why don't we switch seats so you can sit next to Richard?" my wife suggested.

We did. It was now Jane's mother on the aisle, then me, Richard and Stephen.

"Ask Dad if I can go and get a drink," Stephen blared in Richard's ear.

"Stephen wants to know . . ."

"The answer is no," I replied.

"Dad says . . ."

"I heard him," Stephen grumbled.

"Ouch!" Richard exclaimed.

"What's going on?" I asked.

"Stephen pinched me."

"I did not."

"You did so — right on the arm."

"Both of you, stop it. And Richard, sit up in that seat. What are you doing on the floor?"

"I'm looking for something."

"For what?"

"My gum. When Stephen pinched me I dropped my gum."

"Shhh!" said a voice from the row behind.

"Sit between the boys," my wife whispered.

Richard and I switched seats.

The arrangement didn't last long, however, because Richard allegedly reached behind me and gave Stephen a shot.

"We've got to keep the boys as far apart as possible," my wife finally decreed.

For the last time we all got up and changed seats — Stephen on the aisle, my wife, me, then Richard.

Like I say, watching my daughter's first dance recital was truly one of the most moving experiences of my life.

First bra

Why is it we can remember the dark moments of life so clearly? Every word, every detail . . .

It was the morning of June twenty-sixth, precisely at 7:30 (which is when we always get up). And the members of the family were gathered around our bed.

That's because it was Jane's tenth birthday and she was opening her gifts.

A yo-yo from Stephen. Bubble gum from Richard (his

favourite flavour, graperoo). A sleeping bag from us. Cash from her grandparents.

And, from her grandparents in Montreal—a bra?

My God!

My little Jane! My little pigtailed Jane!

Why it seems only yesterday she was doing double dutches in the side drive.

And it was.

At first I thought it was all a ghastly mistake. My daughter is growing up but out is an entirely different direction.

Surely the bra was intended for Jane's mother, perhaps as a belated anniversary present. Or . . .

But no. The tag on the bra definitely indicated it was for Jane.

And Jane was clearly delighted even though at this stage, the only thing in double figures is her age.

Her brothers (especially Richard) howled at the sight of the bra and threatened to tell all their friends.

I put a stop to that.

My wife's parents may put ideas into Jane's head but they're not going to put ideas into the heads of a lot of ten-year-old boys, not if I can help it.

Later, Jane and I had a heart-to-heart talk and she agreed the bra was a little premature.

"I probably won't need one till I'm twelve or thirteen," she informed me.

"That's right," I responded. "Remember, your grandparents live in Montreal. Ten-year-olds mature much faster down there."

How much longer can I hold the floodgates against time?

I don't know.

Two weeks ago Richard (who is seven) came into the house filthy and my wife announced she was going to give him a bath.

Richard was mortified.

He finally agreed his mother could give him a bath under one condition—that he be permitted to wear swim trunks in the tub while she was doing the scrubbing.

What's happening to my babies?

Seven times eight

The most difficult thing to swallow around our house these days is supper.

No it has nothing to do with the quality of the food — my wife still cooks with the average of them.

And my appetite is sound as a yen.

So what's the problem?

My daughter Jane.

Jane is everything a father could hope for in a ten-year-old girl — tidy, polite and built straight as a stick.

However, our dream child does have a tiny flaw: mathematics.

More specifically, Jane doesn't know her times tables, especially her seven times table.

If you want to track it down further, Jane hasn't any idea what seven times eight equals.

Jane can tell you how much Karen's father makes (with bonuses), where babies come from, who in the neighbourhood wears support stockings and why the people at the corner have their house for sale.

For all I know, Jane may have the cure for the common cold tucked up the sleeve of her Charlie Brown sweatshirt.

But she doesn't know seven times eight.

So for the past week at the dinner table we've been firing math questions at Jane.

Last night, as usual, it began with the salad course.

"What's six times six?" I started.

"Thirty-six," Jane snapped back.

"What's three times eight?" her big brother demanded.

"Twenty-four," was the response.

"And five time nine?" I continued.

"Forty-five," Jane answered.

Then Jane's mother came in with the toughie. "And what's seven time eight?"

We all crossed our fingers.

"Fifty-two?" Jane suggested.

"No," we all shouted. "Fifty-six!"

"Jane, before we ruin another meal," I decreed, "I want you to write, 'Seven times eight is 56,' and I want you to write it 100 times."

This morning at breakfast I was able to see the fruits of my crash course.

"What's seven times eight?" I asked Jane.

"Fifty-six," she replied.

It was a wonderful moment.

Unfortunately, her brother spoiled it.

"What's eight times seven?" he asked.

"Fifty-two?" Jane suggested.

You're Number One

For some strange reason there's terrific rivalry among our children.

Sometimes it gets pretty ridiculous.

For example, the other day I caught the three of them arguing — get this — over who had the worst cold.

"My cold's worse than yours, Stephen," Jane was challenging.

"It is not," Stephen countered. "I've been sniffing and blowing my nose all day, so there."

"Well Mom says my face is flushed and I may have to stay home from school tomorrow. Nah!" Jane responded.

"Achoo!" Richard trumped.

That's when I stepped in.

"Who cares who has the worst cold?" I asked. "Is it worth fighting over? Why do you have to make comparisons all the time?"

The lecture (as the kids realized) was about to begin.

"I'm tired of listening to the three of you wrangle over who has the best this or the best that.

"Why do you do it — to get attention?

"You know your mother and I love you all — and equally. As far as we're concerned, you're all Number One. There is no Number Two or Number Three in this house.

"You all get the same treatment.

"So why the arguments?

"Supposing Jane's cold is the worst — and I'm just supposing. So what? Nobody will miss a meal or be forgotten just because Jane needs a little extra care.

"Next week it may be Stephen who has the cold — or Richard.

"But, in the long run, it all evens out.

"Do you understand what I'm saying?

"Don't always look around to see if your sister or brother is getting more dessert, a newer bicycle, a better math mark.

"You'll never be happy if you do that.

"Enjoy what you have — and for heaven's sake, stop competing with each other all the time."

I paused to let my words sink in.

Stephen finally broke the silence.

"I don't compete as much as Jane does," he said.

"You do so," Jane replied. "You compete more, and so does Richard."

"I do not."

"You do so . . ."

Our Christmas letter

Instead of cards, we're sending out a Christmas "letter" this year. This is how it goes.

Dear . . .

With another Yuletide upon us, it's time to bring you up to date on what happened at our house this past year.

The big news was that Gary didn't get the promotion at the office he was hoping for. Nor did he write a book, sign a TV contract or win a daily double at the racetrack.

But the year wasn't a total loss for Gary. He says the eczema on his right leg is just about cleared up and, with only one infected leg, he has cut his scratching time almost in half.

I tell him at his age he's lucky to have any itch at all, ha, ha.

Stephen became a teenager this year. Yes, he turned thirteen this month and he can't wait for his voice to change.

Personally, we feel the same way about his socks.

You probably wouldn't recognize Stephen any more. That's because of the big black thing growing out of his ear. It's called a telephone and he's on it all the time.

We suspected Stephen was growing up this past summer when he asked for his first can of deodorant. Then we discovered he was using it to spray ants in his bedroom. How he could ever find their little armpits we still don't know.

Jane didn't stand at the top of her class this year, but she knows the girl who did, which is something, I suppose.

Her big new is that she made an entire meal for the family and got her Brownie cooking badge. Our big news is that the family survived. Now we all know why the Gourmet does much Galloping.

Richard joined the YMCA on his eighth birthday and immediately signed up for a course in judo and karate.

As far as we can see, the only difference is that Richard still breaks furniture as fast as before, but now he's added grunts.

He certainly is active. And eat! Gary says Richard has the throat of a snake. If it's smaller than a garage, and dead, Richard can get it down with one gulp.

We just wish Richard's teacher would stop sending home notes telling us, "not to worry." We didn't — till we got the notes.

And that brings us to me.

Gary didn't surprise me this year with a new car, as I expected. (I'm still driving the 1966 Mini.) But I did get my fur coat remodelled. Now it's just what I've always wanted — a Persian lamb jacket that, in three years, will be old enough to vote.

I think those are the main highlights of this year so, from us and ours, to you and yours, happy holidays.

— The Lautens

P.S. We think Richard's second teeth are coming in crooked.

Nude is rude

I've seen all sorts of total strangers in the nude — Jane Fonda, Brigitte Bardot, Sally Kellerman, Jackie Onassis, even Burt Reynolds.

But I haven't seen my own children with their clothes off, at least not since they were babies.

Maybe a psychiatrist could explain it.

Why, when the rest of the world is parading around stark naked in magazines, movies, on the stage, why are my kids still hiding behind a towel?

Not only are they unwilling to accept frontal nudity, they reject aft as well.

Take Richard.

Richard is only nine but he absolutely refuses to disrobe in front of witnesses.

Just the other day, for example, I had to get something from the bathroom where Richard was having a bath.

"Can I come in?" I asked through the closed door.

"I'm having a bath," Richard shouted.

"It will only take a second," I promised.

"Couldn't it wait?" he wanted to know.

"No," I said.

"Well . . ."

"Richard, let me in."

"Okay," he surrendered.

"Richard, the door is locked," I grumbled, rattling the knob.

"Just a minute," he said.

I could hear him get out of the tub, take off the lock, and then make a mad dash back to the bath, to the foamiest corner, I'm sure.

"You can come in now," Richard announced. "But promise you won't look."

Richard's brother and sister are the same.

Richard's brother went through an entire volleyball season without once taking a shower at the school gym.

And Jane props a chair against her bedroom door even when she changes her mind.

For all I know, my children could be covered with suggestive tattoos, or have vines growing from their navels.

Frankly, I'm worried.

"Do you think it's normal for children to be so shy about their bodies?" I asked my wife last evening as we were undressing for bed.

"I can't hear you," she replied. "Can't you wait till you come out of the closet to tell me?"

Hugs

For many years, I've referred to my son Richard as "my partner, buddy and pal."

And he's responded in kind.

But lately there's been a change in our relationship, a sort of cooling off.

Specifically, Richard has been pretty stingy with his hugs lately. Sometimes I go days without one.

This is a great loss because my partner, buddy and pal dishes out neat hugs. Lots of squeeze and life.

Oh, he still likes me to scratch his back every night before he goes to bed, especially right in the middle.

However, the hugs are definitely in short supply.

This morning, I decided to broach the subject at the breakfast table.

"Richard, how come you don't hug me as often as you used to?" I asked, getting right to the point. "Aren't we still partners, buddies and pals?"

"Aw, dad," he replied, looking very embarrassed.

"Is it because you're nine and think you're too old for that 'kind of stuff'?"

Richard didn't answer, but I could see I had hit the nail on the head.

I then launched into a defence of hugs.

"Hugs are okay, Richard, no matter how old you are. Just because you hug some one doesn't mean you're a sis.

"Why, your mother and I hug, jet pilots hug, Darryl Sittler hugs, Prime Minister Trudeau hugs, your teacher hugs—I bet even Captain Kirk hugs.

"All it means is that you like someone and that isn't wrong."

Richard didn't look up so I kept on going.

"I know you're a seconder at Cubs and you weigh seventy-three pounds, and you don't need a nightlight any more, and you can stay up now until 9:30, and you can reach the top of the doorway if you stand on tiptoe.

"I know those things, Richard.

"But I'm forty-five and I need hugs. I especially need them at the end of a tough day when the world seems to be going nuts.

"So how about it?

"Can't you spare one hug a day? Not a crummy little hug. I mean the real thing so I can wrap my arms around you for a minute or two."

Richard finally looked into my face.

"Okay, Dad," he surrendered.

And then he added, "But not in front of my friends, okay?"

Obviously Richard is growing up and, I guess, so am I.

It's rotten.

You know what?
What?

Our Richard must think I'm the most stupid man in the entire world.

Every day he asks me the same question about 135 times — and I never have the answer.

The question is, "You know what, Dad?"

Richard uses it to start, carry on and finish all of his conversations.

He repeats the phrase so often I'm not sure if he's my son or my Sony.

Yesterday, for example, Richard broke into the house just bursting with good news.

"You know what, Dad?" he began.

"No, what," I replied.

"George and Peter and Michael and me have a new club, and you know what?"

"What?"

"We're building a neat clubhouse down the creek, out of wood, and you know what?"

"What?"

"We're going to make money by collecting bottles and papers and doing jobs around the house, and you know what?"

"What?"

"We're calling our club The Rats and I'm president, and you know what?"

"What?"

"Jane wants to join our club because we have a neat crest and a clubhouse and everything but she's a girl, and you know what?"

"What?"

"Girls aren't allowed to join the Rats, and you know what?"

It was at that point I surrendered.

As gently as possible, I explained to Richard that he should tell the story without interruptions.

"It's your story," I reminded. "And I'm dying to hear it."

"But can't you tell me without asking if I know what?"

"Richard, I don't know what. I don't expect to know what in the future. And, if I ever knew what in the past, I've forgotten now.

"So just tell me about The Rats and the clubhouse and Jane."

Richard was ready to continue with his story when I reminded him one more time.

"Remember," I said, "I don't know what."

"Well, Dad," Richard responded eagerly, "guess what?"

"What?" I said.

Flu facts

If you're a mother, these things are guaranteed to happen when one of your children gets the flu. . . .

The little one will wake you at three o'clock in the morning, breathe all over your face, and announce: "I think I'm going to be sick."

The flu victim will then dash for the bathroom—and not quite make it.

Your husband will sleep through the incident.

When you call the doctor in the morning, he won't be in; his nurse will be busy; but the girl on the switchboard will tell you there's a lot of it going around and she'll send over a prescription.

The messenger from the drug store will want $9.75, and not have change for a $10 bill.

The brothers of the flu victim will complain because the flu victim has the small TV in her bedroom, is getting all the ginger ale she wants, and doesn't have to go to school.

The flu victim will have barely enough strength to shout, "Mom!" seventy-eight times during your favourite daytime TV serial.

The family dog will spend the entire day on the flu victim's bed, taking turns licking the flu victim's popsicle.

The $9.75 prescription will upset the flu victim's stomach and it will cause the flu victim to throw up all over her bed.

Classmates will send the flu victim a get-well card.

The get-well card will be ten feet long and the flu victim will cry until you drop everything and paste it up on her bedroom wall.

When you're halfway up the stairs, the telephone will ring; it will be your husband asking how the flu victim is feeling.

The flu victim's brothers will ask if they can have the flu victim's bike if she dies.

The flu victim's temperature will peak (101.5) about a half hour before you're supposed to leave for the dinner party you've been looking forward to all week.

You'll have a domestic scene when your husband brings home a large chocolate bar, with nuts, as a special treat for the flu victim.

Your husband will say, no, he won't clean it up if anything happens.

The flu victim will say she's feeling a lot better, and can she, please, come downstairs and watch television with the rest of the family.

The flu victim, after a week at home, will go back to school.

You'll breathe a sigh of relief.

At three o'clock in the morning, the flu victim's brother will wake up, breathe all over your face and announce: "I think I'm going to be sick."

5

Zits Are the Creator's Way of Saying "Get Off the Phone"

A difficult stage

I'm going through a very difficult stage in life — my son's teens. I've been affected in dozens of ways.

For example, before Stephen turned thirteen and entered high school, I spoke normally; my pitch was steady, my tone firm.

Now my voice is changing.

It goes up and down a hundred times a day, especially during the dinner hour which Stephen spends on the telephone talking to his friends.

Stephen only has to ask why he can't drop French seventy-five to eighty times and my voice cracks all over the place.

Yesterday, while discussing why I didn't want him to blow up the basement with his chemical set, my voice hit a note high enough to shatter a beer mug.

In short, when I open my mouth these days, even I'm surprised at what comes out.

Stephen's teens have also ruined my complexion.

Just a few short months ago my skin was the envy of the office. It may sound immodest, but my cheeks were probably in the top ten in Metro Toronto.

Now I've got a hive as big as a dollar (a paper dollar) on my forehead.

It's from watching Stephen eat, and eat, and eat. Frankly, I can't afford it. I have the terrible feeling he's digging my grave (pauper's) with his teeth.

Another thing I've discovered since Stephen turned thirteen is that I've become terribly insecure about sex.

When Stephen was little, I had no hesitation about catching his mother as she bent over the dinner table and giving her a pat on the shoulder.

Not any more.

Stephen has taken all sorts of courses on family life and now I'm sure he can spot a fondle a mile away.

So I keep my hands to myself. If he finds out patting girls on the shoulder is loads of fun, it won't be from me.

Shy?

I don't know how to act around his friends any more. They don't seem interested in talking about beef prices or how many miles to the gallon I'm getting on the Vega.

And they're too big to offer a cookie while they wait for Stephen.

Fortunately, I'm not going through this difficult time in my life alone.

Stephen realizes the teen years are difficult ones for a father so he is being extra patient.

Just the other day he gave me this comforting thought, "I won't be a teenager forever, Dad."

Thank God he's understanding.

For your ears only

My wife called me aside a few days ago and whispered words that have caused fathers to weep since time began.

"Your daughter wants her ears pierced," she said.

"You mean our little Jane who only yesterday was skipping rope in the driveway, carrying around a rag doll wherever she went, and learning to tie her own shoelaces?" I gasped.

"That's the one," my wife answered. "What do you think?"

"But she's only a child," I protested. "It can't be more than a year ago — two at most — that I changed her diapers, walked her after her two a.m. feeding, burped her over my shoulder . . ."

"Jane is twelve years old and you never did those things. That was my job."

"That's beside the point," I insisted. "Jane's too young to have her ears pierced."

"Her friend, Karen, has her ears pierced."

"Pierced ears are just the beginning," I warned. "Next come the tattered jeans, music blaring from some top forty radio station, dates with boys with long necks and spotty complexions, a subscription to *Cosmopolitan*, green eye shadow — God, there's no telling where it will end!"

"All she wants is to pierce her ears. My ears are pierced, you know."

"Sure, but you were twenty and married when you had it done. At twenty, you're mature enough to handle stud, dangly, even hoop earrings. But Jane just got out of Brownies.

"Can you imagine what would happen if she got into a fight with one of her brothers and they got a finger in one of her earrings? They'd stretch her ear lobe down to her waist," I said. "Or else they'd snap it until she got dizzy."

"I think you're right," my wife replied.

"You do?"

"Yes, but I wanted to make sure how you felt before Jane talked to you. She's waiting outside now."

"Why do I have to tell her?"

"Because you're her father and you feel strongly about a twelve-year-old getting her ears pierced."

"Okay, tell Jane to come in," I said, "and leave us alone."

After a twenty-minute talk with Jane, I emerged with the announcement, "I've got some good news and some bad news."

"What's the bad news?" my wife asked.

"After hearing how much it means to Jane, I've agreed she can get her ears pierced."

"What's the good news?"

"In return, Jane has given me her word she won't get married until she's at least thirteen."

I always was a hard bargainer.

How you get zits

Our Jane is thirteen and all she wants from life at this time is a good complexion. Every morning she examines her face for blemishes, or zits, as her friends call them.

Just the other day she asked me how a person gets zits and, naturally, I didn't lose the opportunity to make a few points.

This, I told Jane, is what causes a bad complexion:

1. Listening to Elton John records at full volume while father is trying to read the paper, nap, or breathe.

2. Sitting on cold benches at the shopping plaza.

3. Leaving the house in the morning without making your bed.

4. Karate-chopping a person of the opposite sex, like a

brother, across the throat while he is eating a grilled cheese sandwich at the kitchen table.

5. Neglecting math homework.

6. Being on the telephone more than twelve times in any one-hour period.

7. Wearing eye shadow.

8. Not walking the dog when it's your turn.

9. Allowing a person selling religious tracts into the house and saying that your parents are home and you'll get them.

10. Locking yourself in the bathroom for twenty minutes in the morning when your father is in a hurry to get to work.

11. Riding on the back of a moped with anybody, but especially if he has metal studs in his clothes and wears a T-shirt that has rude words printed on the front.

12. Having more than fifteen friends in your bedroom at one time.

13. Not calling at four o'clock to say where you are.

14. Tight jeans.

15. Tight anything else.

16. Sleeping in past eleven o'clock on Saturday morning.

17. Riding a ten-speed bike that cost 100 bucks over curbs.

18. Getting up from the dinner table and not taking the dirty dishes over to the sink, rinsing them off, and then loading the dishwasher.

19. Asking more than fifteen times why you can't stay up and watch the midnight horror movie with Kim.

20. Bursting into your parents' bedroom without knocking.

21. Changing underwear, nail polish, "best" girl friend or locker partner more than three times a day.

22. Popping the retainer in and out of your mouth while other people are eating.

23. Hitting a tennis ball against the side of the house.

24. Not putting things back where they belong.

25. And finally, eating greasy food.

Needless to say, I expect to come up with other causes of bad complexion in the days ahead, but this, at least, is a start.

Rah deal

Our Stephen came home early from school yesterday and of course his mother wanted to know what was wrong.

"Nothing," he said. "They're having a rally in the gym for the game tonight so I came home."

"Why didn't you stay?" his mother asked.

"Aw, Mom," he replied, screwing up his face in disgust.

Stephen considers pep rallies uncool, like wearing a hat, kissing relatives and taking public transportation, and his mother knows it.

"You should have more school spirit," his mother persisted.

Perhaps I should explain that Stephen's mother was one of those people who went through high school with a letter stencilled on the seat of her knickers.

In fact, if it hadn't been for my wife, when the Saltfleet High cheerleaders turned their backs to the crowd and bent over, they would have spelled S-L-T-F-L-E-E-T. Her "A" made all the difference.

Stephen, however, is unimpressed.

"Mom, I'm not going to hang around the school yelling my head off like a loony."

That was too much for my wife. She knelt on one knee and started to go through the old Saltfleet locomotive: *"Give me an S, give me an A, give me an L, give me a T . . ."*

"Mom, stop!" Stephen begged.

". . . give me an F, give me an L, give me an E . . ."

"Mom, people will see you!"

". . . give me an E, give me a T—Saltfleet! Saltfleet! Rah, rah, rah!"

Stephen groaned and buried his head under a chesterfield cushion, but his mother wasn't finished.

"Blue, white, gold; blue, white, gold; they're the colours we uphold; hit 'em high, hit 'em low; Saltfleet, Saltfleet, go, go, go!"

"Stop, please!" Stephen pleaded, mortified beyond description.

"We're not rough, we're not tough, but, boy, are we determined!" his mother shouted, putting on her cute-as-a-button smile and gazing into a non-existent grandstand.

"Mom!" our teenaged son yelled. "Don't!"

Mom, however, kept sss-boom-bah-ing and phi-ki-sighing up and down the living room floor.

"Themistocles, Thermopylae, the Peloponnesian War; X-squared, Y-squared, H_2SO_4; the French verbs, the Latin verbs, Archimedes' Law . . ."

In desperation, Stephen turned to me and with a look of helplessness in his eyes said, "Dad, can't you say something to Mom?"

"Cartwheels!" I bellowed. "How about a cartwheel?"

Poor Stephen. Next pep rally he'll stay at school, where its comparatively quiet.

Father of the babysitter

Life has cast me in a new role — that of father of the babysitter.

Believe me, looking for a babysitter (a job I had for years) is easier than having one right in your own home.

Our Jane got a call from a couple seeking her services as a babysitter after one of Jane's friends had recommended her.

Well, Jane is thirteen, responsible, and a graduate of the neighbourhood YMCA's babysitting course.

But, up till then, she had never babysat anyone but her younger brother. That is, she had babysat, but not for cash money.

So Jane's mother and I were a little nervous about her first babysitting job.

"What do we know about this couple?" Jane's mother asked.

"Are they decent, reliable people? After all they do live almost four blocks away."

Jane admitted she had never met her prospective employers, but her friend Tammie said they were wonderful people.

Tammie, I pointed out, also approves of Elton John, and I wouldn't want my daughter spending the evening in his pad.

Anyway, the deal was made and Jane agreed to babysit last Saturday evening after a promise from her employers that they wouldn't be late. (As Jane's Al Eagleson, I felt that was an important point to include in her contract.)

When the car pulled into the driveway to pick up Jane, all members of our family raced to the picture window.

"Get the licence number of the car," I ordered Jane's older brother as I smiled through the window at the fellow behind the wheel. "And take down the guy's description, too."

Jane's brother nodded, and did as he was told.

"What do you think of him?" I asked Jane's mother as we both waved, still smiling, at our daughter as she got into the car.

"At least he isn't wearing a black cape," Jane's mother replied, showing all sorts of teeth at the stranger.

"Isn't there someone in the back seat?" I demanded, beaming my warmest grin at my daughter's first babysitting customer.

"Yes, it looks like two little girls," Jane's mother shot back. "They must be the children she's babysitting."

"That's a good sign," I replied as the car backed out and drove away, and I made a mental note of the car's colour and the luggage rack on top.

Of course we stayed home ourselves, near the telephone. We wanted to be available if Jane needed us. After all, one of her charges could swallow something, or refuse to go to bed.

Shortly after eleven o'clock, the same car drove up to our house and Jane got out.

All of us lined up by the window again, smiled some more — and then whipped to the door to greet Jane.

"How did it go?" I asked.

Jane said it was fine. She didn't have any trouble, she made $3.25 and (in response to my question) no, she didn't smell anything on the man's breath.

In short, Jane enjoyed it.

It appears I'm destined to spend a lot of my Saturday nights smiling through my picture window, taking down licence numbers and staying home.

Frown at the birdie

The fastest way to wipe the smile off a boy's face is to take his picture.

Our Richard has just brought home his class photograph and, wouldn't you know it, there he is in the back corner, looking (again) like an escapee from Kingston Pen.

He's wearing a tatty jean-jacket, a T-shirt that appears to be a veteran of 345 performances with a road company of *A Streetcar Named Desire*, and a scowl that could sour powdered cream.

In short, any casual observer would get the impression that this is a kid who'd steal rubber tips from the canes of little old ladies.

But how can I complain? Every other boy in the picture looks exactly the same.

At a rough guess I'd say the boys' rows in the photograph represent at least $15,000 in orthodontics, but not one of the little fellows is showing so much as a tooth, let alone an entire corrected overbite.

If I didn't know better, I'd say they had been taking glowering lessons and were under orders not to smile on threat of death.

Meanwhile, in the other two rows of the class photograph we have sixteen winsome, bright, cheerful, sunny little girls, each one looking as if she had just stepped out of a Jello ad.

Hair brushed, dresses pressed, smiles in place, they exude sweetness, charm and cleanliness.

What is it about a Kodak that turns little girls into angels, and does everything but put a number under the faces of their male classmates?

Our Richard is in grade six, so this is his seventh class photograph and in each one he could pass the screen test if Hollywood was looking for someone to play John Dillinger.

And our Jane (who is in grade eight) has never been snapped from a bad angle, or caught with anything but laugh lines around her eyes.

Having lived with both since day one, I know the truth of the matter in each case is somewhere in the middle.

There are days when Jane can deliver a vicious knee to the small of the back with the best of them and Richard has been known to break out in a warm grin at the breakfast table (Jane doesn't usually talk till noon), and even change his underwear without being told.

But you'd never guess it from their class pictures.

Instead of pouring millions into research to develop pictures in sixty seconds, give us brighter colours, and make it possible to take photographs in the dark, it would be wonderful if the camera industry would concentrate its efforts on turning out a lens that doesn't make every little boy look like a hood on the lam.

Just once I'd like a picture of our Richard I didn't have to hide in the dresser drawer.

Jane bares some

Excuse me if I look pale. I've just seen our Jane's graduation dress. It's stunning, chic, glamorous — and those are just a few of the things wrong with it.

Believe me, I realize Jane is almost fourteen (next month) and that a person doesn't graduate from public school every day and get her final report card at a buffet-dance.

But bare shoulders?

Mind you, I've only seen the first fitting and Jane's mother still has some sewing to do, but I've been informed a higher neckline isn't scheduled.

Of course I realize Jane is growing up, but why can't Jane and her mother realize that a daughter's first formal is a big moment in a father's life?

I'm not sure if I'm ready to accept a halter top, *décolletage*, and a gown that shows my Jane's shoulder blades.

I was rather hoping for some prim bit of business with long sleeves, a turtleneck, and a loose-fitting top, something you could wear to a Sunday school rally or a Brownie picnic.

But this number makes Jane look, let me say it right out — attractive.

It's got a fitted waist, these awfully tiny shoulder straps, and a design at the front that could have come from France, for all I know.

I've even been informed (because I asked) that Jane doesn't intend to wear a T-shirt or blouse underneath. Where there's no dress, there'll be Jane!

Why couldn't Jane and her mother have broken the news to me gently, shown me something first that exposed Jane's elbow, or perhaps even a flash of her Adam's apple.

But to go from blue jeans and a Snoopy sweatshirt to this in one giant leap is too much.

Believe me, I'm no old silly who wants his little girl to stay a little girl. Of course I want her to grow up and wear pullovers and one-piece bathing suits, but not just yet.

After all, Jane is still, well, a little girl.

Didn't she bury a tiny bird in the backyard last week with a carefully printed tombstone that read, "Here lies the body of a little bird that never got a chance to fly. God bless him."

Does that sound like a person who should be going to her public school graduation in a formal that shows her shoulders?

I mean, she should still be skipping in the side drive, and asking me to tuck her in at night, and making leaf charts, and

begging for a few more paragraphs of *Cinderella* before turning out the light, and asking for pony rides on Sunday afternoon, and wiggling baby teeth for my benefit at the dinner table, and . . .

How can it be that my little Jane is wearing formal dresses, and going to her first real dance, and talking about somebody named Wayne or Donald, or some such?

How can it be that fourteen years (next month) have gone so fast?

No can do

It's a sad day when a father is unmasked to his daughter as a mere mortal and not some sort of superhero who can make all her dreams come true with a snap of the old fingers.

Up till now I've been able to preserve the image with our Jane.

No noise in the basement, snowboot zipper, ketchup bottle top, rough friend, nor dreamy outfit was beyond my ability to investigate, open, unscrew, reprimand, or provide. Galahad was my middle name, and the pedestal my address.

Ha!

One word from my Feather (as I called her for years) and I would fly into action with my unbelievable courage, strength, cheque book, etc. And her problem would be solved, or at least glossed over.

However, I am undone.

Jane has come up with a request which even this devoted slave cannot answer.

Well, it isn't exactly a request but the other day I asked Jane: If she could have anything in the world she wanted, what would she ask for?

Without blinking so much as an eye (blue), Jane, who is only a few months short of her fifteenth birthday, replied, "Hips."

"But you've got hips," I pointed out.

"I mean, you know, real hips," Jane responded.

Alas, Daddy does know. Jane wants to be stacked, built, to have the kind of figure that causes truck drivers to pile their semis into telephone poles, and think it was worth it.

Sob! Yes, my little Jane wants all of that.

Personally, I'm opposed; in truth, if I had my way, I'd cut out a couple of curves Jane already has. The last thing a father needs is a knockout daughter.

If Jane wants hips today, what will it be tomorrow — a waist, creamy shoulders, for heaven's sake, terrific thighs? Where will it end — and, please, don't answer that.

How simple it was in the old days to be Jane's hero. All it required was a maplenut cone, a boost up to the water fountain, the skill required to untangle a shoelace, the answer to seven times eight.

But hips?

What happened to my little girl who only wanted me to find the eyes to her doll, and stick them back in? Where is the child who only asked to have her brother's face removed from her elbow?

I may be a little longer in the tooth but I can still give a horsey ride on my foot, cross my eyes (always a hit in the past), provide change for the bubble-gum machine, or sit through a Walt Disney movie featuring a dog that talks, performs nuclear experiments, or reads minds.

Is all that talent to go to waste now?

Can't I bring down the house any more by pretending the din-din on the spoon is an airplane? Has my daughter lost interest in looking up my nose when we have company? Is it no longer enough to pull out a sleigh from behind the back as a surprise, or a Snoopy barrette from an inside overcoat pocket?

Hips?

I get the impression that this Daddy has just fallen flat on his abracadabra.

Well, Olympus was nice while it lasted.

Will people talk?

I never thought I'd live to see the day when a little thing like a kiss from a gorgeous female, delivered in broad daylight in front of a few hundred witnesses, would leave me blushing and giggly.

But that is exactly what happened the other morning on a busy downtown street corner in the middle of the rush hour.

What is significant is that the kiss was planted on my cheek by my daughter, Jane.

Ordinarily I can take a smacker from family without so much as a blink, but Jane has become quite a looker this past year.

(Can you imagine the coincidence? My two sons are the best-looking boys in the world, and my daughter has a clear lead among females. Surely that's something for *The Guinness Book of Records*.)

In any case, Jane and I were walking down the street and, when it came time to make a left to school, instead of the usual wave and "See ya," Jane gave me the embrace.

Mind you, it was my birthday.

But Jane was just in mid-pucker when the thought entered my mind: Will the people witnessing this scene realize Jane is my daughter, and I'm her father, and, well, it isn't one of those May-December things?

When Jane was just a kid (approximately six months ago) I could have thrown myself into the peck with gusto. Other than the concern about whether Jane might be eating licorice and leave a mark on my face, or get bubble gum on an eyebrow, I had no deep worry.

However, Jane is about as tall as her mother now, has a dimple guaranteed to drive men wild, and possesses the good legs that are a tradition in our family, even among the women.

Why, just the other day Jane's mother reported our daughter got "two toots and a woo" on the way home from school, the toots being saucy blasts from horns (a panel truck and a moped) and the "woo" being the comment of a motorist waiting for a traffic light to change.

So you see it's not just the biased report of a proud father, although I spotted her good looks even that first day in the nursery when she was sucking the back of her hand, and needed changing.

However, that is all past. What about my role in the future as Jane's father?

In a dim light, and at a distance, if I haven't had too difficult a day at the office, I could easily pass for eighty-five or eighty-six.

Should a man looking that age risk his reputation and accept kisses on the forehead from a young doll who reads Sixteen magazine, no longer has feet in her pyjamas, and gets toots and woos on the way home from high school?

Should he put his arm around this young dish when they cross an intersection, share a joke in a department store, carry the family capon home from market Saturday morning, or do a dozen other things together?

Well, should he?

Yes.

My days as the Number One man in Jane's life are numbered, and I'm going to enjoy them while I can.

A twelve-year-old boy is . . .

Many of us have, were, or know, a twelve-year-old boy. In case you've forgotten what a twelve-year-old boy is like, let me refresh your memory.

A twelve-year-old boy forgets to bring home inoculation notices from school.

A twelve-year-old boy never gives his sister enough room in the back seat of the car.

A twelve-year-old boy is a master at moving his lips during music class at school, and during hymns at church, and never making a sound.

A twelve-year-old boy wants his mother to buy a certain kind of cereal because there's a plastic rocket launcher inside.

A twelve-year-old boy doesn't like to eat the cereal that comes with the plastic rocket launcher.

A twelve-year-old boy doesn't like it when somebody thinks it's his sister talking on the telephone.

A twelve-year-old boy goes to his first school dance, and then climbs up the basketball backboard to get away from the girls.

A twelve-year-old boy cleans up his room by stuffing everything under his bed.

A twelve-year-old boy always has a friend whose mother lets him keep gerbils in a cardboard box in the basement.

A twelve-year-old boy never wants to grow up and be an accountant.

A twelve-year-old boy hangs around his big brother's friends whenever they'll let him.

A twelve-year-old boy cannot read without putting his feet up on the back of the chesterfield.

A twelve-year-old boy, when asked why his teacher wants to see his mother or father, replies, "Beats me."

A twelve-year-old boy has feet that sweat a lot.

A twelve-year-old boy can bruise your forehead, step on your foot, knock over an end table and spill your coffee just while giving you a goodnight kiss.

A twelve-year-old boy hates it when the Bionic Man embraces a woman, or any of that other mush.

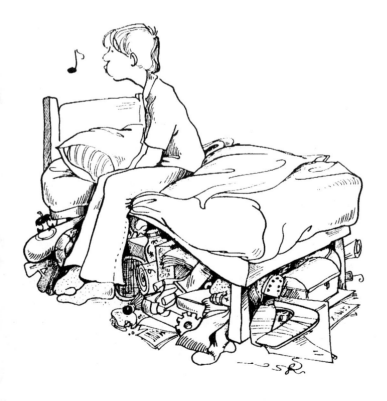

A twelve-year-old boy won't wear the sweater Aunt Maude sent him.

A twelve-year-old boy asks for the comic section first so he can read Spiderman.

A twelve-year-old boy would just as soon not discuss the Life Course he's taking at school from the health teacher.

A twelve-year-old boy insists he didn't have anything to eat after four at his friend's house.

A twelve-year-old boy thinks it's dumb to wash any part of him that doesn't show.

A twelve-year-old boy always leaves just enough milk in the pitcher so somebody else has to get up and refill it.

A twelve-year-old boy likes to look at himself in the mirror, and make faces, when he's sure nobody else is watching.

A twelve-year-old boy rolls up his art work in a ball and brings it home in his hat.

A twelve-year-old boy doesn't understand all the fuss about race, religion and that stuff.

A twelve-year-old boy always orders the green ice cream with the brown bits.

A twelve-year-old boy takes French because his parents say he has to.

A twelve-year-old boy sometimes, if you're lucky, will let you give him a hug, provided nobody's looking.

A twelve-year-old boy is pretty special.

Hair today, gone tomorrow

There are all sorts of landmarks in your son's life—his first words, his first faltering steps, his first tinkle in the proper facilities, his first day at school, his first ride (without help) on a two-wheeler, his first night away from home.

Well, our Stephen (who is seventeen) has reached another important first: His first moustache.

Several weeks ago he announced his intention to grow what we used to call a cookie duster.

Something neat and aristocratic in the David Niven tradition, not one of those long, flowing jobs that look as if they need a quick run-through with the Lawn Boy.

Of course his parents were crushed.

Our little tot with a moustache? It seems only yesterday we were asking him to stick out his tongue and lick the hankie so we could take the smudge off his face before meeting Grandma.

Stephen, the little mischief who, when walking down the street, would suddenly relax, hang between Mommy and Daddy's hands, and demand a swing?

Yes, that Stephen.

(Come to think of it, it was Stephen's brother, Richard, who liked to drop like a rock and pull your shoulder out of its socket when you least expected it, but I don't want to go back and rub out that second-to-last paragraph.)

However, we took the news bravely and said whatever Stephen wanted to put on his lip was okay with us just as long as I didn't have to feed it, and his mother did not have to vacuum it Saturdays.

After assuring us on both counts, Stephen then proceeded to grow his moustache, sort of.

After skipping the area in question with his Remington for a couple of days, Stephen asked if we could see any sign of a luxurious growth sprouting up.

Frankly, he had a better moustache the last time we had grape drink, but we did not want to dash his hopes so we said the bristles were clearly visible when he stood in the light a certain way, and called him Santa Claus.

Each morning we went through the same ritual and his mother went so far as to say "ouch!" when he kissed her on his way to school, and suggested she may have been scratched by his stubble, which pleased him enormously.

Deep in my heart, though, I knew Stephen's dream was doomed. He has my complexion and colouring, and I couldn't grow enough hair on my lip to make a toupee for a gnat.

We're just not the hairy kind, a characteristic that made my mother very proud and caused her to hint that anyone so smooth of cheek must have royal blood somewhere in his veins. Kings, apparently, only have to shave every other day.

Undoubtedly you've guessed the end of this rather sad story.

Apparently Stephen finally saw the hopelessness of his cause because yesterday at breakfast he informed his loved ones, plus his brother and sister, "I've decided to shave off my moustache."

With all of the compassion at her command, his mother asked, "When are you going to do it?"

"I did it two days ago," Stephen said accusingly.

Apparently that last "ouch!" wasn't necessary.

Dating rules

The most pressing question on our Jane's mind is: When will she be old enough to date? Our daughter will be 15 in a few weeks and wants to know.

To answer her question, I've drawn up a little table.

The age Jane can date is . . .

If the guy rides a Harley, wears an SS helmet, leather boots and jeans that have not been washed since 1973, and has a disgusting tattoo on his arm: 87.

If he carries a package of ciggies in the sleeve of his T-shirt and considers *Laverne and Shirley* an intellectual experience: 78.

If he's a member of a political party dedicated to the overthrow of the government, and makes bombs in his basement for a hobby: 71.

If he has a van with "Don't laugh, mister, your daughter may be inside" painted on the side, with more than two words misspelled: 64.

If he plays his transistor on the beach or in the park loud enough to be heard by people with serious hearing problems, and low-flying pleasure craft: 57.

If he has more than twenty-eight pounds of hair: 51.

If he has shaved his head: 50½.

If he belongs to a religion that requires the sacrificing of goats in the mountains, painting your face blue, or dancing on a street corner while playing a saxophone: 45.

If he talks out loud in movies, rattles his popcorn bag, makes rude remarks during the love scenes, and slouches in his seat during the playing of O Canada: 41.

If he gave his mother a litre bottle of Baby Platypus last Mother's Day, and a set of blue plastic wine glasses: 39.

If he wears more cologne than his date: 37.

If he considers it a big night out to go downtown and look at the window displays of revolvers, rifles, war surplus machine guns, grenades, etc., or just make skid marks in the nearest school yard with his VW: 32.

If it's his dream to grow up and one day open a string of body rub parlours: 31.

If he got less than four on his last algebra exam: 29.

If the picture he gives his girl friend for their wallet has a number at the bottom, and includes both a front and side view: 28.

If he makes derogatory remarks about Australians: 27.

If he picks up the family pet, Sarah, by the neck, tail, or the hair in the armpits, and says it doesn't hurt her: 25.

If he wears earrings, or cheers for the Toronto Argos: 22.

If his hockey teammates call him "Animal," and the coach only lets him on the ice when the score is 7-1, either way: 21.

If he knows more than 47 waiters in the downtown area by first name, or is referred to as "Cold Hands" by more than eleven topless barmaids: 19.

If he breaks out laughing when his date's father talks about how difficult things were when he was young, and how he used to walk twelve miles to school and back: 18.

Finally, Jane can date at fifteen — IF the boy's name is Prince Andrew, and I have a talk with his mum and dad first to make sure he comes from a nice family.

What could be fairer than that?

Suits me to a "T"

Our Jane is at the age (fifteen) when she considers herself mature enough to wear a T-shirt with printing on it.

Daddy is not so sure.

Most of the slogans I've read on T-shirts I wouldn't want plastered across my daughter's chest. They have far too much, well, tang.

However, I am not an unreasonable man.

I've told Jane she can wear a T-shirt, provided she clears its message first with me.

Is that unfair?

Of course not.

In fact, here's a rather lengthy list of slogans I've already approved for Jane's T-shirts:

Born To Be Home By 10 o'clock
10:30 At The Latest

Cocoa Power

No, Non, Nyet And Nein

My Father Has A Black Belt
And A Vicious Temper

If You Can Read This
You're Much Too Close

Our Family Dog, Thor, Thinks
Strangers Are Delicious

No, We've Never Met

The Waltz Is A Lovely Dance,
Don't You Agree?

Vatican City Beach

My Cousin's In The RCMP,
What's Yours Do?

Don't Read This

A Knee Delivered To The Pit
Of A Smart Aleck's Stomach
Can Hurt Awfully

Animal's Sister

My Scream Can Be Heard
For Over Two Miles

Yes, I Can Date
But First You Have To Ask
My Daddy, Clark Kent

Did You Know Kissing Can
Cause Concussion?

My Godfather's Name Is Vito

Mormon Tabernacle Choir

If You Want A Good Time,
Don't Call Me

Is Your OHIP Paid Up?

Little Sisters Of Charity
Motorcycle Club

No Foolin'

One, Two, Three Strikes —
You're Out

Philadelphia Flyers'
Ladies Auxiliary

No Speak Romance

I Sell Life Insurance

This T-shirt Is Equipped
With A Burglar Alarm

If You're Planning A Wild Party
Phone 324-2222

There you have it — about thirty slogans I'd be willing to have printed on our Jane's T-shirts. Surely she can find one to her liking.

By the way, that phone number is for the Toronto Police Department. I hope the sergeant on duty won't mind taking Jane's calls.

Richard speaks!

Our Richard is thirteen and I've come to a landmark decision: He's now old enough to talk directly to clerks in stores.

As any parent will immediately realize, it's another watershed in our lives.

Up till last Saturday, the "baby" in our family always conversed with salespersons through his mother or father.

Of course there's nothing wrong with his voice and he does have a tongue.

But traditionally that's how it's done. In the presence of a parent, children and clerks never speak to each other.

On the weekend, however, I took Richard to the neighbourhood department store for a pair of slippers: We went straight to the shoe section.

"Yes?" the clerk asked.

"My son needs a pair of slippers," I informed the clerk.

"What size?" he asked me.

"What size do you take?" I asked Richard, who was standing right beside me.

"I think about an eight," Richard stated.

I looked at the clerk "About an eight."

"What colour slipper would you like?" was his next question.

"What colour, Richard?" I inquired.

"Blue," Richard answered smartly.

"Blue," I told the clerk.

"Any particular style?" the clerk asked me.

"Any particular style?" I demanded of my son.

"No, just as long as they don't have slippery soles and won't mark the floor," Richard said.

"No," I responded to the clerk, "just as long as they don't have slippery soles and won't mark the floor."

The clerk nodded and went into the back room, returning in a moment or two with several boxes of slippers. He slipped one on Richard's foot.

"How is that for fit?" he asked.

"How is that for fit?" I relayed to Richard.

"It's a little tight," Richard commented.

"It's a little tight," I informed the salesman.

The clerk slipped it off. "Will he be wearing socks with the slippers? Those are pretty heavy socks he has on," he commented.

"Will you be wearing socks with the slippers? Those are pretty heavy socks you have on," I passed on to Richard.

"I like heavy socks," Richard stated

"He likes heavy socks," I repeated.

"We'll try a half-size larger," the clerk suggested. "How's this?" he asked me after putting it on Richard's foot.

"How's . . ."

I broke in mid-sentence. I looked at Richard—128 pounds, taller than his mother at five feet, six inches—and I made the breakthrough.

"Richard, you tell the clerk," I said. "You two can talk to each other."

Richard was taken aback but he looked at the clerk and said, "Fine."

"Better try the other one," the clerk advised Richard directly.

Within five minutes it was all over, and it didn't sound as if the sale were taking place in an echo chamber.

It's the end of an era, I guess.

Next time we're at a restaurant, I'll even have to let Richard give his own order to the waiter. That's the ultimate.

I just hope he takes the hint if, when he orders the expensive filet, he feels a kick under the table.

Fathers know second best

Every occupation seems more complicated these days, but no job has increased in difficulty more than that of father.

A few years ago a dad had to teach his son how to catch a ball, make a wooden sword from two sticks, tie a tie, and keep his head in so he didn't fall out a car window on the way to Niagara Falls.

That was about it.

Thanks to the tremendous advances made in the male lifestyle, that has all changed.

This morning, for example, Stephen (who is eighteen) came to the breakfast table with wet hair. He had just washed it.

"Why don't you use the hair dryer in my room?" I asked.

"When I use the hair dryer, it blows up my hair and I look as if I've put my finger in an electric socket," he said.

"It won't," I advised, "if you leave your hair a little damp, put the dryer on a cool setting for a few seconds, and then brush your hair."

See what I mean?

A father has to know these things if he hopes to raise a sturdy son who can cope in the modern world.

Junior doesn't want you to show him the secret of whittling a stick, or playing "My Old Kentucky Home" on a harmonica he bought for fifty cents at the corner store.

He couldn't care less that you have a terrific card trick that nobody can figure out.

So you can make a toy tank out of a thread spool, a matchstick and an ordinary elastic band?

Big deal.

What a son wants to know now is if he can get away with Springtime in the Rockies after-shave on a heavy date, or is Tahitian Musk definitely better for after-five wear?

Yes, yes, it's wonderful to know all the choruses to "Row, Row, Row Your Boat," but what goes with a brown corduroy jacket, tan slacks, and an expensive floral-patterned Mr. Harold sports shirt? Pukka beads? A plain 10K gold chain with astrological sign pendant? Or is the basic silver rape whistle more fitting?

A father is supposed to have the answers to these difficult questions.

Can you fix a pocket calculator? Do you know a decent place to get hair styled inexpensively including shampoo? Will a headband make a person prematurely bald? Do you know how to advance a calendar watch?

Does medical research have anything significant to say about tight pants? What's the weather like during the March school break in Moscow? Will a beef bourguignon stain come out of a surplus German army combat shirt with water? How much would it cost to motorcycle across South America?

Believe me, playing father gets tougher every year.

Just a few days ago Stephen bought a blue dinner jacket with brocaded lapels from a discount clothing store for fourteen dollars, and they tossed in a dress shirt (with 1962 style collar) as a bonus.

The next day Stephen asked if it was too dressy to wear to Mr. Thornton's class, and if it would look right with his khaki pants — the ones held up by the leather belt with the World War I army buckle.

I said it would be fine but, between you and me, it was strictly a guess.

Until Stephen asks me something simple, like how to make a beanie out of an old fedora, I'm basically winging it as a father.

A date's dad . . .

Thanks to our Jane (who will be sixteen next month) I've assumed a new role in life, that of father of the date.

Of course it's strange to me but so far I've found out . . .

A father of the date, when a boy arrives at the front door, does not yell up the stairs, "You'd better move your cheeks. Dreamboat is here."

A father of the date does not bring out baby pictures.

A father of the date does not ask a boy to take off his shoes before he comes in, even if the mother of the date has just waxed the floors and is in the mood to kill at the first sign of dirt.

A father of the date does not make pimple jokes.

A father of the date does not ask a boy about his parents' marital status, his marks in math, if he's started to shave yet, or what kind of a career he has in mind for himself when he gets out of school and is able to support a family.

A father of the date does not tell stories about how tough things were when he was young, and how he had to get the date's mother home by 11:30 when they dated.

A father of the date does not straighten a boy's necktie on first meeting, or offer him a Kleenex for his pocket if he sniffs.

A father of the date does not armwrestle, attempt to lift said date over his head in a display of strength, or make pointed remarks about Donny Osmond being too young to marry.

A father of the date does not refuse to let the happy couple out of the house until the boy gives his word that the van parked out front is not his.

A father of the date does not notice braces on teeth.

A father of the date does not send the date's little brother into the front room every fifteen minutes to see what's going on.

A father of the date definitely does not ask a boy if he'd like to watch the Stanley Cup playoffs on TV with him rather than going out.

A father of the date does not let his knees buckle visibly when he learns which movie the boy wants to take his daughter to.

A father of the date does not say John Travolta stinks.

A father of the date does not mix up boyfriends and call them, gasp, by the wrong name.

A father of the date does not examine corsages for price tags.

A father of the date does not greet a boy while wearing a sweater with the elbows out, even if it is a favourite.

A father of the date does not make a big scene just because the stereo is on full and the heavy furniture on the third floor is vibrating.

A father of the date does not peek out the front window for a better look.

A father of the date does not flick porch lights.

A father of the date does not holler down the stairs when it's just a little after midnight, "It's time your friend went home."

And, finally, a father of the date does not add, "After your friend has gone, let the dog out in the backyard for a whizz."

Being a father of the date is quite a challenge.

Handling teen calls

The other evening the telephone rang and a lovely female voice asked, "Is Stephen there?"

As it happened, our eldest wasn't, so I said, "I'm sorry, he's out."

I should have left it at that.

However, I broke the cardinal rule of being the father of a teenager while answering a telephone.

"Is that Debbie?" I asked.

Boom, crash and thud.

As soon as the words were out I knew I had made a terrible mistake.

"No," was the rather chilly reply. "It's . . ."

Of course it was a totally different name, the name of somebody who obviously didn't know Debbie even exists or, if she did, wasn't happy about it.

What a fool I am.

With three teenagers in the house, I should know you never mention a name over the phone and give away a son's (or daughter's) secrets.

You say, "Hello, there" or, "Hi, I'm sorry but you missed Stephen. Is there any message?" You can even say, "He's out but he won't be long."

But you don't cough up a free name and put your teenager in possible hot water with someone he's probably told is the only one in his life.

When will I learn?

I am pretty good now in that I never say, when a teenager at our house gets a call, "He (or she) is in the bathroom. I'll take a message."

Bathroom references are "gross."

Also, I never say, "He's over at Bill's. Maybe you can reach him there."

Giving away a teenager's social calendar is just as taboo as giving away a free name. You've got to be noncommittal. "Stephen will be sorry he missed you" is okay. Ditto, "Jane was talking about a movie, but she may have changed her mind," a statement that gives her lots of leeway and will not stand up in a court of law.

On the other hand, a teenager expects his or her father to pump as much information out of a caller as possible.

The absolute minimum is (a) who is calling, (b) the time of the call, (c) where the caller can be reached and (d) the sex of the caller.

You can forget about (a), (b) and (c), but heaven help if you flub (d).

Establishing the sex of the caller is absolutely vital and any father who misses out on that one is definitely in trouble. Unfortunately, when your teenagers have friends whose voices haven't changed yet, it isn't easy.

Other things a teenager expects a father to learn are:

Was the call (in your opinion) to invite said teenaged son or daughter to a party, school dance, etc., or did the caller sound like someone who only wanted the title of the book required for the French course.

As a guess (in the case of a call for a teenaged daughter) would you say the caller was probably six feet tall with a clear complexion?

Why do you think the caller didn't leave a number and, in your estimation, do you think he (or she) will call back if said teenager sits by the telephone for an hour or so?

The pressure of being the father of a teenager is enormous when the telephone rings and sometimes you just want to let it ring rather than risk making a mistake.

Fortunately, with teenagers in the house you know one thing: the call is never for you.

Behind times

Our Stephen (who is eighteen) came home from a disco the other evening with distressing news: while minding his own business on the dance floor, some girl he had never seen before reached over and pinched him on the bum.

According to the account we received, the assaulter was about twenty, had a dynamite figure and gave Stephen a cheeky grin when he turned in total surprise.

Fortunately, Stephen was with a date, so the whole sordid business went no further, but Stephen's mother and I were seething, of course.

Can a young lad no longer boogie in safety on the hardwood surfaces of this city? Must he keep his wits about him and his vitals protected even during the intricacies of The Bump to make certain no lusting female, half-crazed by the sight of his plunging Pierre Cardin loungewear, takes unwanted liberties with his person?

For someone of my generation, it's totally unthinkable. Why, when I was Stephen's age, a male person could fox trot, waltz and dip to his heart's content in the school gymnasium without fear of being womanhandled every time he box-stepped past a dark corner. In all my years of swinging and swaying with Sammy Kaye, not once did I have to ward off the impudent grope or the lecherous pat. Women respected men for their minds then, and understood when we told them we were "saving" ourselves for marriage.

No more apparently.

"Perhaps this young creature mistook you for somebody else," I suggested hopefully to my eldest. "Or else it was an accident."

"I don't think so," Stephen replied. "I think I can tell a deliberate pinch when I feel one, and she definitely smiled at me."

"You don't suppose she was in the middle of snapping her fingers to the music when your bottom happened to get in the way, do you?"

"No."

"Perhaps she works in a clothing store and was feeling the texture of your trousers. That's how they do it you know, between the fingers."

"She pinched more than cloth," Stephen insisted.

"This is even worse than I suspected," I said. "If you eliminate the music and the cloth, it means she was interested in only — my God! Thank heaven you were with somebody. If you had been alone, it's anyone's guess what might have happened to you."

Stephen shot back an answering nod to indicate he had, indeed, thought about the possibilities.

Unlike other males his age who might have wept and made their complexions blotchy after such a harrowing experience at the hands of a female stranger, Stephen remained composed and I was proud of him.

"I don't want this one unfortunate incident to change your attitude toward women," I cautioned. "There are lots of them out there who can control their hands at a dance and not get out of line. However, as a precaution, I think you should take some preventative steps to avoid similar pawings in the future."

"Like what?" he asked.

"First, I'd buy trousers that are a size or two too big. You're just asking for trouble if you wear form-fitting ones in front of some sexually-liberated, twenty-year-old female who is only interested in a one-night stand.

"Next, for extra protection, put a thick hankie in the back pocket of the baggy trousers. Not only will it give you a lumpy appearance that should be as good as a cold shower to any female out for a good time, it will provide protection in the event she still tries to get fresh during a Barry Manilow number.

"Finally, try not to turn your back on a female if she is pawing the floor with one foot, has steam coming out of both nostrils and spits in her hands as she walks in your direction. She's obviously up to no good."

Stephen said he would weigh my words carefully because, "I don't think any one in the country knows more about turning off women than you do."

It was difficult holding back the tears. It's not often an eighteen-year-old son pays his father such a glowing tribute.

No toys for Dad

The years have a nasty way of sneaking past and if I needed a further reminder all I have to do is look at the children's Christmas lists.

No longer do they painstakingly print out requests in inch-high crayoned letters to Santa at the North Pole asking for a "bingy" (Stephen's word for a toy xylophone he had his heart set on fifteen or sixteen years ago) or a doll that wets herself.

That day, alas, is long gone.

Stephen this year wants Santa to cough up the necessary for a Pro Drivers course and, as a stocking stuffer, insurance coverage for the heady hours when he slips behind the wheel of the family Chevelle and heads for the favourite disco with a lovely dish beside him.

Daughter Jane has opted for dance lessons — modern jazz stuff — and some knockout Danskin outfits that will cause spectators to tumble out of their balcony seats when she does her stuff.

Even Richard whom I counted on to ask for a Dinky toy car he could run across the living room carpet and say "brrrum, brrrum" on Christmas, yes even trusty Richard has requested grown-up stuff — a cord suit, Brut hair shampoo, a couple of neckties. He might just as well have plunged the knife all the way in and asked for a razor.

What has happened?

It seems only yesterday that Stephen was prepared to feed Dancer, Prancer, Vixen and Comet, too, if need be, for an entire year if dear old Kris would only leave a Big Bruiser truck under the holiday spruce.

He was just as nuts about getting a Man From U.N.C.L.E. gun, the one with the secret opening in the carrying case through which a clever lad could fire a plastic bullet at evil men bent on world conquest.

Jane never aimed higher than an Easybake oven, one which she could use to turn out hard cookies and brownies, eats no decent daddy would ever refuse even if it did mean sharp abdominal pains for the next 24 hours.

And Richard? Was he the one who promised to be good for the next thirty-seven years if only he could get a Secret Sam outfit and the wonderful Gunfight at the OK Corral set?

He was definitely enraptured by the Popeye punching bag that sat on the floor and was bigger than he was. How many flying leaps he took at that Christmas present I couldn't even guess, but 300,000 wouldn't be far out.

And now it's come down to driving lessons, dance outfits and crummy neckties.

Of course I realize that by Christmas day they will be nineteen, sixteen and fourteen years of age.

But is that any reason to turn their backs on Silly String, Leggo, Ready Ranger sets, Mr. Action, the immortal Johnny 7 kit, Hot Wheels and all the other items that set their hearts soaring in past Christmases?

If Stephen, Jane and Richard aren't interested themselves, they should at least consider Daddy.

What am I going to do on Christmas morning, play with Richard's new shirt or see if I can get Stephen's driving brochure to fly across the room?

I wonder if the missus would like a Darth Vader helmet.

Scoops

Jackie and I are alone in the house for the first time in nearly nineteen years, all three children being away on vacation, and it's made a tremendous difference in our lives.

Here are just a few things we've discovered:

You can kiss without anyone saying, "Cut that out."

You can turn on the radio and get the same station you had on when you turned it off, and not a blast of rock 'n' roll.

You can spend an evening at home and never hear the telephone. Ditto the front door bell.

Two bath towels can last an entire day.

You can serve liver and bacon (with onions) and not get a barrage of "Yuk!"

You can serve dinner AFTER 6:30, even as late as 6:35, and the world will not necessarily come to an end.

You can get something on TV besides *Laverne and Shirley*, *Monty Python* and reruns of *Adam 12*.

A mother can try as hard as she wants but she cannot cook for two people and, if she makes chili, it will last anywhere from nine days to two weeks.

A quart of orange juice can be placed in the refrigerator at

4 o'clock and still be there at 6 o'clock, with no sticky spots on the kitchen floor.

A person can pick up the newspaper and find the comic section, even if the edition has been in the house for over sixty seconds.

Besides holding coats, books, wet bathing suits and bicycle parts, the chesterfield in the front room can be used to sit on.

The family dog can find ways to put in the day without having anyone blow up her nose with a straw or, during a deep sleep, shout "Bow Wow!" in her ear.

You can step into a bathroom without somebody bellowing, "How long will you be?"

You can get all your socks back washday.

A person can go twenty-four straight hours without having to say, "Don't you think you should have put a paper on the floor first?"

It is also possible to spend garbage night doing something other than scraping gum off the bottom of a wicker wastebasket with your fingernails.

You can sleep through an entire night without keeping one ear open to make certain everyone's in, and the front door double-bolted.

You can buy enough ketchup.

You can get yourself a treat at the market (black cherries, for example) and not be forced to hide it at the back of the refrigerator behind the broccoli.

A pair of jeans can fit on a clothes hanger as well as on the bedroom floor.

A dinner can be stretched out past six minutes.

A conversation can be held around the breakfast table without a single mention being made of driving lessons, and the absolute necessity of having same as a birthday present.

You can shop at the supermarket with $100 and not run short.

An adult can go twelve minutes without discussing somebody's complexion problems, and still not suffer any withdrawal pains.

There is such a thing in the world as leftover pie.

You can dress without going to somebody else's closet to retrieve your belongings.

Without too much effort, it is possible to balance on all four feet of a kitchen chair.

Finally, we've discovered our stereo can be turned down.

Be still, my heart!

A farewell to little arms

Our Stephen was introduced to readers of this journal on February 27, 1963. He was three years old then and proud Papa was bursting out in paragraphs for the new employer.

Stephen, I reported, liked to stand by the record player, fiddle with knobs in best mad scientist fashion, and announce to all within listening range, "I'm going to blow up the 'erf."

Whenever I had a cold, he'd reach to my lips, squeeze shut his little fists, and assure Daddy, "I've got the germs." He'd then throw them to the ground, and jump up and down, presumably breaking their little necks.

When Stephen was somersaulting on the front room rug, he was "upside down," when he was standing, he was "upside up."

If he got mad, he didn't shout and holler. He merely stared into your face and said, "I'm giving you my eyebrows."

Why all the nostalgia now? Why the memories of a little boy who usually skipped five when he counted? Why the warm reflection of that day on a Florida beach when, after playing long enough in the ocean, Stephen asked his father to "pull the plug" and make the water go away?

Well, Stephen is eighteen now and leaving for Europe on his first big adventure. He'll be gone most of the summer, touring Britain, Holland, Belgium, France, Austria, Germany, Italy, Switzerland.

He has a Youth Hostel card, a Eurail pass, money saved up from his job this past year at the supermarket, a passport, the addresses of a few friends.

Yes, he's well prepared.

But somehow old Dad still hates to let go. For heaven's sake, it was only a twinkling of an eye ago that we let him out of the house with a piece of paper pinned to his coat that said, "Please leave me outside!" so he wouldn't talk his way into a neighbour's for a cookie.

And now he's off to see the world, a young man now, with no message pinned to his shirt but all kinds of hope under it.

He's finished high school where he and a friend started a newspaper and acted as its editors-columnists-business-managers-typists-layout men and chief worriers.

He's been on television as a member of the school's *Reach For The Top* team; he was in a musical at the old high school, on the chess team, and he and some friends have just made a mini-movie based on a skit he helped write.

Next September he'll be at university and . . .

I remember when Stephen used to hold up old popsicle sticks and conduct "interviews" with Fat Stuff (his sister Jane who was only one at the time, and not exactly a glib talker).

I remember his first birthday party when, with his usual sense of the dramatic, he took his first steps and crossed our grey rug without a helping hand.

Now it's an ocean he's crossing and there will be thousands of moments in the weeks ahead when I'll wonder where he is, and if he's all right.

Of course he will be. He's a fine person, bright, kind and a joy to have around the kitchen table at the end of a day.

Still, there'll be mornings when I'll look at the office telephone and wonder why it doesn't ring and a cheery voice ask, "Would you like company for lunch, Dad?"

Dad always does.

No Sex Please . . .
We're Married

1

Introduction

An introduction to a book is supposed to give the reader a taste of what is to follow so let me get to that bit of business immediately.

The articles here were written over a twenty-year period (from the early '60s to 1982) and concentrate on the main woman in my life, my co-vivant — dare I say it in this liberated age? — my wife. Her name is Jackie and I fell in love with her twenty-six years ago. Even better, we also fell deeply and meaningfully in like. As experts in the old man-woman thing know, like is very important if you want a relationship to last 125 or more years, which is my plan.

If I had to describe the one thing that makes me want to be home when the streetlights go on it's Jackie's sense of humour. In a phrase, she makes me laugh. And I hope she makes you laugh, too, because this book is mostly about the woman I refer to as the Resident Love Goddess.

Illustrations are by my friend Lynn Johnston, best known for her internationally acclaimed comic strip, For Better Or For Worse, but also illustrator of my last book, *Take My Family . . . Please!* Lynn managed the drawings while in the midst of planning a move with her dentist-husband and their children from Lynn Lake, Manitoba, to a new home in northern Ontario. No artist ever laboured under more trying conditions, and I appreciate it.

What else?

Oh, yes — the title.

When I started putting the material together, I asked my family for suggestions, always a dangerous approach if you know my family. My eldest (Stephen, who is now twenty-three) thought *Not Adolf Hitler's Diary* had commercial possibilities. Richard (who is eighteen) voted for *His and Herpes* just because he thought it had a nice ring. Daughter Jane (twenty-one) approved *Tee Hee For Two* and also leaned toward something a little naughty, *Oh, What A Lovely Pair!*, as a tribute to her mother and dad.

From the office came *Yes, We Have No Nirvanas* and *Everything's Coming Up Neuroses*. My wife's preference was *Love At First Laugh* or *The Party's Never Over*.

Finally, we settled for the title you see on the jacket — *No Sex Please . . . We're Married*. Even if you don't like it, I suggest it's better than Richard's second choice, *I Do, We Do — But No Dog Do*.

I should point out these stories appeared originally in the Panorama section of the defunct *Canadian Star Weekly* and in *The Toronto Star*. Some of the facts have been updated for 1983 but I've chosen to leave some stuff as written. Do not accuse me of being lazy. If you could be reported once more at ten years less your real age, wouldn't you leap at the chance, too? This is written, you see, by a happy man whose only regret is that it has all gone much too fast.

Gary Lautens

July, 1983

144

2

In the Beginning . . .

Why can't a woman remember like a man?

Usually I've got a pretty good memory. For example, I can remember my first car (a 1947 Ford), my first kiss (her name was Joan and it was 1945), my first job ($3 a week in 1941 for putting up baseball scores at the Hamilton *Spectator*).

Oh, yes, I can recall details from way back.

But I can't remember the first time I mentioned marriage to my wife. I don't remember proposing.

Let me explain right away that I don't drink or smoke pot, nor have I been struck on the head by a blunt object recently.

So that's not it.

I just don't remember. And, as a result, I have to depend on my wife to fill in the details about how I got married.

"Let's get this straight," I said to her the other night. "Explain to me how I wound up married."

"We've gone over this a hundred times," she replied. "Let's not do it again."

"Just once more," I begged. "For the record."

"Very well," she surrendered. "It was in 1956 . . ."

"I can remember 1956 perfectly," I said. "That was the year

Edmonton beat Montreal for the third straight time in the Grey Cup. Jim Trimble was coaching the Hamilton Tiger-Cats and . . ."

"That's right," my wife interrupted. "The Tiger-Cats were running their contest to select Miss Tiger-Cat and you were one of the judges."

"So far, so good," I encouraged.

"You sat next to me at a luncheon—I was wearing a brown outfit with matching hat," my wife continued. "It was the twenty-first of October."

"I remember the contest," I said. "You and a girl named Garee Nash were tied for first place and I voted for Garee Nash to break the deadlock."

"That's right—she got the fur coat," my wife stated. "And I wound up with you as a consolation prize."

"You seem to have skipped something," I complained. "I don't remember running up to you and saying, 'Take me! I'm yours!'"

"Of course you didn't. You asked me out for dinner and a hockey game about a week later. You had a cream sports car and . . ."

"Get on to the part where I asked you to marry me," I suggested.

"You didn't ask me that night," my wife stated. "You asked me to marry you on our third date."

"Are you positive?" I asked.

"Don't you remember? We had been out to a movie. It was in November. And we were parked in your car in front of my place. You said . . ."

"Tell me exactly," I demanded.

"You said, 'If I had my way, there'd be something on that finger of yours.'"

"Maybe I meant gloves," I said. "After all, it was November and that was a cold car."

"Silly! You meant an engagement ring."

"Is that what I meant?"

"Of course."

"What did you say?"

"I was shocked," my wife recalled. "I told you we had only had three dates and it was nonsense to talk about marriage. Besides, I was only eighteen. You were twenty-eight."

"So I dropped the subject," I added.

"You wouldn't take 'no' for an answer," she contradicted. "I asked for time to think it over but you were too overpowering."

"I wish you'd explain that," I said.

"You sent flowers, candy, notes," my wife revealed. "Then, on December 2, you gave me a magnifying glass—and a diamond ring."

"What did you do?" I wanted to know.

"I didn't want to accept it. We hadn't known each other even two months."

"So you gave the ring back?"

"I wanted to," my wife informed me. "But I knew that would break your heart."

"Oh," I said.

"You set April 6 as our wedding date and said you couldn't live a moment longer without me," my wife concluded. "I didn't have a choice."

Anyway, that's the way it happened.

And, if you don't believe my wife, ask her mother.

Behind every successful man is a goof-off friend

Some people get ahead in this world through marriage and, although I'm not proud of the fact, I'm one of them.

In fact, marriage and promotion were virtually simultaneous in my particular case.

I know what you're thinking—that I married the boss's daughter or at least a very close niece.

But that wasn't how it was at all.

The girl I married worked as a secretary in a soap factory and the contacts she had were with Mr. Clean, not Roy Thomson or John Bassett.

Still, if I hadn't got married, I'd probably still be chasing ambulances and writing obituaries for ninety bucks a week.

Just for the record, let me explain what marriage did for my career in journalism.

I can remember getting up on my wedding day, throwing open the window to let in the morning sunshine, and thinking to myself, "Should I, or shouldn't I, jump?"

Like every other bridegroom, I felt that the idea I had six months before (the idea of getting married) didn't seem nearly so hot now that the actual day had arrived.

I made a mental note of all the drawbacks of getting married — the expense, the problem of getting into the bathroom for the rest of my life, the pain of having to give up my own room and Mom's cooking.

I then put down all the reasons why I should get married.

The best one I could think of was my wife-to-be's father. He is 6 feet 3, 220 pounds, a former football player, and a very poor loser. It seemed to me that I stood a very good chance of going through life with a fist sticking out the side of my face if I didn't go through with the marriage.

So I started to get dressed.

The wedding ceremony was scheduled for the early afternoon and it came off without a hitch except for the fact that my wife wore a silky dress and she kept slipping off the satin cushion when we knelt in front of the minister.

First she'd slide to the right, then to the left. Finally, she compromised by putting one knee on the cushion and anchoring the other on the floor. It gave her a 20-degree list to starboard but that didn't bother my wife. A girl doesn't have to be on the level to make it legal — as long as the guy says, "I do."

After the church service, we went downtown for the reception, where we had all the trimmings: a big cake, a lovely buffet, and a bunch of relatives glaring at each other, trying to figure out who got the best of the match.

It was a good party and still going strong when my bride and I finally left around six o'clock to start our car trip to Florida, where we spent our honeymoon.

Still confused?

Well, so was I when I got back from Florida and found I had a new title, new responsibilities, and a fatter pay cheque waiting for me at the office.

On the honeymoon, my wife promised she'd take me to the top. She pointed out that behind every successful man there's a woman — but frankly, I didn't expect such quick results. I thought I might have to wait a day or two before making my mark in the newspaper game.

But here I was, not back in the office fifteen minutes and already climbing toward the executive washroom.

Then I found out why.

Naturally, I had invited a lot of my friends to my wedding and the reception that followed.

One of them (as I discovered) had so much fun at the reception that he didn't go home for several days — or to the office.

To put it mildly, the office was furious.

Anyway, I got his job.

So now you know how I found fame and fortune through marriage.

It sure beats night school.

The funny things that happened after dark

It's been years since my wife and I moved into our first home — a two-bedroom bungalow in the suburbs that cost $11,500. And we only lived in that house a short time. But I'd still like to explain a few things to my old neighbours, wherever they are.

Like about the lights.

Our lights used to flick on and off at the strangest times. For example, the house might be in complete darkness by seven o'clock in the evening. On the other hand, every bulb in the entire place was often ablaze at three a.m.

That sort of thing can disturb any block and I wonder now what the people around us used to think. Did they figure we were running an all-night diner on the side? Did they suspect we were operating on European time? Or did they merely put us down as eager newlyweds who didn't rate sleep very high on our list of priorities?

I suspect the latter.

In any case, I want to put the record straight and tell the old neighbours just what was going on in the house they whispered about.

In the first place, I should explain that my wife and I practically went from the church to the bungalow with no stops in between.

Before we got married, I decided to sell my yellow sports car to scrape enough money for a down payment on a house. No apartment for us. I wanted to start off with a landlord that I like — me.

That was fine except for a couple of things. One was that neither of us knew the first thing about how to run a house. Especially Jackie. For example, it wasn't unusual for my bride to plug half a dozen appliances into the same electrical circuit. That accounted for many of the blackouts our neighbours witnessed. The couple in No. 7 weren't hugging and kissing. They were downstairs in the basement, trying to find the damn fuse box.

Now for the second problem. Jackie had never been away from her parents before and moving into her own home was a strange experience.

To put it politely, Jackie was nervous. She kept hearing noises in the basement and seeing shadows in the yard. When I was around, that was no problem. We could hide under the bed together.

However, it just so happens that I worked a lot of nights at that time. Needless to say, it wasn't much of a life for a bride, especially one who was chicken about the dark. To put it bluntly, Jackie couldn't sleep a wink when I wasn't around to offer at least token protection.

Finally, she made her compromise. We'd go to bed right after she came home from work (Jackie was a secretary at the time) and get up around midnight. Jackie would pack me off to work — and then turn on every light in the place and do housework until dawn.

By the time I got home, the ironing would be finished, the washing would be finished, and Jackie would be finished, too. We'd both collapse in bed for a few hours of sleep and then start all over.

Fortunately, I didn't work every night in the week so sometimes we had normal hours.

But I can remember one neighbour who remarked he had seen me turn off the lights right after supper on the previous night.

"That's the fourth time this week," he commented.

Then he shook my hand, gave me a wink, and bet a dollar that I'd be dead by the time I was thirty-five.

I hate to shoot down the reputation I falsely built up in those years.

But a buck's a buck.

Pledging undying love is a problem

I've got a problem. Our wedding anniversary is coming up and I don't know what to get my wife.

Years ago buying her a present was a snap. All I ever did was look around for some sexy line in Latin or French and then buy a piece of jewellery for it to be inscribed on.

In fact, that's how our romance got started. I got hold of this verse somewhere:

> Omnia vincit amor:
> et nos adamus amori.

Which, translated, means:

> Love conquers all:
> Let us, too, yield to love.

Well, I had that slapped on a silver makeup case before you could say "Rudolph Valentino."

Frankly, I felt guilty sending such high-powered stuff to an eighteen-year-old girl who, up till then, figured the height of romance was being allowed to carry her boyfriend's spikes home from a baseball game.

But I meant business.

The clincher, I think, was a photograph I sent to my wife-to-be that had this simple inscription:

> Toujours et peut-être plus encore.

Yes—"Forever and, perhaps, a little longer."

After that it was just a matter of sticking around to cash in the chips. My Juliet didn't know what the hell I was talking about but she was curious enough to marry me to find out. Besides, she was tired of carrying around the baseball spikes.

That was twelve years ago. And that's the reason I've got the headache.

After twelve years of washing my socks and seeing me prance around the house in my corrective shorts, my wife isn't likely to be taken in again by any inscription, even if it's in Swahili.

My bachelor brother has a surefire gimmick. He sends unsuspecting young things a silver identification bracelet with only his telephone number engraved on the front. But if I pulled something like that on my wife now, she would probably fall over her vacuum cleaner in laughter.

So all my good stuff is out. I can't send her a doorknob (as I did in 1956) and claim I bit it off while waiting impatiently for our next date. The same goes for routine items like huge boxes of chocolates. (Chocolate makes her break out now.) And it's a little too soon to send her a nice cane with a rubber tip and her social security number scratched in the handle.

So here I am stuck in the middle years.

We've talked about going back to the motel where we spent our wedding night—a place called the Golden Gate—and trying to get room 5 again. But it's nearly ninety miles away. Besides, we don't like to leave the kids overnight and it wouldn't be quite the same if we took them with us.

We've thought about getting our wedding party together for a reunion. However, two of them are now divorced; another is a widow; and one of the bridesmaids is pretty pregnant. It doesn't have the makings of a swinging party.

Our TV cost $65 for repairs. I suppose that could always be considered our anniversary present. On the day itself—a Sunday—we could sit around, watch TV, maybe even send out for a pizza after the kids have gone to bed.

We could . . .

What's that jeweller's telephone number again?

Love letters: why don't women throw them out?

After years of marriage, a man is conditioned to face practically anything. He can survive rush hour traffic, a huge mortgage, Top Twenty records, income tax forms and a kid who says, "Do I hafta?" But one thing still brings him to his knees—his old love letters.

For some strange reason, women never throw away a note

written in passion. They adore heavy breathing, provided it comes in an envelope.

My wife, unfortunately, is no exception. Put an X at the bottom of a page of paper and my wife immediately wraps it in a blue ribbon and stashes it in her cedar chest. As a result, she has a bundle of old letters the size of a giraffe's goitre locked away.

And it's embarrassing.

Don't get me wrong. I plead guilty. I wrote all that stuff. Yes, I did say it was an eternity between kisses, that life is empty without her, and that I won't be satisfied until she's mine. I may even have commented on the sky being jealous of the blue in her eyes.

But does my wife have to remind me? If there's one thing a guy doesn't need, it's having a lot of nice things he wrote fifteen years ago thrown back in his face. Certainly I stated I wanted her in my arms. But that was in 1957, before the postal rates went sky-high. You could make a naughty suggestion then for a fraction of what it costs today. Besides, I was only a boy of twenty-eight at the time and didn't know what I was doing.

In any case, those old love letters are coming back to haunt me with a new generation. My daughter Jane (who is nine) has discovered where her mother keeps the literature from our courting days. And Jane would give both pigtails to get her hands on those letters for just fifteen minutes. She'd love to know what the old man had in mind when he was dating.

If she ever finds out, the old image will sure be shot to heck.

3

Suburbia

I just can't afford to become a celebrity

My wife's going to kick herself if I ever amount to anything—
you know, win a Nobel prize for chemistry, write a terrific sym-
phony, quarterback the Argos to a Grey Cup, that sort of thing.

Over the weekend we had a garage sale and Jackie sold my
old desk for $20. It's thirty years old, and we can't take it to the
new house (no room), so she felt it was a fair price.

But what if I become Prime Minister, or discover a cure for
the common cold next week? Jackie will be furious she didn't ask
at least $40 for the desk.

That's a chance you take when you hold a garage sale. You
put price tags on the items, and then keep your fingers crossed
that the original owner (in this case, me) isn't going to ruin everything by becoming famous.

Take our old bed. Provided I don't become the first person to
go to Mars, or score 100 goals in a regular NHL season, the $15
we got for it is a fair price. After all, Jackie had the bed as a child;
we slept in it the first few years of our marriage; and our eldest
has used it the past ten years. So the doctor who bought it (for
his summer cottage) was happy with the deal, and so were we.

However, I'll have to remain obscure to keep it that way. If I go into the movies and become another Fred Astaire, for example, I'll mess up everything.

In particular, I'm going to keep on my toes in the next few years and make sure I don't become the father of any country like George Washington. If I do, you can be sure the doctor who bought our bed will slap a brass plate on the headboard stating, "Gary Lautens, father of Ruritania, slept here," and charge $1 to see it.

If that dark day ever comes, my wife will be so mad at herself for letting a golden opportunity slip through her fingers, she might never speak to me again.

As I watched customers walk out of our garage with easy chairs, wine glasses, books, our picnic table, an old tow rope, garden furniture, pictures, and dozens of other items, I could feel the pressure mount.

Never in my life has failing been so important. Can you imagine what that stuff would be worth if The Who ask me to join their group, or I invent an engine that runs on pollution?

Fortunately, I've been able to avoid celebrity so far, but how long will my luck hold out? What if, by accident, I become a famous general, or get discovered by a Hollywood agent while sitting at the soda fountain in a local drug store? What then?

I just hope my wife's lack of faith in me isn't unjustified.

Passing the trash test

There are moments in life when you put your reputation on the line: risk prestige, image, and good name on one toss of the dice. Trash day in the suburbs is one such moment.

Twice a year you're allowed to put out junk at the curb and have it collected, free of charge, by the city or town. Mattresses, ancient ice boxes, wheelless tricycles — they're all eligible for pick-up.

However, before your discards vanish they're judged by your neighbours. On trash night, every one is out, cruising up and down the streets to see what's up for grabs, and assessing the quality of your throwaways.

Naturally we try to keep up, but it isn't always easy to find something good enough to put out in broad daylight. The best we could come up with this year was a pair of kitchen chairs that have been down in the basement for a couple of years, an old golf cart (but still in working order), a bamboo pole, an empty barrel used for pool chemicals, and a push broom with some bristle showing.

Frankly it didn't compare with the best trash on the street. I think Gards won that honour with a toboggan that looked almost brand new, or it could have been the new people who put out a fold-up bed.

Still, I thought our junk was a good average and could hold its own with most of the stuff stacked on the street. At least we didn't have boring chunks of concrete, or a tacky tire covered with blow-out patches. However, until somebody drives up and picks up your son's old wagon or the deck chair with no seat, you never know if your trash really measures up.

Nothing is more embarrassing than putting out your trash on trash night, and having it still intact next morning when the official pick-up takes place. It means you've really struck out, that not even the neighbourhood kids (who'll pick up anything) want your rubbish.

My wife stood nervously by the front window to see how long it would take for some one to pick through our stuff; she was certain the golf cart would be snapped up first.

Well, she was wrong. The bamboo pole was grabbed about thirty minutes after our curb opened for business, and the cart followed that, and then the kitchen chairs (which were badly ripped and not a hot item, in my estimation).

By morning, when the official pick-up trucks arrived, all we had left at the front of our place was a pail of odds and ends, and my wife never expected them to move.

So she was delighted.

Even better, I gave our kids strict orders not to bring home anybody else's trash because we're in the process of moving and don't need more clutter. Except for a large paper rose, an umbrella that practically works, and part of a skateboard, they followed my instructions to the letter.

These trash days sure are hard on the nerves.

The joys of being alone

At this very moment I'm trying to write a column at home. The kids are at school; my wife is at her exercise class at the Y; and the dog is outside in the yard.

Yes, I'm alone.

Perfect, you say?

Wrong. The racket in the house is driving me up the wall.

Brrr-ummm. Click, click, click, click. Klackety-klack. Chug-a-boom, chug-a-boom. Ker-bang, ker-bang.

My ears are ready to fall off.

The reason, of course, is that I am the twentieth-century man and home is not a home; it's a hydro sub-station. Sure, my wife is at the Y, running her little heart out, doing pushups, and taking a dip in the pool to maintain her body tone. But the housework goes on whether or not she's on the premises.

This, for example, is Monday, and Monday is washday. So, before my wife packed her sweatsocks into her gym bag, she packed everybody else's socks (and other dainties) into the automatic washer. She also loaded the breakfast dishes into the automatic dishwasher. She dumped a few damp things (including a pair of Richard's running shoes) into the automatic dryer. She put lunch into the automatic oven. She set the thermostat on the automatic furnace to click on at 75. (My wife hates to come home to a cold house after working out all morning over a hot barbell.) She checked the automatic humidifier. She adjusted the automatic timer on the radio so she wouldn't miss Gordon Sinclair.

And then she activated the entire system before ducking out of the electronic jungle we call home.

So here I am, sitting in the midst of whirring gears, squirting hoses, and an assortment of switches flicking on and off with no help from me.

The only thing that isn't automated is the typewriter — and I'm supposed to make it work. But how can I concentrate with all this cleaning, washing, etc., going on?

Do they manufacture a transistor that can be implanted in a columnist's nose (or spleen), something the lady of the house can set for 500 words when she's throwing the toggle switch on her other labour-saving devices? I hope so because getting anything done when you're alone in the house nowadays is impossible.

I sure miss the kids, the dog, and my wife. At least when they're around, they keep it down to a low roar.

On middle-aged antiques

Whenever my wife gets her hands on a few bucks these days she rushes out to buy something old for the house. Yes, she's on an antique kick.

Maybe "old" is the wrong word. We can't afford old. The stuff we get is more middle-aged, old enough to vote but not quite old enough to have hardening of the drawers.

This past weekend, for example, she picked up a wash stand at a flea market back in the country. The price on the tag was $150 but my wife, coming from thrifty English stock, WASPed the dealer down to $110.

According to my wife, it's the very thing she's been looking for to fill in the blank spot in the living room. It has everything — wobbly legs, a stone counter top with a big chip in it, lots of stains on the wood, and a missing door handle.

Of course, my wife would have preferred a wash stand with two missing door handles — but that would have been out of our price range.

"Isn't it gorgeous?" my wife asked when she first spotted the treasure. "Don't you just love those old blue tiles across the top of the wash stand?"

I told her "love" was probably too strong a word. "Like" would be closer; "hate" would be dead-on.

Naturally she wasn't listening. She closed the transaction and gave me instructions to load her purchase into the car.

As any one who goes to country flea markets, auctions, or swap shops knows, there is one irrefutable law: whatever your wife buys, it will always be long enough, wide enough, or deep enough to make it impossible to close the trunk of your car. It is also heavy enough to make the veins stand out on your forehead and give you a stabbing pain in the groin.

Anyway, trunk open, kids fighting, wash stand loaded, we zoomed home along the highway at a steady ten miles an hour — "make sure you don't scratch it," my wife cautioned. In the antique game, they only want old scratches, not new ones.

So now the wash stand is in our living room, a mere 2,569 man-hours of sanding, staining, and cursing away from being a gleaming jewel among our possessions.

But I shouldn't complain. If my wife didn't have this weakness for middle-aged, beat-up stuff with wobbly legs, where would I be today?

Rosebuds, pressed flowers, and a flooded basement

During the coldest night of the winter, a water pipe burst in our home and flooded the entire downstairs area — the family room, a playroom, the spare bedroom, and my office. Rugs were ruined, including broadloom put down only a week earlier; floors heaved; the ceiling drooped at a dangerous angle; the TV was doused.

Even worse, Jackie lost her rosebuds.

That may not seem tragic to you but my wife's rosebuds have always been important to her. I must admit, I've grown attached to them too, over the years.

They were taken from our wedding cake, carefully wrapped in plastic, then stored with our other valuables under the front stairs. Because they were sugar rosebuds, we didn't take them out often — but it gave us a warm feeling to know they were there if we wanted them.

So you can imagine the panic on the morning of the flood when Jackie saw the water pouring out of the ceiling and swirling in deep pools on the floor. Ignoring the floating furniture, Jackie wanted to dive immediately for her treasures.

Fortunately, a cool head prevailed. "Turn off the water first," I ordered, handing her a pair of rubber boots. "Then we'll see if we can save your rosebuds."

As it turned out, we were too late. Jackie's rosebuds were goners by the time the water was stopped and pumped out of the house by a crew of men (for a big fee, incidentally).

Picking through the damp rooms after the workmen were packed and leaving, Jackie came up with a soggy cardboard container. Yes — the carton where all the souvenirs of our honeymoon had been stored. The sugar rosebuds were just puddles of coloured water.

"Our wedding invitations are ruined too," Jackie groaned. "Look."

What she held up looked like a clumsy U-boat commander's lunch.

According to Jackie our total loss was (1) four rosebuds, (2) a half-dozen leftover invitations inviting the receiver to the wedding reception of Jacqueline Joan Lane and Gary Lautens on April 6, 1957, and (3) the pressed flowers from her wedding bouquet.

The loss of the floor, ceiling, and broadloom was strictly incidental.

Happily, Jackie was able to salvage some of her souvenirs. For example, the blue garter she wore on her wedding day survived with plenty of snap. So did a blue hanky that was part of the wedding bouquet.

And, after working on them with a warm iron, my wife was

able to present me with some other remembrances of the honeymoon trip.

To wit: a receipt for $6 for room 5 at the Golden Gate Motel (I was nervous when I signed the register and got my address wrong); a written warning from a Florida state trooper for doing 70 mph in a 60 mph zone (it was difficult enough explaining to my mother why it took us six days to cover 1,600 miles without having to explain a speeding ticket, too); a menu from Hollywood, Florida (full course meals, $1.45 up); and, finally, a postcard of the apartment-motel where we stayed by the ocean in Florida ($70 per week), plus a business card from the Polka Dot Gift Shoppe, souvenirs a specialty.

It's going to cost plenty to get everything straightened around at the house but Jackie has only one question on her mind: how come we didn't have rosebud insurance?

Bargain at the cleaners

Don't invite us over for the next couple of days. We can't come. My wife doesn't have a thing to wear. And I'll tell you how it happened.

Yesterday, Jackie decided to take a pair of slacks to the cleaners. And, while she was there, she spotted a sign pasted on the wall.

It said: "Today's special! Any red article of clothing dry-cleaned free with a $3 regular order." Jackie's eyes lit up. "Is that any red article?" she asked the clerk in the cleaning shop.

"That's what the sign says," was the response.

"What time do you close?"

"In about twenty minutes," the clerk said.

"Is the special on again tomorrow?"

"No."

Jackie was in a dilemma. There wasn't time to go home and fetch something — anything — red. But the bargain! That's when the light went on.

My wife realized she did have something red with her — her overcoat. She started to take it off. The other customers gawked.

"What are you doing?" a slightly shocked clerk wanted to know.

"You said you'd take any red article of clothing, didn't you?" Jackie replied.

"Well, yes — but it's zero outside. How are you going to get home without a coat?"

"I'll manage," my wife said.

She emptied the pockets of her red overcoat, picked up her cleaning ticket — and walked out into the blizzard.

That's how she came home — coatless.

"I've just saved $6.50," she announced proudly, shivering in the front hall. Then she explained what had happened.

Thank God the cleaners didn't have a special on articles of clothing in pink with little daisies on the top. I hate to imagine how Jackie would have come home.

The egg man cometh

Somebody's come between my wife and me. It's our egg man. Every Monday morning my wife leaves me in charge of the house while she trots off to her exercise class. And every Monday morning her last instructions are: "Don't get any eggs today."

Thirty minutes later there's a knock on the door. Yes — the egg man. And I buy another tray of eggs. To put it bluntly, I can't say no to the egg man.

Oh, I can get up on my typewriter and lecture the PM, the President, or even the Pope. I'm not reluctant to tell General Motors where to get off. But the egg man is another matter.

Believe me, I try to be firm. I practise saying, "No eggs today, thank you." However, my refusals vanish when I come face to face with my Monday morning visitor. He raps on the back door, comments on the weather, smiles — and the next thing I know I've got another three dozen grade A large on my hands.

Maybe it's the way he pulls his tweed cap down over his ears. Maybe it's the way he talks to our dog. Or maybe he's an amateur hypnotist. All I know is I'm putty in his change purse.

Unfortunately, my wife doesn't understand. Women seldom do, especially those with a refrigerator already bulging with eggs. For one thing, my wife never fails to point out, nobody in our family likes eggs. Except me. To take off some of the heat, I eat eggs as often as I can; but ten to fifteen a week is my limit. Any more than that and I get a curious urge to climb up on the roof at dawn and cock-a-doodle-doo at anything passing in feathers.

Because I can't keep up with the supply, after a few weeks we usually have enough eggs on hand to stage a student riot — unless I can palm off a couple of dozen on mother.

What's the answer?

My wife has threatened to pin a sign to my shirt which reads: "Do not sell eggs to this husband." Or else we could move and hope the egg man never finds me.

Shopping holiday for stay-at-homes

Nobody's going to be more sorry to see the summer end than the Lautens family. For the last couple of months we've been living on something even better than borrowed time. We've been getting along on borrowed groceries. That's the advantage of living on a block where everybody goes away on holidays.

As our neighbours pack up to leave for the cottage or on a car trip, they invariably find something in the refrigerator they can't take with them. It can be anything from half a quart of milk to a chocolate pie with only one piece missing — but rather than throw it out, they want to give it to somebody.

And that's where we come in. We're the "somebody" who stays home in July and August and picks up the district's delicious discards.

For example, just last evening there was a knock on the door about 11 o'clock.

Marion (who lives next door) apologized for disturbing us so late but said she was leaving in the morning and could we use some butter, a loaf of bread, and half a watermelon she had in her refrigerator. We said we'd be glad to take them off her hands. They'll go nicely with the almost-full bottle of ginger ale, the rice pudding, and the fruit tarts we got from Isobel earlier this week.

And I can't wait for Sam and Pat to go on their trip. Pat's usually good for at least one berry pie and her crust is as good as anyone's on the block.

Food isn't the only dividend to stay-at-homes. My neighbour Ed has been working like a slave all year in his garden but he's going to be away for most of this month. So he told me to help myself to his tomatoes, beans, and raspberries. Which I've been doing.

I haven't planted anything more spectacular than myself (and only in the hammock out in the backyard) but I've got all the fresh fruit and vegetables I can handle. Thanks to good old Ed, we've even got flowers on the dinner table these nights. He sure plants a mean daisy.

I enjoyed Ron's football tickets (he's in Florida) and Harold's lawn chairs (he's down east) and Mark's barbecue (he's up north). If I want, there's Clarke's pool and Jim's second car, not to mention every magazine published in the English-speaking world. (We take in the neighbour's mail, natch.)

Frankly, when you consider the high cost of living, I'm amazed that people go anywhere in the summer.

My wife doesn't "work"

Is there anything more embarrassing today than being married to a woman who doesn't "work"?

Take Jackie.

She weaves, spins wool, attends classes twice a week at the Ontario College of Art, and is currently putting together a seven-foot tapestry she designed for the living-room. She also whips up 100 meals a week, irons a dozen shirts, waxes and washes the floors, walks the dog, throws a dinner party once a week.

But she doesn't "work."

She feels a minimum of two foreheads a week (to see if they're warm), listens to enough homework to get a degree from Oxford, runs the family budget, finds things in the basement no other living human being can find, reminds Richard to comb his hair every morning, cheers up Jane when she gets a zit on her face, and refinishes furniture.

She does the shopping, locates the bargains, washes gym stuff, keeps track of everybody's underwear, answers family mail, makes certain nobody leaves a ring around the bathtub, takes care of minor medical problems.

But she doesn't "work."

She cuts hair, cleans the filter on the furnace, clips the dog's nails, provides waltz lessons for male members of the family, vacuums, puts treats in school lunchbags for a noonday surprise, hangs up coats, holds feet when they get cold, provides laughs when needed or not, removes splinters, gives instruction on the application of eyeshadow, announces if it's a boot day, smiles through the recounting of old Monty Python skits, files class photographs.

She doesn't let anyone out of the house without a hug; she tucks Jane into bed every night (even though Jane is fourteen and almost as big as her mother); she knows the postal rates, moves chesterfields, listens solemnly when someone in the house says he or she is going to be prime minister, a famous athlete, or just an astonishing detective (Richard's current ambition); she hangs pictures (eighty on our one wall), sews on buttons, visits art galleries.

But "work"? I'm afraid not.

Jackie lengthens jeans, unplugs plumbing, remembers to serve spaghetti once a week (the kids' favourite), picks out newspaper items that might make columns, does thirty situps every morning to stay trim, explains patiently to Richard why he can't wear the same shirt eighteen days in a row, and makes the Christmas cards.

Mind you, she doesn't jog three times a week now, act as lifeguard at the "Y," or take German at night school, and her university class on great books is over.

But she did broadloom Jane's bedroom, make our front room coffee table (from an old dining-room suite), and (just last week) figure out how to replace the bulb in our slide projector when Daddy had failed.

That is, unfortunately, beside the point.

Jackie does not go to an office, perform brain surgery under OHIP, drive a truck, belong to a union, type up letters, sell real estate, host a TV show, or wrestle at Maple Leaf Gardens.

In short, she doesn't "work."

Mind you, she did "work" the first three years we were married and trying to get a start, but she quit a month or two before she had Stephen.

So she's just a homemaker, wife, and mother now.

Perhaps one day when the kids are a little more grown up, Jackie will "work" again, but in the meantime, I'm afraid she's too busy.

Living next to a work nut

As everybody knows, a man wants only one thing out of life — a neighbour who is lazier than himself. That's human nature.

Unfortunately, I live next door to the work champion of the entire world. This guy has every fault in the book — ambition, energy, industry, and a complete set of tools, which never leaves his hands.

He is a sweat nut and I hate him.

Compared to my neighbour, Pierre Berton is a drifter. Every weekend I just get propped up in a soft chair when my wife says:

"Ed's out raking the leaves." Or, "Ed's rebuilding his sundeck." Or, "Ed's bringing in his corn." Or some other darn thing.

Ed never sits down. His lawn is the first one cut. He catches snowflakes in mid-air before they even land on his driveway. His garage is neat as a pin and his windows (front and back) just sparkle, for heaven's sake. It's enough to make you sick.

Naturally, with that kind of competition, I'm forced to do all sorts of things that I'd ordinarily let slip.

To make things worse, Ed is a "helper." When he sees a tree in my yard that looks sick, he brings over a saw and suggests we cut it down together. He's been after me to put up a sundial I was given barely two years ago. "I'll bet we could do it in a weekend," Ed has told me at least a hundred times. "A little digging, some cement . . ." Most people have consciences; I have Ed.

He ran me ragged all summer but Ed really went too far about a week ago. I was just home from work when my wife said: "Ed's painting his house."

Ed's house was painted only two years ago but, sure enough, he was at it again. And he didn't even have his wife helping him. That's what I call flaunting it.

All evening I seethed. How can a man sprawl on the chesterfield, kick off his shoes, and enjoy himself, knowing that sort of thing is going on next door?

Ed waved and shouted to me that he had mixed up a special water resistant stain for his wooden siding and expected to finish the house in a couple of days. He said we could start my place next. I just smiled—weakly.

Ed wasn't on his ladder the following day and I noticed his special stain hadn't dried. In fact, it was still wet yesterday when a professional painter came over and gave Ed a price on how much it would cost to sand down the house and re-do the job.

Last night I saw Ed inside his house watching TV. It's the first night off Ed has given us in three years and every husband on the block is delighted.

I just hope it lasts.

The writing on the wall

Few groups in society are sadder than those people who go around printing dirty words on walls — except, of course, the even more unfortunate souls who try to erase the dirty words the other group has scribbled.

The other morning I was walking the dog before breakfast when my neighbour Len pulled to the curb, "I hate to be the bearer of bad news," he said, "but somebody's written THAT word in letters two feet high on the side of your house. And it's on the brick."

Yes, between dusk and dawn, someone with a paint bomb had sprayed THAT word on the side of our house.

Of course, when I saw it, my first thought was about the author. Did he or she have an unhappy childhood? Is this his or her way of crying out for attention? Was society really to blame?

My second thought was how to get the graffiti removed before being raided by the morality squad for keeping an obscene wall.

Alas, while thousands of dollars have been spent on delving into the minds of people who express themselves by jotting down naughty things in places where they can be seen, not a dime (as far as I can learn) has been directed to research programs aimed at removing their handiwork from walls, especially those made of rough brick. In fact, the first hardware store operator I called told me flatly, "It will never come off. I'd advise you to move."

"On rough brick?" a good friend answered. "Why don't you add a couple of letters and make it into a nice word, or disguise it in a floral design?"

Unfortunately, although a graduate of a couple of educational institutions, I cannot for the life of me think of a word containing THAT word, at least none that's perfectly respectable. So that idea was discarded, too.

A chemical firm representative said acid might turn the trick. "But it might just clean up the brick and make the letters stand out even more," I was informed.

At that point I was prepared to paint a message under the one left by my mysterious caller, something like: "The preceding is a paid announcement and does not necessarily represent the opinion of this home-owner," and leave it at that.

Then I realized there was one expert on the subject of rude word removal — the janitor at the corner school.

I was right. In his years of obliterating coarse words from walls (so he informed me) he had enjoyed his best success with a product — here he named it — that didn't totally remove the bad phrases but did fade them to the extent they no longer caused a lot of giggling among the children.

Well, I tried it, and after three applications THAT word has almost disappeared. And it only cost $2, or fifty cents a letter.

Which leaves me with one thought for the day: our forefathers knew what they were doing when they decided to keep obscenities short.

Some dirty tricks are too much like work

Our neighbour Bev gives her husband Barry the same present every spring — a load of topsoil. It's amazing how many wives in suburbia do the very same thing. Why any husband would want a huge load of dirt, I don't know, and Barry isn't much help, either.

As soon as the dump truck unloaded its cargo Saturday morning (in Barry's driveway, of course), Barry came outside and walked around the dirt.

"What are you going to do with that?" I asked.

Barry smiled sheepishly, shrugged his shoulders, and didn't have any answer.

"Is that your Father's Day present?" shouted Jim from his yard next door.

Barry's smile was definitely weak as he circled the dirt, piled high enough to challenge all but an expert mountain-climber. Hands in his pockets, he stared at the topsoil, turned over a clump or two with his foot, and then disappeared into his house.

An hour or so later Barry and his wife came out of their house, got into the car, and carefully backed out around the dirt, a very difficult bit of manoeuvring.

They had just driven down the street when my wife came up with a terrific idea. "Wouldn't it be funny if you moved the topsoil while Barry's out?" she said. "Imagine the look on his face if he came home and found a ton of dirt gone from his driveway."

I broke out in laughter. "I can hear Barry now when he telephones the police. 'I'd like to report a load of topsoil missing. That's right — topsoil. It's brown and, when last seen, was about seven feet high, weighs around 2,000 pounds, and has no distinguishing marks or scars.' It would be a riot."

"I bet Jim would go along with you," my wife suggested. "All you'd have to get is a couple of wheelbarrows and shovels. If you start now, you could probably move the entire load before Barry and Bev get back from shopping."

"It would be a great practical joke," I agreed, slapping my knee and giggling so hard the tears began rolling down my cheeks. "With brooms we could sweep up the driveway so Barry wouldn't find even a trace of the dirt. He'd wonder if he had been dreaming."

My wife said we didn't have a moment to lose if we wanted to pull this fantastic gag on Barry.

However, I began figuring out how many shovelfuls of dirt were involved, how many trips (approximately) I'd have to make with the wheelbarrow, the problem I might have finding a place to bury a ton of dirt without Barry spotting it, and if it might bother my back which, up to now, has never given me any problems. It was with great reluctance that I finally abandoned the entire idea.

But next year when Barry gets his annual spring load of topsoil, I fully intend to do it.

Provided it's a nice day, of course, and I can find a shovel.

$100,000 fireplace
— just grate

When we were looking for a house, my wife made only two stipulations: it had to be more than we could afford and it had to have a fireplace.

The first condition was no problem. Every place we looked at met that requirement, with thousands to spare. But the fireplace was another matter.

My wife wanted a big fireplace. Stone. Floor-to-ceiling. Something that would dominate the room and still have charm.

My wife didn't care if the house was made of brick, boards, or corn flakes. The basement was incidental. And the roof could have more leaks than a 29-cent pen.

When my wife stepped into a house, she immediately went to the fireplace. She looked up the chimney. She checked the firewall. She examined the mortar. She asked questions about the draught. And then she'd lean against the fireplace to see if it clashed with her hairstyle.

Finally, she found exactly what she was looking for — a dramatic, cosy fireplace with enough rooms attached to take care of the kids and make meals. Even better, thanks to the easy monthly payments, it could all be mine, provided I live to 186 and walk to work.

Naturally, with an opportunity like that, I snapped it up. I could see us living like a page out of *Home Beautiful* — midnight suppers around crackling logs, shadows dancing on the ceiling, filmy peignoirs, passionate glances shared over the kindling.

I should have my imagination checked because that's not how it's worked at all. The only thing dancing out at me at midnight is garbage. My wife stuffs everything in that fireplace — cake boxes, milk cartons, apple cores, leftover cloth, string, socks too tattered to mend, broken toys.

I live in the only $100,000 incinerator in town.

172

When my wife cleans up after supper, she has a theory: if it won't fit in the dog, it will fit in the fireplace.

I don't know if wood will burn in the fireplace. We've never tried it. But newspapers make a nice flame. Orange peels aren't bad. And the wrapping the bacon comes in is really hot stuff.

Naturally, there are advantages to my wife's trash program. The children, for example, love to see the pretty glow of hot tin cans on a cold night and they think the smell of cooking banana peels is dreamy.

You must come around some night and see our pyre drill.

I give you one word of caution, though. Don't fall asleep in our family room — not unless you're too big to fit in the fireplace.

My wife is a bug for neatness.

Must the car of my dreams die?

According to the newspaper, it would take $4.5 million to save the mighty MG from being phased out this year and going the sad way of the Studebaker, Edsel, and Hudson Hornet.

Alas, a quick check of my own cash flow indicates I am $4,499,987.50 short of the fiscal mark, the holiday having left only $12.50 in my trouser pockets.

Too bad.

If I had the necessary folding stuff, I'd be off like a shot to the troubled British Leyland plant in southern England where the most respected of sports cars is made.

"Here's your piddling $4.5 million," I'd say, dumping the bank notes on a desk top with ill-concealed disdain. "That's a small price to pay for a treasured dream."

Yes, that would be the strategy if I wasn't a little short myself 'til payday.

My first car was an MG — a TF model in racing ivory with wire wheels, red leather upholstery, a 1250 cc engine, plastic side curtains and a top speed of just over 80 mph. It cost me $2,400 in 1954 and was brand, spanking new.

On summer days I'd flop the windscreen flat, take off my shoes (the foot pedals were a little too close to be operated with size 11½ shoes), and seek out remote country roads where I could let her out and practise my "drifts" around sharpish corners.

Oh, what enchantment that was, little nuts and bolts shaking out of the dash at unexpected moments, the accelerator chattering at the idle under stockinged feet, a top that could be put up in the event of an unexpected cloudburst in less than fifteen minutes, provided you had help.

And then there was the heater.

The MG of that era was for purists and, of course, came without soul-softening frills like defroster or heater. However, I weakened when it became difficult to see the road through puffs of January breath.

A makeshift heater used in ambulances was installed in the cramped cockpit and, except for falling off at regular intervals, it worked fine. Better it should fall off than a vital part of my anatomy was my philosophy.

How I smirked at fake sports cars like the Thunderbird or Corvette when I tooled around town in my MG. How I lorded it over those who had springs in their cars and trunks for luggage.

For heaven's sake, the MG I drove had hardwood in its frame.

And the only mechanic I'd allow near it was a Brit named Harry Shute, a very tweedy type who always had a scarf around his throat and employed a stethoscope when listening for engine noises.

By George, those were the days. We MG drivers waved to each other on the road, many with gloved hands (although I never went quite that far). And we talked about mysterious things like RPMs, then quite unknown to owners of North American machinery.

Once a man (whose identity I won't disclose) put a garbage can on top of my MG as a gag, causing the canvas roof to droop down like a beige goitre. I would never have forgiven him but I wanted to marry his daughter.

Which brings up Jackie.

I would be driving that MG yet, I suppose, polishing the chrome, doing my own lube work and waxing the bonnet 'til I had houseperson's knee, but it was my only asset when I popped the question, the one about marriage, I mean.

So, at the risk of breaking your heart, I must reveal I sold the car for a down payment on a love nest, love nests going for $10,500 in those days. That was 1957.

Over the years I thought I might get another MG one day but the closest I've come is a Dinky toy model Jackie included in a Christmas present a few years ago.

Now, unless I find $4,999,987.50 on the street on the way home tonight, the dream of owning an MG will be over for a lot of us.

However, as my mother-in-law likes to sympathize, "by the time a man can afford a sports car, he doesn't look good in it anyway."

Song of Myself

98-pound weaklings —look out!

I go to the gym three times a week but I suppose you've already guessed. Fabulous bodies like mine don't just happen. They require a lot of work.

Of course having these enormous muscles isn't all fun. They are responsibilities, too. You have to go to the beach every Sunday and kick sand in the face of 98-pound weaklings and steal their girl friends. You have to leap tall buildings with a single bound (I find the tighter the leotards, the better the distance on those leaps). And you have to put up with people who confuse you for a movie star in one of those secret agent, bang-bang, action films that the English turn out. (Three times this week I was mistaken for Inspector Clouseau and twice for Elsa Lanchester.)

All this can be yours if you will only follow the proper workout schedule. The best way to start a workout is with a laugh, which explains the locker room where men take off their clothes. A man wearing only a double-breasted grin can't take himself too seriously and he immediately forgets his troubles at the office. He becomes a boy.

Put him in a pair of shorts and some sneakers and he will do all sorts of silly things. Which brings up running. At our gym the instructor believes in running. He talks about it by the hour. He feels everybody should run a mile or two a day.

All you need for running is two clever feet and one dumb head, he explains as he blows his whistle and lets us loose like a pair of whippets. Then he goes back in his office and reads magazines. Every now and then he comes out and checks our mileage by the distance our tongues are hanging down our chests. Unless you have a good excuse, like dropping dead, he expects you to run until your tongue falls over the laces of your tennis shoes.

As the survivors straggle in, he looks them over and states in a loud voice (it has to be loud to be heard over the thumping of hearts) that he just wishes the Russians could see us. "They don't realize what they're up against," he shouts.

We just lie there, remarking to each other how much he looks like Adolph Hitler and wondering if he'd accept a plane ticket to Argentina on his birthday.

Then we do some push-ups, clutching desperately to the floor so that we don't fall off. Sometimes we throw our legs over our heads (beginners get two throws) and touch our noses in all sorts of awkward places.

The hilarity lasts about forty-five minutes.

Some of us tried to get an insurance machine, like the ones at the airport, installed at the entrance of the gymnasium, the idea being that you could put in a quarter and be insured for the duration of the workout. But no company will touch it. They said they'd want to give us mental examinations before they'd even talk about insurance.

Anyway, we keep it up, three noons a week, running nowhere, filling the air with feet, bottoms, and profanity. Of course we can't do any other physical activity since we are always resting for the next workout. Besides, I have this sore knee now.

But it's worth it. The instructor said the workouts would make us live longer and it seems that way already. Some days are unbelievably long. He also says it will improve my wind. Right now, he claims, he would be willing to bet that nobody in Toronto has more wind than me.

Yes. Step a little closer. I could be persuaded to let you feel my muscle. It just came back from the dry cleaners.

Keeping fit

I've never felt better in my life, thanks to fitness classes. Three times a week I go to the gym. I run; I do push-ups; I play volleyball.

There's only one problem with being fit: I think my marriage is falling apart. You see, my wife can't keep up with me any more. I first noticed her slowing down a few months ago in the supermarket. She was pushing a grocery cart, holding the baby, and chasing the two other kids around the toilet paper displays.

"You're puffing," I told her at the time.

She admitted she was and asked if I'd mind holding the baby for a while.

I told her I'd love to. But I couldn't.

"I've got to go to the gym today," I reminded her. "Fitness classes don't do you any good unless you're fresh and relaxed."

"I'm sorry," she said. "I forgot."

I suppose the same thing happens a hundred times a week. My wife will be scrubbing the floor or putting up a bookcase or moving the chesterfield and she'll ask me to give her a hand.

"And risk pulling a muscle in my back!" I answer. "I've got a volleyball game today and it may mean a spot in the playoffs for the team."

So my wife does it herself.

Sometimes she asks me to carry something heavy into the basement after I've been to the gym. Of course I'm too tired by then. Besides, you're just asking for trouble if you exert yourself after a stiff workout. A sore back could put my training program back a week or ten days.

Right now I'm resting because I have to be at the gym in five hours. My hand's steady. No circles under the eyes. Biceps perfectly relaxed.

But you should see my wife! I'd call her but she's outside shovelling snow. Her hands are red and rough. She has a stiff neck from trying to lift the washer. And lines are creeping into her face. It will take her three hours to clear out a driveway that should be done in two, two-and-a-half at most.

And she'll come in pooped. She'll probably fall asleep by ten o'clock after she does the dishes, sews on the curtains, and puts the kids to bed. And there I'll be, raring to go.

"Why are you tired all the time?" I asked her last night. She couldn't hear me, not until she switched off the vacuum.

"What did you say?" she answered.

"I said, why are you always tired?"

"I don't know," she admitted.

"You wouldn't be if you went to fitness classes," I said, turning back to my paper.

Quotes my wife can't resist

Of course there are many things about me my wife finds irresistible — my gracefully rounded shoulders, my high (sensitive) forehead, my double-jointed thumb that provides no end of merriment on bleak November nights, my left knee that I can click if the party is getting dull.

However, it's more than a physical attraction.

Jackie also likes the considerate way I hold open doors for her when she's moving heavy furniture; the way I steady her ladder when she's hanging pictures; the way I stack mail on the dining room table on top of my hat, gloves, and coat so as not to take up valuable space in kitchen drawers; the way I never let the children kiss the dog on the mouth until they've washed their faces first; the way . . .

Well, let me just say Jackie is so gosh darn happy that she often expresses her intention never to get married again if anything happens to me.

And I can tell by the way her lip quivers when she says it she isn't kidding.

Having pointed out my good points, I think it only fair to add, however, that there is one thing about me that Mrs. Lautens doesn't like.

It's the way I read to her.

Lately, for example, I've been reading the paperback edition of Lester Pearson's memoirs and every time I come to a part that I really like (which is pretty often) I read it aloud to Jackie.

Last evening, for example, we were in the front room, Jackie going through her favourite daily, yours truly engrossed in Mike Pearson's account of his early days at college, in World War I, and then as a lecturer at University of Toronto.

"Listen to this," I'd say to Jackie, and then launch into a sentence, perhaps a paragraph, but always less than a full page, of the late prime minister's autobiography.

Jackie would look up from what she was reading herself and politely listen. Once or twice she told me not to laugh so much as I read the excerpt, and on one occasion she hinted she'd like me to wait until she finished the particular article she was on.

However, when I interrupted for what I swear was no more than the thirty-seventh time, thirty-eighth if you count the amusing anecdote I related about the time I had lunch with Mr. Pearson, a story my wife hasn't heard for perhaps weeks, well, Mrs. Lautens got pretty huffy.

"Let me finish the paper," she ordered, "or do you want me to start reading interesting things to you out loud, too?"

Of course I was shocked.

To show my disappointment at her attitude, I immediately took my feet out from behind her back where they were getting warm and sat straight up on the chesterfield. I know it was pretty cruel, but a man doesn't like to be stopped when he's in the middle of reciting a really topnotch chapter of a book.

Fortunately, I'm not one to carry a grudge.

Undoubtedly tonight, when I'm back reading the book, I'll give Jackie a second chance to hear me quote particularly clever phrases and guffaw over Lester Pearson's days in Hamilton, or some such. That's the kind of forgiving guy I am.

Maybe I should twist my nose first and make the cartilage pop. That always puts Jackie in a good mood.

Locker room Valentine

Every Valentine's Day my wife surprises me. She surprises me with paper hearts. Paper hearts, you may point out, are not especially surprising. And I agree. But it's where my wife pastes the hearts that catches me by surprise.

Last Valentine's Day, for example, I picked up my electric razor and discovered it swarming with tiny red hearts. The February 14 before that, my typewriter got the heart treatment. Over the years, I've had paper hearts stuck to lunch bags, place mats at the table, my morning newspaper, and even my forehead.

So you can imagine how I felt when Valentine's Day rolled around this year. I awoke with only one thought: where would Jackie strike this time? I shaved as usual. No hearts on my razor, the bathroom mirror, or my face. At breakfast, the grapefruit checked out and the scrambled eggs were unmarked. The kids were okay. (Yes, she's decorated them, too.) Ditto the dog, the toast, our front door, the tube of toothpaste, my copy paper.

By noon, my nerves were beginning to crack. I knew Jackie had a heart somewhere up her sleeve — but where? Finally I came right out and asked: "Okay, where have you hidden the hearts this year?"

Jackie looked hurt. "That's what's wrong with you," she said, "you're too suspicious."

By the time I left for the Y and my usual little workout, I was ready to agree. Valentine's Day was fast fading — and still no hearts. However, I was half into my gym clothes when the guys in the locker room began to snicker. Then guffaw. I looked down to see the source of their merriment. Yes — Jackie's paper hearts. They were all over my athletic supporter.

If Jackie had to boobytrap my gym equipment, why couldn't she at least have picked on my socks?

Love match I can do without

Mrs. Lautens has signed me up again for tennis lessons, a decision which shows how much faith she has our marriage will last. On my list of favourite things to do, I'd rank tennis about 198th, just behind parachute-jumping, taking a correspondence course in root canal work for fun and profit, and letting a killer shark snatch sardines from between my lips at some marineland extravaganza. Tennis is just not my game.

But Jackie refuses to take my word, claiming deep down I love it. Why is it wives insist they know more about their husband's views on vital topics like tennis, square-dancing, broccoli, and what tie goes best with the brown suit than we do? It's amazing how many times I come to a decision about something only to be corrected by the missus, who tells me that's not how I feel at all.

Anyway, back to tennis. Mrs. Lautens is certain once I learn to hit the ball and serve with a style that doesn't bring Karen Kain in *Swan Lake* instantly to mind, I'll thank her for signing me up. Of course, she said this the other times she filled out the coupon and sent in the cheque, too, and so far the seething romance (the one I'm supposed to have with tennis) hasn't surfaced.

One thing I have against the game, I think, is the fact tennis players are so picky. Unless you can get the ball back over the net, they don't want to play with you. One or two complete misses and they remember a previous engagement or claim it's time to take an insulin shot or something equally fake.

I wouldn't hazard a guess how many tennis players I've met on the court — once. Let them master the mysteries of the forehand or the complicated business of keeping the ball inside the white lines and they only want to play somebody named

Pancho who struts around with four racquets under his arm and a headband above his ears. Snobs.

Tennis gets no marks from me either for being a sport populated with people who look about seventeen years of age and have figures that suggest they wouldn't know a banana cream pie if they swatted it. Who needs the competition? What I'm looking for is a game where a mature man with thin hair, white legs, no reflexes to speak of, and a waist that knows its way to Frank Vetere's pizzeria can look good.

Okay, end of complaining.

This year we're taking lessons for a second time (although he will deny it to anyone who has seen my backhand, a swish followed by a loud, "I'm sorry!") from Peter Dimmer. We didn't even have to use false names to enroll, which indicates he is even-tempered or loves a challenge.

To make sure I didn't run off to Brandon to cover a sewage convention or stop breathing in a clever attempt to convey a saving impression of death, Jackie didn't tell me about our first tennis lesson (last night) until the last possible moment. When I got home, my tennis stuff was laid out and Mrs. Lautens informed we could only have a bowl of chicken soup for dinner because we were due on the court in one hour.

"The last time we had a lesson you had chili for dinner (how can wives remember details like that?) and it upset your stomach," she said. "We'll go light at dinner for the next two weeks while we take our tennis lessons."

Sixty minutes later, I was swinging vainly at a tennis ball and having, what my wife assures me, was the time of my life. Apparently nothing makes me happier than a sore shoulder and gulping for breath.

But to end on a happy note I should point out one thing: the tennis class is split in four groups — the Wimbledons at the top, the Queens at the bottom. Purely out of seniority, the instructor has allowed me to move up to the second-from-bottom group, the Forest Hills. At least when he asks the Queens to stand up this year, I don't have to respond. I'm not insensitive, you know.

5

It Happens to Everyone

The world's foremost "A" expert

If I ever get on one of those quiz shows with the fabulous prizes, I don't care what they ask — provided it begins with "A." That's my specialty. In fact, I may be the world's foremost "A" expert.

Abscesses, absinth, accordions, acetylene, and Achilles tendons are no mystery to me. And what I could tell you about adenoids should be worth a trip (for two) to Hawaii or an automobile on any TV game show.

The secret of my expertise when it comes to "A" (A, first letter and first vowel in the English alphabet . . . derived from ancient Semitic script . . .) is simple: my wife can't refuse those encyclopedia "bargains" at the supermarket — the ones that start you off with Volume One (A-Amer) for fifty-nine cents.

Unfortunately, subsequent volumes soar in price, sometimes as high as $2.49 each. Or they appear on store shelves the very week that meat is up, or sugar doubles. In any case, we never get as far as Volume Two; our book case is filled with twenty or thirty encyclopedias—but all Volume One.

Naturally, it's rather limiting. I can locate Aberdare, Aberdeen, Abilene, and Adapazari on any decent map. Not even Lake Agassiz is beyond my grasp, But I haven't a clue where to find Boston, Chile, Davos, or Ecuador, let alone something as remote in the alphabet as Zambia.

Perhaps it's only my imagination, but I also suspect the people who write encyclopedias don't put their best bits in Volume One. They seem to save all the interesting people for the $2.49 volumes. For example, the fifty-nine-cent introductory job never has anything about Shakespeare or Hitler or Rasputin. Instead we get essays on Abd-al-Aziz, sultan of Morocco from 1894–1908; on Niels Abel, 1802–1829, Norwegian mathematician; and on Lascelles Abercrombie, 1881–1938, British poet.

No offence, but those are hardly superstars; their names seldom pop up at cocktail parties where you're trying to make an impression.

But, alas, it's my fate to be forever stuck at the front of the book. Just this past weekend my wife was shopping and picked up (for fifty-nine cents) the first volume in an encyclopedia of wildlife. Of course we will never get to Volume Two, let alone Volume Twenty-Two.

But if anyone wants to know about aardvarks, aardwolfs, abalone, accentor, or addax, I'm your man.

The unkindest cut

The universe may be unfolding as it should but in this fast-changing world there's one thing every man wants to remain the same—his wife's hairstyle.

We can face a new ice age, adapt to population explosions, even find our way around downtown Toronto when they build a new one every weekend, but God help Mr. Armand when he starts fooling with the missus' bangs. Hubby wants every hair to be in its proper, and usual, place, and that goes for the part, too. For heaven's sake, we all need something to cling to, even if it's just a familiar cowlick or a shade of Miss Clairol we've learned to love over the years.

You can imagine my chagrin, then, when my wife came home the other day with her hair cut short enough to qualify for a YMCA membership. She didn't have enough hair left for a gnat to run barefoot through, let alone a forty-seven-year-old man with size eleven shoes.

"What happened?" I asked, expecting to hear that my wife's head had been caught in the coffee grinder at the supermarket, and that a large settlement was on its way. Unfortunately, the news wasn't that good.

"I was sitting at the hairdresser's and I decided to change my hair," she said simply.

"After only nineteen years of wearing your hair the same way you decided to change it?" I gasped, unable to believe my ears. "But I liked it the old way."

"This will take less work," was her casual reply.

I was so furious I could have sucked my arm and bruised myself. What a frivolous, selfish, rotten thing to do to me! Jackie's hair was the one constant in my life, and now it's gone!

Worse still, everyone who sees her new hairstyle tells her — now get this — they like it. Even husbands who would put their fingers in an electric outlet and stand in a bucket of water if their wives came home with the same thing.

So far Jackie has been informed the new hair cut makes her look (1) younger, (2) much younger, and (3) young enough to pass for my daughter. I'd be worried about the flattery turning her head if I weren't more concerned about what's outside.

What's next? Wigs, colour rinses, expensive falls, frosted tips, for God's sake? Where will it end?

I'm not one of those men who wants to nail his wife's foot to the kitchen floor and Crazy Glue a frypan or broom in the palm of her hand. Certainly not. I want my wife's soul to fulfil itself, her spirit to soar free, her mind to challenge the great unsolved problems of mankind. But I wish she'd leave her hair alone.

With my luck, I'll just be getting used to this new hairstyle around the turn of the century, and she'll change it again.

Darling, don't take my side

If my face looks cranky today and the smile definitely forced, it's because of a rather nasty experience I had in bed last night. After twenty years of marriage, the missus came up with the most outlandish suggestion in all our 7,300-plus nights of sleeping together. She wanted to change sides.

Yes, just like that, with no warning, without so much as a "now-don't-get-mad-but," Jackie wanted to change.

Of course I was thunderstruck. Since 1957, and room 5 at the Golden Gate Motel near London (Ont.), the left side of the bed has always been mine. There was never any question of that. Whether in Leningrad, Paris, Rome, London, Vienna, or something really exotic like a Day's Inn on the way to Myrtle Beach, that has always been the sleeping arrangement. Me left, Jackie right.

Why this bizarre suggestion to change sides? Because (Jackie claimed) she could feel a draft coming from the register on her side of the bed. On grounds as flimsy as those, she wanted to tamper with tradition, upset the normal way of doing things, and take my (left) side of the bed. Oh, what fickle creatures women are, changing their minds after a measly decade or two of successful sleeping habits.

Being a gentleman, I agreed to the switch, but I knew the arrangement would never work. A confirmed left-side-of-the-bed sleeper cannot be bounced around and still zonk out before he gets to the third sheep.

Of course I was right. First off, I stretched out my left foot, expecting as usual to find nothing but a lot of empty space. Instead, it collided with another foot—my wife's—which normally wouldn't be there. What a start that gives you, especially

when it's dark and your left foot has enjoyed over twenty years of comparative freedom and an occasional dangle over the side of the bed.

It's also jarring for a left-side-of-the-bed sleeper to turn on his left shoulder and suddenly come face to face with another face, a face your subconscious tells you should be on the other side.

Changing bed sides in mid-marriage is just asking for trouble, if you ask me. How can you possibly get the necessary eight hours when the clock-radio appears to have drifted to the other side of the room and what you push down in your stupor to see the time is your wife's nose? How can you keep your good temper and drift off for a snore when you reach over for the customary goodnight kiss and fall out on the floor instead? For heaven's sake, how can anyone climb into the arms of Morpheus when he knows, if he has to go to the bathroom in the middle of the night, he may make his usual turn and wind up in a closet by mistake, with unfortunate results?

No, it's wrong and, after almost two hours of tossing and turning on the wrong (right) side of the bed, I had to shake my wife and tell her to give back my proper side. She'd have to put up with the draft. Which she did with some fuss, I might add, and an elbow I don't altogether consider an accident.

So I am two hours' short in my sleep today, and grumpy.

Instead of all that business of "love, honour, and cherish" in the marriage ceremony, I knew I should have got Jackie to promise me the left side of the bed, 'til etc., etc.

She may forget a name but . . .

Jackie has a real knack for forgetting names. Whenever she meets someone, old friend or new, the thing she usually finds on the tip of her tongue is her foot. Names just elude her. First names, family names, nicknames — names.

To my wife, every one has the same name — "there" as in, "Hi, there!" Mind you, she also forgets telephone numbers, how to get to places she's been, what time the kids said they'd be home for supper, and if she turned the stove off.

But Jackie does have a good memory when it comes to dresses. In fact, I'd say she has total dress recall. Mention any wine and cheese reception, Sunday brunch, office party, sit-down dinner, or birthday bash in the past two decades, and Jackie can tell you what dress she wore. More impressive, she can tell you what the other women there wore, too.

How can it be? Here's a person who can't remember she put buns in the oven to heat up an hour and a half ago, but she knows instantly she was wearing her mauve dress (the one with the mandarin collar) the last time we had dinner with Isobel and George in 1974. Oh, yes, and that Isobel had on her blue Ports suit, a white blouse, and a bracelet with twenty-three charms.

Jackie may boob on a brooch or miss an accessory like a belt, but when it comes to the big stuff — cocktail dresses, pantsuits, evening gowns, wedding rings — she has total recall.

Before we go out for the evening, my wife likes to know who may be there so she can pick her wardrobe accordingly. Heaven knows she's no clothes horse. Some of Jackie's things date back to high school days. But she lives in dread that one of the dinner guests may go home saying, "Jackie Lautens wore that same outfit the last time we saw her, too." That, apparently, is my wife's concept of Hell. So she has developed this fantastic ability to remember exactly what she was wearing the last time she met "what's-his-name" or even "what's-his-name's wife."

Is it a trick memory? I pride myself on having some sort of talent for recollecting the past, but I couldn't for the life of me tell you what I was wearing the last time we were at a party together. It was either my blue suit, or my brown one, but I couldn't tell you which.

Even more amazing than Jackie's phenomenal memory is the reaction I get when I tell people about it. The other day I mentioned to a woman at the office how Jackie can recall perfectly what she had on at every social gathering we've ever attended.

"Can you imagine anyone knowing what she wore to all those parties, and what the other women were wearing, too?" I asked.

"Certainly," the woman replied. "Doesn't everyone?"

Well, the men I talked to were astonished.

The washer socks it to me

My cousin Diana has some pretty strong views about socks. Men's socks. According to Diana, no matter how many socks you put in a washer, you always get one less out. Diana has put socks in washers in Winnipeg, Toronto, New York and in Chicago where she and her husband Morley (and two children) now live and it never fails. Dump in twelve socks and eleven come out; sixteen become fifteen; eight become seven; well, the number doesn't matter.

What is happening across the world is that the supply of men's socks is reduced by one sock every time somebody does a load of wash.

Diana has no theory about what happens to the sock in

question but she knows it isn't a matter of which detergent you use. She's tried them all and the effect is invariably the same. The obvious conclusion is that washers are designed to consume one sock every time they're turned on, but Diana is willing to leave explanations to science.

Her chief concern can be summed up in a few words: what are you supposed to do with the surviving sock of a pair? Her off-the-top answer is a sock exchange. Diana figures the newspaper should have a page put aside for readers interested in matching up all the single socks they've got at the bottom of their laundry baskets.

As she sees it, a person could list surviving hosiery in a notice like this: "Available for immediate occupancy, one black cushion-sole sock (ankle-length), one executive grey polyester-and-cotton sock (calf length), one Argyle sock in showroom condition, one sports sock with fewer than twenty miles on it, one subdued patterned sock used only to walk to church Sunday. Can you match or deal? Reply Box 999."

Diana feels such a sock exchange would serve a real need in the community and get the solitary footwear of the country moving again. People are so desperate to find a solution to the problem, Diana feels, they wouldn't object to wearing somebody else's sock if the thirty or forty unmatched socks in the typical closet can be transformed into fifteen or twenty usable pairs.

Until the sock exchange becomes a reality, Diana is trying an experiment. She has started buying her husband socks with little dome fasteners near the cuff. Before dunking them in hot suds, Diana simply snaps them together and, while she still loses one regular sock per wash, so far none of the snapped-together pairs has gone missing.

My own wife attacks the problem more directly. Jackie restricts me to identical black, elastic-top socks so that I've always got a matching pair, at least until I'm down to one sock. And she stitches a thread of blue wool in the cuff so she can separate mine from our sons'.

There are no flies on girls from Hamilton Beach.

Sit-ups in bed, Honey?

The big problem with having had only one wife is not having anyone to compare her with. For example, is it normal for a woman to do exercises every morning in bed? Under the covers? Usually while her husband is still trying to catch that last valuable wink of sleep? That is how it is at our house.

Moments after the alarm has gone off, there is a great writhing and thumping, bouncing and kerplunking on our Beautyrest. Jackie is doing her daily dozens again. She does sit-ups, knee twists, leg raises; she touches elbow to knee; she crosses her hands back and forth like a semaphore signaller on a sinking ship; she rotates her head. In short, Mrs. Lautens leaves no sternum untouched.

And, as I mentioned earlier, she goes through all this while still under our duvet. That's because, as she explains, it's too cold to do exercises in the bedroom itself, especially on the floor. Hence her choice of gym.

Anyone dropping into the little scene from another planet would naturally assume what was going on under the blankets was an athletic event, or worse. But it's only Jackie.

Frankly, if I get caught in bed during one of her exercise sessions, I can develop motion sickness very quickly. It's like having a team of Swedish trampoline artists for a bedmate.

But Jackie insists what she is doing is perfectly natural and not unusual at all. How can I argue? It's like when she tells me ironing is only a rumour started by busybody women who like to make trouble. Or that a thick layer of dust on the furniture preserves the wood and makes end tables last a lot longer. Or that taking off your shoes when you come into the house is proper behaviour, even if you do slide in your socks and fall down the stairs a lot. Or that kissing and fooling around when the kids are out causes warts. Or that men who can get an extra day out of a shirt go to heaven faster than men who don't. Or . . .

Well, there's quite a long list of things Jackie has told me in the twenty-three years of our married life, including the one that if a wife doesn't get to Myrtle Beach for a holiday at least once every other year, the husband goes impotent.

Anyway, with only one wife to my name, how can I tell if Mrs. Lautens is acting like a perfectly normal member of that honourable profession? Do all married women tap dance in the kitchen during breakfast and sing, over and over, the first three words only of every song lyric ever written? Do they all have freezer compartments in their refrigerators with items that may have been there dead a decade, or longer? Do they all consider having their back scratched part of a husband's regular chores and give you a dirty look if you stray even the slightest off course? Do they all want to hammer 13,000 holes in the walls to hang up pictures? Do they all whip up the thermostat when nobody's looking?

Do they, to conclude on the same inquiring note we started, do they all do exercises at 7 a.m., under the covers, in cosy bed?

Those people who have been to the altar, or other, several times may have a quick answer, but when your experience is limited to one (1), the best you can manage is a profound shrug.

The great crockery caper

Life can surely hold no more thrills for Mrs. Lautens. The Resident Love Goddess has reached a personal Everest that makes all else pale in comparison.

Let me put it this way. Jackie wouldn't trade what happened this past week for a date with Robert Redford, a guarantee from Bjorn Borg to help with her backhand, drinkie-poos with Ken Thomson and a tour of his wallet, or the name of a hairdresser who doesn't lean. What took place in the past seven days is even better (in her estimation) than having a burglar break into the house and steal her iron.

Okay, no more suspense. This past week my wife went out and bought a new set of kitchen dishes. For the first time in twenty-three years of marriage, we now have dinnerware that actually matches! The dinner plates are all the same, likewise the bread-and-butters, the tea plates, salad bowls, cups and saucers. Even more breathtaking, there aren't any chips out of the crockery. This is brand new, grade A stuff.

Practically since day one of our life together, Jackie has had a dream, a dream that we would one day have kitchen dishes that didn't look like leftovers from an Animal House movie.

I said she might just as well dream of winning Lotto Canada or even coming home just once after the kids have made their own supper and finding the kitchen clean. Nobody, I pointed out, ever has fewer than the remnants of four patterns of kitchen dishes on the go, and to have three dinner plates and two nappes that match at the same time (our best previous record set in 1974) is about as much as any couple with a family can hope for.

The words didn't deter Jackie. We kept eating from surviving dishes of a wedding set given us by cousin June, on dinnerware retired from active service by relatives and no longer wanted, from plates that came with detergent ("Bonus Inside!"), from cereal bowls the gift of grateful service stations after a spring special, oil change and lube job. And there were other saucers and the like whose history had been long lost in the mists of time.

But amid the cream plates with maroon flowers, the blue ones with stylized chickens, the bowls with the bear cubs on the bottom, etc., my wife kept the faith.

About a week ago, a department store had a special on kitchen dishes and, without telling any one, Jackie ordered a full six-place setting. She felt we were at last mature enough to handle matching dinnerware with smooth edges.

When we sat at the kitchen table that evening, the new stuff was laid out in snowy splendour. There wasn't a crack in sight. Believe me, it was an emotional moment. Jackie was so choked up she barely could say, "Anyone break one of these new dishes and I'll kill them."

Where the old stuff has gone I don't know, probably into the basement where it will stay until one of our kids goes off on his own and needs a starter set(s).

In the meantime, it's pretty elegant dining off kitchen dishes that are the same colour, shape, and design. Of course, our kitchen glasses still don't match. However, I don't think even Jackie dreams that big.

Cave space rearranged

I don't know of any words that strike more terror in a grown man's heart than the ones Mrs. Lautens whispered over the telephone the other day. There I was at the office, minding somebody else's business, which is a journalist's regular line of work, when the main woman in my life called and said: "I've rearranged the furniture in the front room."

It was devastating. If she had informed me our daughter had run off with a tag team of touring midget wrestlers, I would have felt awful. If she had stated our son was toying with the idea of buying a suitcase-size radio and walking down the street with it turned full blast to CHUM, I would have been terribly depressed. But rearranging the furniture in the front room? That is definitely going too far.

A man likes his front room to stay the way it is. He wants to come home after a hard day in the trenches, throw himself down, and be reasonably certain of landing on a chesterfield. He does not want to find himself sitting on a magazine rack with the TV guide poking up his never-you-mind.

Is that too much to ask of life?

Apparently.

Jackie adores switching furniture, even though our front room is only nine feet wide, twelve if you count the hallway, which really is cheating.

What caused this latest rearrangement of the life goods is a pew purchased (for $40) from our church, which is in the process of being torn down, sob. Mrs. Lautens wanted a souvenir of St. Andrew's, the one on Bloor St. near Church, where our children have spent many an hour pretending to sing hymns, especially Richard.

So off we had trotted, Père Lautens and the two male off-spring, to unbolt the pew and bring it home under the watchful supervision of Foreperson Jackie.

(Where, I ask, are the libbers when it comes time to get on a dusty floor and reach behind a radiator to wrestle with a screw covered with 78 layers of shellac and driven in crooked by the world's strongest human being?)

Of course, I thought that would be the end of the suffering part, but when Mrs. Lautens got the pew into its planned spot (our hallway), she decided next day only a complete reshuffle of our belongings would do.

I whimpered and whined when I got the news over the telephone, pleading with the missus not to give me another of her patented surprises, the kind that cause the few hairs left on my head to sit down and write suicide notes.

It was to no avail, however. Everything, as threatened, was changed around. The sectional chesterfield has been broken up, the bamboo bench and matching chair are in the kitchen with a plant (they have become part of the resident decorator's "tropicana" motif), and whenever I get up from the purple chair I bump my head on a lamp that wasn't there before.

The personal cave sure isn't what it used to be in the good old days, about a week ago.

I'm afraid the old church pew is hearing language it never heard before, but how would you like to automatically put down a cup and find you've missed the coffee table by four feet?

Spaghetti tradition cut short

All of us in the Lautens household are facing the cruel fact that one of our great family traditions has been laid to rest forever. Never again, it seems, will Jackie cook too much spaghetti for dinner.

For nearly twenty-five years Mrs. Lautens has prepared too

much spaghetti for the eager faces around our dinner table. It's something we could count on.

Jackie can size up any crowd in rice pudding, gauge a platoon if necessary in hamburg patties, make the french fries work out to the final fry. But spaghetti has been her downfall since she first learned the mysteries of that delicious food from Danny Pugliese's mother in Welland.

For some reason, when my wife looks at spaghetti before dumping same in boiling water, she invariably comes to the same conclusion: there isn't enough. So she plops in more. As a result, we've always wound up with enough leftover spaghetti to feed the entire cast of a Puccini opera, plus every citizen of the city of Naples whose family name ends in "i."

At a guess, I'd say we have spaghetti once a week, or fifty-two times a year. Even calculated at twenty years, that works out to 1,040 spaghetti dinners that Mrs. Lautens has over-estimated. And not once has the Sun of my Life come even close to getting the amount right. (When you're exposing a woman's spaghetti faults, a little flattery never hurts.) In short, her record is 0–1,040, with not even a tie.

Invariably, after every spaghetti dinner, Mrs. Lautens looks at the bowl in the middle of the table, still heaped high enough to challenge Steve Podborski in a cup downhill, and begs: "Can't anyone help out?" To eat even another mouthful at that point would be dangerous to everyone's health, not to mention the brickwork, so we always decline, leaving Mrs. Lautens to vow that next time will be different. But it isn't.

As I say, this has been going on throughout our married life, but at Christmas our Richard gave his mother a special present — a spaghetti measurer.

The little plastic gadget cost less than $3 and Jackie used it for the first time last evening. She put in what the measurer claimed was the right amount of spaghetti for five people and, what do you know, it came out dead on. Stephen, Jane, Richard, Jackie, and I each had just the right amount of spaghetti—and there wasn't a single strand left in the bowl!

Mrs. Lautens was really pleased with herself as we cleared the table, commenting that not having spaghetti left over was a new and wonderful experience. For the first time she wouldn't have to put spaghetti in the refrigerator for two or three days, and then throw it out. (Throwing it out immediately offends her sense of thrift.)

Naturally, we're happy about Jackie's triumph, too, although it's always sad to see any family tradition bite the dust. I wonder how long it will be before Richard asks for seconds, just to see the panic on his mother's face when she looks at an empty spaghetti bowl.

6

No Sex Please . . . We're Married

Mama Bear's nightie

I'm not one to complain but I did blow my top the other evening when my wife came to bed.

"Where are you going?" I said as she walked into the bedroom.

"To bed," she announced.

"I thought you might be going to the North Pole," I commented.

"What do you mean by a crack like that?" she wanted to know.

"I mean you're dressed as if you're going to the North Pole. You look like Smokey the Bear."

"You never used to talk that way."

"You never used to dress that way," I answered.

For those of you who weren't there to see for yourself, I must describe my Aphrodite as she climbed into bed. She was wearing a pink nightgown (flannelette) which hung down to her toes and was generous enough to make a lovely awning. On her feet she had wool socks and on her head there was a net. Underneath it all, well, your guess is as good as mine.

"Where's your dog team?" I muttered.

"What's that supposed to mean?"

"Nothing. It's just that the last time I saw anybody dressed like that he was behind a dog sled," I said. "Or was he pulling it?"

"Can I help it if I get cold feet?" she stated.

"Up to your ears?"

"Yes, up to my ears, Mr. Wise Guy. Why don't you save your nasty remarks for your reader. Or do you have two of them now?"

"You look like a clothing drive," I insisted.

"If you didn't keep this place so darn cold during the night I wouldn't have to wear all this stuff," my wife countered. "If you weren't so cheap you'd turn up the furnace a little higher."

"It's healthier around 60 degrees," I said.

"Only if you're a sirloin steak," she countered. "Or a rump roast." And here she gave me a withering glance, which I ducked, of course.

"Whatever happened to that nice blue nightie you had?" I asked.

"That was seven years ago," she said. "It's a cleaning rag now. Besides, when I get up in the middle of the night with the kids, I want to be warm."

"But you don't wear that much clothing when you go to church," I protested. "Has the romance gone from our marriage?"

"It has until spring — or you turn up the furnace," she admitted.

So we just sat there, staring at each other, my wife unwilling to admit she was wrong.

"Supposing, just supposing, we turned up the furnace a little higher at night," I finally said when it appeared that bribery, not logic, would carry the day. "Would you get rid of about ten pounds of what you're wearing and come to bed in something more feminine?"

"Try it and see," she whispered, pulling one sock tantalizingly off a toe.

The next night the furnace was set at an expensive 70 degrees when my wife said she was going to get ready for bed. In a few minutes she reappeared wearing a white negligee, all frills and laces and tiny straps.

"Well?" she asked.

"Come closer," I ordered.

She did.

We looked into each other's eyes. She into mine. Mine into hers.

Finally I spoke.

"How much did it cost?" I asked.

I think it was the wrong thing to say. Or maybe she was planning to wear the wool socks to bed with her new negligee anyway.

Never too late to celebrate

Each autumn there is a social event called The University Homecoming. The Old Grad returns to his alma mater to savour the past, to cheer once more for the Football Twelve, to revive spirits laded by a world of annual reports and graphs and ugly profits, to drink deeply again from the fountain of learning—oh, yes, especially that. Some swallow so eagerly they cannot move by halftime and must be carried home.

It's good to get away from sordid business, to rejoin the academic life where, except for an annual pledge, a donation to the library fund, a gift for retiring professors, and a contribution to provide sneakers for the basketball team, money is never mentioned.

Last weekend was homecoming at McMaster University (which is my old college despite rumours you might hear, unfounded denials spread by faculty members). It was a moving occasion—walking through historic halls some of which date back to almost 1950, sitting in a windswept stadium where many of the great men of intercollegiate sport once played, invariably with visiting teams, looking into wave after wave of friendly faces and asking that great question of every reunion—"Who's that?"

It was particularly nostalgic because it was my birthday weekend, too. "I know why you're getting me out of the house," I said to my wife at the football game. "You're planning a surprise party. Right?"

"Aren't you always?" she said.

"Say, there's a girl I took out when I was at school . . ."

"My, she looks old," my wife said. "Here. Hold the baby."

"Why is it every time I see a girl I used to know you ask me to hold the baby?"

"Coincidence," she ensured.

Later we left the park (McMaster won 38–0 and my son beat my wife, three hot dogs to two).

"Everybody's hiding behind the furniture at home, eh? They'll jump out and say, 'Surprise!'"

"How did you guess?" my wife replied.

Well, there wasn't anyone at the house—just a birthday card from my insurance man who asks often how I'm feeling.

"Here's a package," my son advised.

It was a present from my mother-in-law, a book on Italian art, the very thing my wife has wanted for months. "When's the party start?" I asked.

"Any minute now," my wife said.

"C'mon. Drop the act. I know you planned a surprise party."

"That's right," she said. "How about a quick supper—bacon and eggs?"

We ate silently.

My mother called. "I ordered a birthday cake," she said. "But there was a mixup. The one I've got says, 'Happy Birthday, Gary—aged two years.' It belongs to a lady out in the suburbs. We've got to deliver it and pick up yours."

"Okay," I said. "Anyway, happy birthday to me—aged thirty-five."

The evening went pretty fast. It was seven o'clock in no time. Then 7:15 and 7:30 and, finally, nearly quarter to eight.

"Guess I should stay dressed up," I suggested hopefully.

"Why not get comfortable," my wife said.

So I did. I can bluff, too.

It was getting pretty late. Almost 8:30. "We could catch a show downtown," I mentioned. "Should do something. Or would you rather stick around, just in case somebody drops in. Ha, ha." The laugh wasn't very convincing.

"A show would be fine," my wife said. "Should I get dressed?"

"Never mind. I'll just read." So I sat there.

"The babysitter tells me she thinks she's got chicken pox and wonders if she's given them to the kids," my wife mentioned.

"When I was single I always had a birthday party," I replied. "I got a cake, too. With candles."

"That's nice," she said.

"Here I am thirty-five and nobody cares."

"Your insurance man does."

"Oh, I think I'll go to bed."

"Why don't you? It's almost ten o'clock."

"Okay, I will."

Just then there was a knock on the door. About twenty-five people burst into the house and they said "Happy birthday." My wife brought out the lunch from down in the basement and I got one barbell, a genuine teakwood yo-yo, a bottle of Greasy Kid's Stuff, a jar of pickled pimentos with a candle on the jar . . .

Somebody had an accordion and played polka music. The girls kissed me. (The baby was in bed so I didn't have to hold her.) My mother brought in the right cake and squeezed me and talked about the first night I was tucked under her arm—"I told the doctor I wanted a girl but I didn't care if it was pups just as long as he got it over with," she said.

"Were you surprised with the party?" my wife asked after the company had gone.

"Naw," I said. "I wasn't worried a bit."

"Did you get everything you wanted?"

"All the important things."

And we stood there, holding hands.

"Big mush," she said.

Romance on the sofa

Nothing is more embarrassing than being caught necking by your parents, especially if your mother is a Methodist. But that's what happened to me Sunday.

Let me make it clear that, ordinarily, I don't neck on Sunday. Sunday I cut the grass and watch football on TV. However, this Sunday I lost my head. The kids had gone to Sunday school and the house was quiet when I suggested to my wife, "Now that we're alone, why don't you slip into something more comfortable?"

"Like what?" she asked.

"Like the chesterfield, beside me," I responded.

"Aren't you going to cut the grass?" she wanted to know.

"Later," I snapped. "Come here!"

"Let me stack the breakfast dishes first," my wife replied.

"To heck with the breakfast dishes," I said, flaring my nostrils. "We've only got an hour."

I grabbed my wife by the hand and pulled her to the chesterfield where I proceeded to cover her forehead with kisses. The next thing I heard was somebody in the front hall.

"Anybody home?" a voice asked.

Yes—my mother.

My wife jumped up like a shot. Her hair was mussed and the strap from her apron was down over one shoulder.

"I knocked but nobody answered," my mother explained as she came up the hall steps into the front room. My father was three steps behind. "The door was unlocked so . . . ."

Then she spotted my wife trying desperately to rearrange her hair and adjust her apron straps.

"Oh," my mother said. "Oh!"

"I . . . I . . . I was just stacking the breakfast dishes," my wife blurted, slipping on her shoes.

Thinking quickly, I said, "Hi," looking mother straight in the shoulder. I never unflared a nostril so fast in my life.

They stayed for an hour, but it wasn't a relaxing visit. I knew that they knew what we were doing. And they knew that I knew that they knew what we were doing. But nothing was said.

However, I wish mother hadn't giggled as they backed out of the driveway to go home.

Lighting my wife's fire

It's a good thing I'm not a bachelor. I could never pass the physical. Just the other night I tried to light my wife's fire and the only thing that almost went up in flame was the house. Here's what happened.

I got home late, the kids were in bed—and I was feeling romantic. "Why don't you slip into something comfortable," I suggested to my wife, "and we'll have supper by the fireplace."

"What do you have in mind?" she queried.

"Oh, a little beef fondue, some candlelight, and a million kisses for dessert," I replied, sinking my teeth savagely into the shoulder strap of her apron and emitting a low animal groan.

"Okay," my wife agreed. "Get out the fondue burner and I'll be back in a few minutes."

"Every second will seem like an eternity," I vowed, bringing out the grade A material.

In ten minutes she reappeared wearing a backless jumpsuit, a hint of her best perfume, and a blue ribbon in her hair. She was also carrying a plate of chopped meat and a pot of cooking oil.

"She walks in beauty like . . ." I began.

"You'd better start the burner," my wife interrupted. "This is heavy."

"The heat from a thousand suns couldn't equal the flame that burns in this heart for you," I vowed. "It feeds on . . ."

"The burner?" my wife reminded.

"How do I love thee? Let me count the ways," I recited as I filled the burner and struck a match.

That's as far as I got. The whole damn table-top caught fire. With only candlelight to work by (and my glasses being upstairs) I had apparently poured too much fluid into the burner and it had overflowed. The only thing being shish-kabobed was the furniture.

"Stand back!" my wife shouted. She handed me the pot of cooking oil while she proceeded to beat the flames with a damp cloth from the kitchen.

Unfortunately, I got so excited I forgot about the cooking oil in my hand and tipped the pot while backing away from the fire scene. After my wife got the flames out, she noticed a peculiar gleam on the floor. Yes — cooking oil. And about a half inch deep, or so it seemed.

Using paper towelling, my wife got down on her hands and knees and began sopping up the oil, which had also splashed on the wall, the sewing machine, and my shoes. In about forty-five minutes, everything was more or less back to normal.

"My love's more richer than my tongue," I started up again.

"Knock it off while I get my wind back," she said, slumping in a chair.

Somehow I don't think seduction is my line of work.

Thin people are sexiest

Diet experts say thin people are sexy people. Well, take it from the soft voice of experience, they're right. Since Christmas I've lost nineteen pounds—I'm down to 163, my lowest since college. And, in the process, I've become a bottomless reservoir of passion. All I do in my spare time is smother my wife with tight-lipped kisses.

Take last night. We were watching television when a food commercial flashed on. It was for a gooey dessert. "Do they have to show this sort of thing on TV?" I demanded. "Don't they know I'm hungry enough to eat an end table?"

"Why don't you make yourself a snack?" my wife advised.

"You know I can't eat between meals!" I replied in astonishment. "I've already had as many calories as I'm allowed for the day."

"Then don't watch the commercial if it bothers you."

"How can I help but watch it? There it is right under my nose—a picture of banana cream pie covered with whipped cream and sprinkled with . . ." I ran up to the TV set and licked the screen.

"Why don't you drop over and visit Bill?" my wife suggested.

"Bill's wife is too good a cook. She'd offer me something and I might not be strong enough to refuse."

"Then go downtown."

"I can't. None of my clothes fit me since I lost the nineteen pounds," I grumbled.

"Why don't you get new clothes—or have the old ones taken in?" was the next question.

"Because I'm not sure I'll stay at 163. I don't want to spend a lot of money on clothes until my weight settles down."

"If you don't want to watch television, visit friends, or go downtown, what do you want to do?" my wife asked.

"Let's neck," I said.

"We necked last night," my wife reminded. "And the night before that. I've got ironing to do."

"I don't like necking any better than you," I told her, "but it keeps my mind off food."

And that's why people on diets are so sexy. In fact, if I stay on this diet much longer, I'm going to lose another 124 pounds. My wife says she'll leave me.

Sex secrets for sale

Like many others, ever since Shirley MacLaine made a bundle for talking about her affairs, I've been trying to assess how much my personal sex secrets would be worth. So far, this is how I've got it figured out.

Item: on our first date, I distinctly remember driving my future wife home and saying in a low voice, "It's time to get down to some serious hand-holding." Which I did. Total value for any future sex book: thirty-eight cents.

Item: neither Jackie nor I can remember our first kiss but Mrs. Lautens says it took so long for me to make a move she was beginning to think there was something wrong with me. However, we think the kiss came on our third date and both agree we were wearing overcoats, snow boots, mufflers, gloves, etc., at the time. Bidding price for scandal purposes: seventy-five cents.

Item: goodnight kisses during the courtship were limited by several factors. One: as soon as we drove into the side drive, Jackie's mother always flicked the veranda lights on and off. In fact, for a time I thought Jackie lived in a lighthouse. Value of anecdote for sex excerpt: twenty-eight cents. Two: if we did get as far as the front hall, Jackie's mother regularly shouted down the stairs, "It's time Gary went home and you came to bed." Value to potential book publisher: fourteen cents. Three: Jackie's father weighed 220 pounds and enjoyed bending storm doors in two to indicate to his daughter's boy friends how he felt about hanky-panky. Market value for raunchy newspaper syndication: nineteen cents.

Item: we courted in a sports car, an MG, with the emergency brake in between the two seats, no heater, plastic windows that didn't fit, and it was the dead of winter. As a hot scene for possible film or TV series: four cents.

Item: during the entire romance, I had a runny nose, the unfortunate result of taking secret swimming lessons every morning at the YMCA so I wouldn't be unmasked to the blushing bride on the honeymoon (in Florida) as a nonswimmer who had to bob around on an inner tube while the light of his life was doing half-gainers from the highboard. I learned to swim in time but the sneezing put a definite crimp in the hugging and kissing department. Probable porno value on open market: nine cents.

Item: we got engaged in Buffalo, N.Y. Romantic value to world-wide distributor of literary rights: 0.

Item: when the subject of the honeymoon comes up, Jackie's favourite story concerns a police officer who stopped us on a Florida highway and was going to give us a ticket for speeding until he learned we were honeymooners. That was the highlight of the trip, Mrs. Lautens insists. Price TV station would pay for the explicit details: twenty-seven cents.

Item: the groom (me) still has the actual honeymoon pyjamas in the dresser drawer. A gift from his saucy bride, they are white and are covered with little red hearts and tiny owls that are saying, "Whoo do you love?" Value as a teasing chapter in a reveal-all volume: twenty-three cents.

Item: the only garter belt in the house is the one used by me years ago to keep up the hockey stockings in an industrial league. Possible bid from photographer interested in snapping the owner (still me) wearing same: two cents.

And that's it.

Believe me, when sex secrets are going for $1 million, it's pretty discouraging to think your own best stuff is worth only $2.39 (Canadian).

Putting the bite
on romance

The old self-image is in tatters today. The spring has gone from my step and I'd have to get some colour in my cheeks to pass as pale. I've just found out my kisses leave something to be desired. It's a crushing blow.

Over the years I've always considered myself pretty good at kissing. Maybe not Olympic gold but certainly above average. Let me put it this way: I've never had any serious complaints about my pecks, smacks, busses, etc. No lawyer's letter at least.

However, the other morning I learned that in the osculation profession I could be charged with carrying at least a semi-dangerous weapon. It seems this front tooth of mine (the one on the right) sticks out and can cause mischief if a person isn't careful.

How I found out was a little roundabout. I was talking to Mrs. Lautens about daughter Jane, who had braces on her teeth several years ago but is complaining her front teeth are getting out of line again.

"Jane thinks they should be re-straightened," Jackie informed me.

I pointed out that (a) Jane at seventeen has never had a cavity, (b) her teeth look fine to me, (c) the first orthodontic experience set Daddy back over $1,000.

"Besides," I said, "my front teeth are a little crooked and may be a teeny bucked, but they've never bothered anyone."

"Except me," Jackie blurted.

That's when the whole sordid story came out. Under direct questioning, Mrs. Lautens confessed the tooth I prize so much during the corn season, the one I use to peel oranges and snap off ketchup bottle caps, well, THAT tooth was not always a joy to the kissee.

"Unless a person knows what she's doing, she could bruise a lip pretty badly kissing you," the love of my life stated.

As the words fell, I could feel my fang creep back into the dark recesses of my mouth. Oh, the shame! Oh, the ignominy!

"Why did you wait twenty-three years before mentioning it?" I asked. "I could have kissed you on the other side of my mouth, the safe one."

Jackie indicated the tooth in question added a certain element of danger and excitement to our relationship but it certainly wasn't something she'd recommend for beginners like Jane. We decided to let the family dentist look at Jane's mouth and go along with his expert decision.

However, life has not been the same for me since the accidental disclosure of my dental shortcomings. Guilty memories have been flooding back. In my madcap youth did I innocently leave a trail of battered lips in the wake of my rogue tooth? Was this the real reason Norma didn't go out with me on second date, not because (as stated) she had a previous engagement in Bolivia? Did Elsie refuse to let me kiss her fingertips in that playful romp for fear I'd sever a major artery and end her career as catcher for the class softball team? Was I first pick at Hallowe'en parties for my ability to spear bobbing apples out of a tub rather than because of my personality? Are there dozens of women walking around at this very moment with highnecked dresses because of an impression I made on them years ago?

I suppose it's something I'll learn to live with. In the meantime, I'm not going to kiss anyone unless they can prove their OHIP is paid up, and they sign a release.

I'm pretty warm stuff in bed

I'd like to say Mrs. Lautens admires me for my mind, but what she really likes about me is my warm body. And, please, no tittering.

If I had a dollar for every time Jackie jumped into bed on a winter night, shivered up to me, and asked, "How come you're so warm?" I'd be having lunch today with Conrad Black instead of in the office caf.

To be straight about it, Jackie doesn't care that I use my fingers when adding numbers, or that I sometimes get my grammar wrong. As long as my body stays warm, she'll never leave me.

To the Resident Love Goddess I'm worth my weight in fifty-cents-off coupons. She wouldn't trade me for fifteen minutes' free shopping at Eddie Bauer, not in the weather we've been having lately. Jackie is always cold and will admit the only time from October to April she's goosebump-free is when she cuddles up to The Warm Body in bed.

I don't mind when she puts a cold foot on me, wraps a blue arm around my thermal shoulders, or uses my back as a toaster for some personal bit verging on frostbite. Like Old Faithful, I am only too happy to do missionary work among the teeth-chattering and share my warm. In fact, I'm rather humbled to see the circulation and colour gradually return to Jackie's nose and cheeks.

Within a few minutes Mrs. Lautens is cosy and warm, and nodding off, undoubtedly to dream about walking in the hot sand of some tropic island, or stretching out on the most expensive deck of a cruise ship in the Caribbean.

Why I was chosen by some Unseen Hand to be the possessor of a warm body, I don't know. It's a mystery which, perhaps, no human dare explore. The plain fact is I have a warm body, just as some people have thick mops of hair, a baby toe that bends under, or the ability to wiggle their ears. Cold doesn't bother me.

Having a warm body is a responsibility, of course, and not one I take lightly. I'd never exploit my warm body or use it except for the betterment of mankind. For example, no matter what kind of marital spat Jackie and I might have had, I'd never threaten to take my warm body away, even though it would mean her immediate capitulation and victory for me, especially if there's frost on the windows.

When the thermostat for the evening is down to 55, and the wind's howling, I know I have an unfair advantage. It would be cruel to resort to the ultimate weapon on a person who, without your warm body, could be a human icicle in a matter of minutes.

No, my motto is: no argument is worth winning at the risk of another person's life, or chilblains.

How many others in the nation have been blessed with warm bodies, I don't know. But I do know it's our duty to make sure the less fortunate come through February, and without turning into popsicles or momsicles in the process. My only regret is that I have but one warm back to give to the missus. Still, it gets her through the night.

7

Aquatic Adventures

How a kiss turned Prince Gary into a frog

Men do all sorts of things for the love of a woman. Edward the Eighth gave up his throne for the woman he loved. Macbeth gave up his peace for the woman he loved. Romeo gave up his family — and life — for the woman he loved.

But I gave up my rubber duck for mine. And greater love hath no man than that. Rubber ducks, as you may realize, don't grow on trees.

But it was more than that. My rubber duck represented security. It comforted me in troubled waters. It was like a beacon to me. More important, it kept me from drowning whenever I was in water deeper than my nose.

You see, when I met Jackie, I was a confirmed nonswimmer. Oh, I had dabbled here, waded there. But swimming wasn't my cup of tea. Some people look at water and see beauty, mystery, and challenge. My reaction to water for the first twenty-eight years of my life could be summed up in two words: "Glub, glub." I hated water.

But there I was, going out with this blonde girl who had been raised on a beach, a girl who had water on the knee and everywhere else for the first eighteen years of her life. She considered Esther Williams a landlubber.

Anyway, when we began talking about marriage and honeymoons, Jackie mentioned she would like to go to Florida for a vacation.

Well, as it happened, most of our courting was done during the winter months and Jackie didn't know that the only thing I could do in the water was play dead—and very effectively.

Male pride what it is, I had two choices: I could either throw Jackie back and bait my hook for something that didn't go splash. Or, I could learn to swim.

The choice wasn't easy but I finally decided if anybody was going to give me mouth-to-mouth resuscitation, it was going to be Jackie.

So I started to take lessons. Every day through the dead of winter I'd go over to the YMCA and practise sinking. And I got to be very good at it. With very little practice, I was soon able to duck my head under water, to open my eyes under water, and even hold my breath under water. It wasn't until about the tenth lesson that I figured out the whole trick of swimming was to stay above water. As I recall, a lot more than my pride was swallowed those months. I had enough chlorine in me to open my own pumping station.

But after weeks and weeks of pretending the water was my friend (I knew darn well that the water hated me and was just waiting for a chance to swallow me whole) I finally managed enough of the dog paddle to feel qualified to make the trip up the aisle.

In case you're wondering, I didn't exactly dazzle my bride on the honeymoon with my aquatic skills but I was at least able to go wading without the services of my rubber duck. Nothing ruins the heroic image of a man faster than a lot of bubbles coming from his nose at the bottom of the ocean. It puts an awful crimp in the honeymoon, too.

After we got settled into the routine of marriage, swimming wasn't very high on our list of things to do. In fact, as far as I was concerned, it came right after flying to the moon and learning how to play the musical saw. For almost ten years I was able to keep up the little game. I wouldn't even watch Lloyd Bridges on television. That's how far away from water I kept.

However, three summers ago I got hooked into buying this home with a swimming pool as part of the deal. My wife couldn't have been happier if I tossed her a fish. So, at age thirty-seven, I had to start all over again—kick, gasp, kick, gasp, kick.

All the kids can swim now like their mother. They do the crawl, the breaststroke, the butterfly.

And me? Would you believe I was once a handsome prince until along came this pretty girl who kissed me and turned me into a frog?

Croak! Croak!

The amazing Lautens spa

I am certain that long lines of pilgrims will soon be forming in front of my home and that the name Lautens will one day rank with Pasteur, Banting, and Salk in the medical texts. Or, perhaps, I may put Lourdes or the Ganges right out of business as pilgrimage spots. That is, if the police don't nab me first for practising medicine without a license. You see, I'm operating a clinic.

It wasn't supposed to be a clinic. It was supposed to be a swimming pool. But it didn't work out that way. I was always under the impression that a swimming pool was filled with water. Fortunately, I found out better. A swimming pool is filled with chemicals. Chemicals to kill germs. Chemicals to kill algae. Chemicals to kill fungus, rot, and blight of every description.

Up until now, I've only used chlorine and muriatic acid, shaking in enough every day to keep my backyard bathtub kissing sweet. No bad breath for this Flipper. However, the good man who supplies my pool needs has convinced me I've only been half-safe. He's just sold me a third chemical which, when added to the other chemicals, even prevents and treats athlete's foot. He says you can now eat off my pool, it's so clean.

My pool bubbles. It gleams. A mouse fell into it the other day and was dead before it hit bottom. Now that's what I call antiseptic.

I'm sure you could bathe in my spa and be cured of boils, sprains, toothache, fallen arches, and that curious rash you have on your stomach. Undoubtedly crutches and eye glasses will soon be heaped beside my diving board, silent tributes to the miracles wrought by modern science and the dog paddle. After a refreshing dip, I myself notice a tingle in my muscles. The silver fillings in my teeth are left glistening. And I have a general feeling of well-being.

Each day I go out and feed my pool, tossing in chemicals by the handful and listening to the little bacilli go "Ugh!" as they keel over in a death rattle. I'm so pleased I may even have a particularly splendid cocci I bagged just last week stuffed and mounted for the fireplace.

To make sure I get the right mixture (one pail of water for every 35,000 gallons of chemicals) I even have a testing kit and, so far, my pool is in perfect balance.

Only one thing worries me. The more I swim, the shorter I get. Do you think you could learn to love a man who is two feet, three inches tall and hasn't got athlete's foot?

How to kill a swimming pool

Usually our swimming pool doesn't turn green until the middle of July. Once it didn't die until almost September. But this year we established a new record. Our water developed terminal algae by the first week in June. It turned up its toes before we had a chance to dunk ours. We didn't need a lifeguard in the backyard. We needed a medic who could treat swamp fever.

How did we manage it? Frankly, I was baffled too. It was more than strange; it was Erie. Naturally, I called George. George is the man who takes care of two things — my swimming pool and my savings. George can't understand why I complain about my salary. He can get along on it very nicely.

"George," I reported, "the pool has turned green."

"Are you putting in chlorine?" he wanted to know.

"Of course," I told him.

"Double the dose," George instructed, "and call me in the morning."

I did as he said but by morning the pool still looked like a subdivision for frogs.

"This calls for drastic action," George agreed. "You'd better super-chlorinate. Throw in four times the usual amount."

I did. Nothing.

"Have you tested the pool?" George asked when informed of the lack of results.

"Yes," I said, "and I don't get any reading."

George confessed he was stymied.

"Could the chlorine lose its potency over the winter?" I suggested. "It's been in the garage since last September."

"I never heard of it happening," he replied. "Maybe I'd better come over and take a look at your water."

"Yes — and bring $38.95," I stated. "I want a refund on that chlorine you sold me. It's no damn good." Then I hung up.

Later in the day I was working in the garage, getting the

de-humidifier set up for summer. And I couldn't find the calcium stuff that goes in it to absorb moisture. Pow! It hit me. Last winter I needed a place to keep the calcium — so I used an empty chlorine pail. What I'd been dumping in the pool was . . .

Well, our water may be green, but it's very dry. I'd better call George.

Midnight swimmers

I'd like to explain about the party you saw at my house the other evening. I know. It looked bad. You can't have seven lovely girls in bikinis running around the backyard at midnight without starting a few rumours, I suppose. But I'm innocent. So help me, it wasn't my idea.

I give you my word this is how it happened. My wife and I were watching the eleven o'clock news on television when there was a knock on the front door. When I answered it, there were these seven girls — hardly more than children, really — standing in the doorway. They were wearing short coats as far as I could make out because an awful lot of leg was showing. I admit that. Anyway, one of the girls spoke right up: "Mister," she said, "could we go swimming in your pool?"

What was a fellow to say? You can't turn away seven needy girls from your swimming pool, especially at eleven o'clock at night. Naturally, I agreed.

I asked them if they had a place to change and they said that wasn't necessary. They whipped off their coats, and they were standing in their bikinis before I could say, "Golly willickers!"

Don't ask me how they arrived at my doorstep. Maybe they go door-to-door every evening looking for a place to swim. All I know is that I had never laid eyes on them before.

When I got back in the house my wife asked who was at the door and I explained how these little tykes had asked to go swimming.

"That's nice," she agreed. Then she took a look at them herself from the back window.

"Tykes!" she exclaimed. "They're sixteen or seventeen if they're a day."

I told her I didn't get a good look at them and that she might very well be right.

Anyway, there I was with a pool full of young girls, splashing and diving, giggling and showing their form on the diving board. Naturally, I can only guess at what they were doing. Other than checking the chlorine level of the pool, turning on the lights, asking them if the temperature was just right, handing them towels, taking them soft drinks, and making sure they were good swimmers, I didn't go into the backyard once.

My wife was nice about it, too, once she understood. In fact, she didn't say another word the rest of the evening.

Shortly after midnight I had to go out to tell the girls that I was going to bed and that they had better take one last splash before the lights went out.

They did.

Maybe that's what woke you up — all the laughter and noise.

They dried themselves off, thanked me over and over, and then walked off down the street in their bikinis, their coats hanging from their shoulders.

And that's all there is to it. I swear.

Naturally, I invited the girls back any time they're passing. It makes you feel warm inside when you can help a fellow human being like that. Besides, seven is my lucky number.

Mother, will you come out to swim?

Why does a man slave to put in a swimming pool? Is it for his children? Is it to avoid the headache of driving north weekends to some faraway cabin to escape city heat? Is it for investment purposes, or prestige? Of course he says it's all those things.

But the real reason we men put in backyard swimming pools is because we think we'll get a chance to skinny-dip with the wife. No use denying it. As we sign the contract with Foamy Pools Ltd., we can picture ourselves cavorting starkers with the missus in a spanking new 40-by-20, playing like baby seals in the moonlight while the rest of the world sleeps, or whatever.

Now isn't that a lovely thought!

Well, you've hardly had time to turn on the taps, and send the cheque to Foamy Pools, before you learn your wife has no intention of joining you in your midnight swim. Especially without a stitch.

You can make all sorts of pretty speeches about the joy of swimming *au natural*, the thrill of doing the Australian crawl or even backstroke with nothing between you and the sky but stars, the freedom of taking the plunge without something by Speedo or Jantzen tugging every-which-way.

You can say all those things. You can even promise not to snap your towel at her.

No matter.

Wives want no part of a skinny dip. Daddy can do whatever he wants; she'll stay inside, buttoned, hooked, and zipped up.

In the eight years we've had a swimming pool, my wife has turned down suggestions of a midnight skinny dip on the grounds that it's too cold, it's too warm, it's too dark, it's too late, it's too close after dinner. She has complained about having a headache, not knowing where her beach towel is, and that she was expecting a phone call.

She has also said she didn't want to miss Johnny Carson (who evidently was having a particularly good show that night), that Richard had a little fever and might want a glass of water at any moment, that the neighbours seven doors down were having a party and might see, and that the streetlight across the road was giving off too much light.

Once, so help me, she said she couldn't go skinny-dipping at 11:30 at night because she had ironing to do.

At a rough guess I'd say I've suggested a skinny dip to Jackie 800 times, and 800 times I've been unsuccessful.

So (you're asking yourself) why don't I give up, get rid of the pool, and forget about skinny dips? Simple. Whenever Jackie turns down my invitations to a little midnight swim, she always finishes with the same phrase, "Maybe tomorrow night."

Well, it isn't a definite "no."

8

Broken Legs and House Husbandry

On becoming a ski racer

For thirty-nine years I've been able to go through life with one proud boast on my lips: No. I don't ski. It's been a major accomplishment. I could fail ink-blot tests, fit square pegs in round holes, climb the TV antenna and bay at the moon—but not a hospital in the world would ever commit me, not when they found out I was smart enough not to take up skiing.

Well, I've fallen. Don't ask me why. Maybe my father dropped me when I was a baby. Perhaps I nurtured a secret desire to wear plaster and have people write funny things on my hips. But there I was, agreeing to fall down some mountain I hardly knew—and pay for the privilege. I couldn't believe my dumb lips. Why should I take up skiing? I don't even like hot buttered rum.

Anyway, the first job was to put on the ski clothes which, to put it mildly, fit rather tight. In fact, when I put on the ski pants, I felt like a loaded slingshot. If my braces ever slipped off my shoulders, I knew I'd be accordioned to death. Then came the wool shirt, the sweaters, a thick hat, a heavy jacket, a scarf, goggles, boots, and two pairs of mitts.

My friends asked me if I could move and, when I assured them

I couldn't, they pronounced me ready to go skiing. They carried me to the beginner's hill (designed for small children, expectant mothers, and sissies) and I got my first lesson in self-destruction. Skiing, I've learned, is to North Americans what kerosene is to Buddhist monks.

The instructor, a fellow named Ron Sadist, spent the first thirty minutes telling me the best way to enjoy skiing. He told me, for example, that skiing is more fun if you don't run into tree stumps at 40 mph. He also said there were limited laughs in sailing over cliffs and holding onto the tow rope too long. He told me how to fall down, how to get up, how to slip out of skis in an emergency, and what to do while waiting for the ski patrol to pick me up in a toboggan.

"What do you do when your hands get cold?" I asked.

"You jump up and down and say, 'Isn't this fun! Isn't this fun!'" he explained.

I tried it but it kept coming out, "I must be nuts. I must be nuts."

Finally I was ready to be launched. "I hope I don't break anything," I said to him.

"If you break anything, make sure it's a leg," he warned. "Everything else is rented."

Down I went. I skidded. I slid. I did something called a snow-plow. I also sagged. But I got clear down to the bottom without sitting down.

Triumph!

On the tow going back up the hill, I said to Ron: "How much would it cost me for boots, harness, and, maybe, racing skis?"

A glorious ski weekend

I was bitten by the ski bug about a month ago so you can imagine how excited I was when I got a chance to borrow a friend's cottage in the mountains last weekend.

"Boy, oh boy! Are we going to have fun!" I announced

to my wife when I got home with the good news.

My wife never answered. It's amazing how she can conceal her enthusiasm even at moments like these.

"We'll pack the kids, drive 475 miles, and be skiing that very day," I enthused. "I'll arrange everything."

All we needed was skis, boots, harness, poles, goggles, wax, waterproofing, sweaters, parkas, mitts, après-ski ensembles, and a rack to carry everything on the car roof. In the past, I always rented. This time I bought the works. It cost a bundle but when you're going to have that kind of fun, who worries about money?

The day we left home, it was pouring rain. "Boy, oh boy! Are we going to have fun?" I repeated gamely. "I can't wait to get to the mountains and see all that snow."

My wife just gave me a friendly glare and told the kids to stop fighting in the back seat, or she'd throw them out the window at 60 mph. (She's great with that child psychology stuff.)

When we got to the mountains, it was still raining. "Never mind," I said. "It's going to turn to snow overnight and we'll ski tomorrow." The next morning it was still raining.

"We'll get our boots adjusted, wax the skis, and check our gear until the snow starts to fall this afternoon," I suggested bravely. "And then—zoom! Are we going to have . . ."

"I know—fun," my wife interrupted. And then she ran off to stop the children from feeding the baby—to the animals outside.

I have to admit even I was getting discouraged. It rained when we went to town for supplies. It rained during dinner. It rained that evening. And we were down to our last day.

"The temperature's almost freezing," I pointed out as we went to bed. "Just another degree or two and we'll be sliding . . ."

My wife was already asleep so I never finished my Knute Rockne speech.

When we woke up in the morning, there it was — snow, glorious snow! And the hills were only a twenty-minute drive away!

"Get dressed," I ordered. "We'll be the first ones on the tow. Boy, oh boy! Are we going to have fun?"

225

"Think so?" my wife replied, pointing to the road. Or where it was supposed to be. We were snow-bound.

The ploughs came past at four o'clock that afternoon—just in time for us to get a really good look at the ski hills on the way home.

Now I'm lady of the house

I'm the kind of guy who worries when his wife goes out for an afternoon of fun and comes home with her underwear tucked under her arm. I know it's silly but that's how I am. So you can imagine how my forehead wrinkled the other day when Jackie opened the front door.

There she was, exactly as when she left—but with her underwear in a neat roll under one arm and a friend (female) under the other.

"Hi," Jackie said.

"I thought you were skiing," I responded.

"I was," she agreed.

Just then part of her underwear fell out of her grasp and landed on the floor.

"Have a good time?" I asked.

"No . . . not exactly. . . ."

"Jackie had a little accident," her friend interrupted. "We had to take her to the hospital for X-rays and, well, Jackie can tell you the rest. Good-bye."

Exit, one friend.

"What happened?" I asked when we were alone.

"I was taking just one more run before coming home and I went down the smallest hill and I hit some deep snow and I fell and they had to call the ski patrol and they brought me down the hill on a toboggan and they took me to the hospital and the doctor thinks I have a hairline fracture in my knee and I feel just awful," she said.

"Thank God!" I said. "For a minute I thought it was serious."

"It is serious," my wife blubbered.

"Not as serious as I thought it was," I told her. "By the way, your underwear is dragging on the ground."

"Those are my long johns," she explained. "After the X-rays, I couldn't get them on again."

With a little help from me, Jackie limped to bed—and that's where she is right now. She's got her leg propped in the air and her après-ski outfit consists of flannelette pyjamas and a plaster cast from her thigh to her ankle. If I didn't know better, I'd swear I was married to Angelo Mosca or Whipper Watson.

I'm in charge of the house so it's my job to help the kids get dressed, prepare breakfast, do the dishes, sweep up, go to the office, get home early, make (or buy) supper, answer telephone calls from people wanting to know how Jackie is, get the kids to bed, do a little dusting, etc. And then, at night, I sleep on a spare cot so that Jackie's knee won't be jiggled while it heals.

Today I had an uncontrollable urge to get Jackie's skis and throw the rotten things out on the front lawn in a gesture of defiance.

Revenge!

But then I remembered how much they cost and discarded my plan. Everything has a price apparently, even my righteousness.

A lesson on using a refrigerator

It's taken forty-one years but I'm finally getting the real low-down on how to run a kitchen. Every evening my wife props up her broken leg on a kitchen chair and gives me instructions on how to prepare dinner, what pots to use, which button on the stove to press, etc. Last night's lesson was on the use of the refrigerator.

I was cleaning up when my wife asked, "What are you doing now?"

"I'm taking the mashed potatoes we didn't finish at dinner and putting them in the garbage," I answered.

"Wrong," my wife chided. "You don't throw out mashed potatoes like that."

"What do I do with them?"

"You get a plastic baggie out of the top drawer and put the mashed potatoes inside of it."

"Then what?"

"You put the mashed potatoes in the refrigerator. They'll keep."

"There's only a spoonful or two left," I protested.

"When you're running a kitchen, you've got to learn not to throw out perfectly good food," my wife advised.

"But . . ."

"Don't argue—just put the mashed potatoes in the refrigerator."

"All right," I surrendered.

It took a couple of minutes but I scraped the mashed potatoes into the bag and prepared to put it away.

"Very good," my wife encouraged. "Now, while the refrigerator door is open, see if you can reach the plastic bag at the back of the middle shelf."

I said I could.

"Throw it in the garbage," came my next order.

"What's in it?" I asked.

"Mashed potatoes."

"Let me get this straight," I pleaded. "Do you want me to put mashed potatoes in the refrigerator, or to throw them out?"

"Both," she said.

"If you've already got cold mashed potatoes in the refrigerator, why don't you just let me throw out the ones left over from tonight's dinner?" I suggested.

"Because tonight's leftover potatoes are fresher than the leftover potatoes I've already got in the refrigerator."

"Then when will you throw out tonight's leftover mashed potatoes?"

"Probably next week," my wife admitted.

"We never eat leftover mashed potatoes at any time," I pointed out. "Why do you bother wrapping them up and putting them in the refrigerator?"

"Because I hate waste," my wife explained. "By the way, don't throw out that gravy. Get some plastic wrap and a jar and . . ."

Wife's crutches an added weapon

I thought my chances of finally winning a domestic scrap (after thirteen years of marriage) would be immeasurably improved after my wife broke her leg skiing. After all, how tough can a 124-pound blonde be, especially if she has to hop on one leg to catch you?

The answer is plenty.

As it turns out, the accident has added just one more weapon to my wife's arsenal of tricks. You'd better make that two weapons — both crutches.

Not only do the crutches keep her up, they keep the rest of us down. The other day, for example, the kids were tearing through the house just slightly faster than the speed of sound. Now, ordinarily, you have to wait until they tire a bit — and then tackle them before they get their second wind. Not any more. My wife just sat calmly on the chesterfield — and stuck out a crutch when the little tykes made the turn into the kitchen a good six feet away.

Pow! They were down like bowling pins.

"Stop running," my wife ordered, wiggling the rubber tip of her crutch under their noses.

The rest of the morning they were very subdued. Wouldn't you be if you had a mother with a twelve-foot arm span?

Nobody or nothing is safe any more. We were in the family room the other evening when my wife spotted a spider crawling on the ceiling. Zap! She crutched him to death without getting

out of her chair. The poor little fellow didn't know what hit him.

Thanks to her crutches, my wife is sort of a Hardwood Pimpernel. She's here, she's there, she's everywhere. Believe me, it's dangerous being married to The Fastest Crutch In The East. Just yesterday my wife and I were discussing something and, since I'm the more mobile at the moment, I was confident I'd get the last word in.

". . . and that's final," I suggested, turning to make my exit.

"I'm not through yet," my wife said. And she plunked her crutch down on my foot.

I couldn't move. Only after she got in her say did my wife lift the crutch and finally release me. It sure put a dent in my ego.

However I've got an ace up my sleeve. Some night when my wife's not looking I'm going to infect her crutches with Dutch elm disease. Let her explain that to the health department.

The stumbling gourmet

My wife's knee and I have two things in common: we're the sole support of my wife. And we're both sore at this moment. But there the comparison ends.

For example, the knee has been getting nothing but rest since Jackie had a skiing accident. On the other hand, I haven't sat down once since she took a spill and landed on her two most sensitive points — her pride and her kneecap.

The doctor claims the injury isn't serious — just a slight fracture. However, I can't say the same for me. Thanks to that knee, I'm bushed, bothered, and beleaguered. Everything has given out, including my temper.

To be perfectly frank, I'm not crazy about Jackie sliding down mountains on a pair of expensive fibre-glass runners in the first place. If I had wanted to marry Jean Claude Killy, I'd have asked him. What I wanted was somebody who was soft, cuddly, and a good cook. Unfortunately, at the moment, what I've got is a partner who, with her leg wrapped up in plaster and an elastic bandage, looks like a cross between a Canadian and an Egyptian mummy.

What does that mean to me? For one thing, from failing hands I've been thrown not a torch but an apron. I'm in charge of putting enough grub inside my kids so that they won't keel over at recess with malnutrition and cause a big scandal.

Alas! This is one gourmet who doesn't gallop. Stumble might be the better word. If James Beard ever saw what I do with food he'd probably lay a charge of assault and battery — or arson. I can get by breakfast all right. Cornflakes, toast, orange juice, and a vitamin pill each. Ditto lunch. How much talent does it take to make a peanut butter sandwich that will glue a kid's mouth shut so he can't ask for dessert?

But supper is my Achilles heel. Isobel has sent over some tidbits. So have my mother, Pat-down-the-street, and Carlo (who runs a takeout pizza place). My trouble is I can never get things ready in the proper order. For example, Isobel's chocolate pudding was just at the right temperature before the roast my mother left me was cooked.

What do you do in a case like that? We ate chocolate pudding as an appetizer and then dug into the meat course, forgetting completely about the vegetables, which weren't done until about eight o'clock that evening. It was like putting on your underwear after you've pulled on your trousers — but, when you're hungry, who cares?

Well, the kids for one.

They don't seem to have an appetite for roast beef after they've polished off a couple of bowls of chocolate pudding. They said the gravy tasted like Hershey bars. I couldn't even tempt them with a late snack of boiled potatoes and beets served up just before they went to bed.

Happily, I've discovered that youngsters love peanuts, which are a snap to prepare, if you can find the red tab on the cellophane package. I don't think serving them three times a day, and between meals, is too much although I do find it strange that Stephen has this curious desire now to hang upside down from the light fixtures. At least he's out of the way.

My other complaint about this skiing injury concerns the sleeping arrangements at our house. Ordinarily, my wife and I share a double bed which, on cold winter nights, has certain advantages. However, because of the sore knee, which hurts even when viewed from closer than ten feet, my wife has taken over the bed completely. After making meals, writing columns, cleaning up, and issuing bulletins to friends on the state of my wife's knee, I'm relegated to the spare bedroom, where the only thing I can wrap myself up in is the cobwebs.

These are dark days for me — and the nights are no fun either.

The joy of charity

Thanks to my wife's broken leg, we have a new standard of living at our house. You'll think I'm gloating but, at this very moment, we have a huge lasagna in the refrigerator, a pan of stuffed steaks waiting only to be heated — and a casserole brimming with mysterious goodies. We also have a lemon chiffon cake, some chocolate chip cookies, two quarts of vanilla cherry ice cream, and a strawberry pie. And that's just today's take.

As it's turned out, the best break I've had in years is the one just below my wife's kneecap in her left leg. I didn't catch on to my good fortune right away. In fact, the first few days after the ski accident were grim, as I may have mentioned.

But then the plaster cast began to pay dividends. First Isobel (who lives around the corner) came over with a dish of spaghetti and her homemade sauce, which I can only describe as the best thing to come out of Italy since pinching.

"I hope you won't feel insulted if I bring over something for you and the children to eat," she apologized, "but I know it must be difficult for Jackie to get around the kitchen."

I assured Isobel that she wouldn't hurt my feelings if she brought over spaghetti (and her homemade sauce) from now till doomsday.

Although I didn't realize it, that was the turning point in my career as a homemaker. As soon as word got around that Jackie was laid up and that I wasn't too proud to accept charity, the food began to pour in. And not just *any* food.

Because they realized their donation to our supper table was being compared with recipes whipped up by others on the street, the neighbours began to outdo each other. Patricia delivered a steaming plate of filet done in some wine sauce that was strictly topflight. Marion turned out several dreamy desserts. Doreen came over one day with a complete dinner on a huge tray, everything from salad to barbecued chicken to homemade rolls to blueberry cheesecake — and she set our table as a bonus.

That's how it's gone day after day. Why, just yesterday, honest, we had *three* main courses brought around to the house.

So now you know why my refrigerator is groaning under the load.

Unfortunately, there is a price to pay for all this high living.

Every husband in the district glares at me when I go past — and I can't blame them. I've been in the same boat. I've watched my wife turn out gourmet meals for somebody down the street and then been forced to settle for hash myself because she's too pooped to prepare anything better for her own.

But now that I'm on the receiving end of all this kindness, not to mention calories, I'm not going to knock it. When the ladies bring over bowls heaped high with mouth-watering treats, a small tear forms in my eye (I can make either eye glisten in gratitude now) and I say, "Bless you." Or, on occasion, I murmur, "Oh, you shouldn't have!" I am careful to say this, however, without conviction. If someone like Isobel asks how my wife's feeling, I sadly reply, "About as well as can be expected, I suppose."

And, after the door is closed and Isobel's gone, I shout, "Soup's on, gang!" And we all race for the dinner table, Jackie included. Jackie is usually first to the kitchen because she (unfairly, I think) uses her crutches to trip the rest of us and hamper our movement.

So you can see what the broken leg means to our stomachs. It's our meal ticket. We are living like kings — and it's costing me only about $6 a week for milk, sugar, ketchup, etc., little items the neighbours (up till now) have neglected to bring.

I don't care what the doctor says. I'm keeping Jackie's leg in a cast till Christmas at least. Why heal a good thing?

A beginner's guide to supermarkets

While my wife is on crutches with her broken leg, I've been doing the family shopping and these are some of the things I've learned about supermarkets:

Shopping carts all have one defective wheel which makes them impossible to steer straight.

Today's "specials" include dented cans of boiled turnip, parts of the cow you never knew it had, and a brand of ketchup your kids won't eat on a bet.

Before you get the chicken checked through, it leaks all over your groceries and down the front of your trousers, causing all sorts of nasty stories to start.

It's possible to get whiplash if rear-ended by a four-year-old pushing his mother's shopping cart.

There is no dignified way for a woman in a skirt to lean over the milk bin and pick up a three-quart jug of 2 percent.

When shopping for a family of five, it's only possible to get pork chops in packages of four.

Large bags of potatoes are invariably on the supermarket floor and can be lifted with safety into your cart only if you have won a medal at a recent weight-lifting competition of international standard, have at least one teen-aged son with you to take the other end, or are wearing a truss or some other recognized support.

The roast in the next person's shopping cart looks better.

Supermarkets place their frozen foods at the most distant point in the store so that by the time you get to the checkout counter you can see it melting at the corners or hear it swishing in the can.

At the fruit counter, there is one rule: if you can reach it, don't take it. (A veteran shopper wouldn't consider taking home a grapefruit unless he or she dug it out from the bottom of the display, and had to get a boost to grasp it.)

Every supermarket has at least one aisle where someone has dropped a bottle (economy size) of salad dressing.

The most friendly clerks in the supermarket are in the fruit section while the most abrupt tend to be in the meat division, possibly because the first words expressed by most customers when they look at the price tag on a package of steaks is, "They've got to be kidding."

Novice shoppers can be spotted trying to figure out whether it's better to buy a five-pound box of Washday miracle for $2.07

and get a bonus towel, another brand not advertised on TV but only $1.65 with a china figurine inside, or let the entire family go dirty for the week.

In the express line-up for eight-items-or-less, there's always a shopper with 18 items, plus a plant.

All checkout girls are named Helen, have a plastic flower on their smock, and ask, "Do you have two pennies?"

Finally, I've learned one thing going to the supermarket: I'm getting stronger every year. Why, five years ago I could barely manage to lift $35 worth of groceries, and now I can carry $70 worth with ease.

Housework and a passionate wife

There's been an amazing change in me since my wife broke her leg and I took over the housework. Just the other day, for example, Jackie came home from her daily therapy session and started across the front hall on her crutches.

"Did you wipe your foot?" I demanded. "I've just waxed that hall and I don't want it tracked up."

"I think my foot's clean," she responded.

"Thinking isn't good enough," I admonished. "I'm not getting down on my hands and knees and scrubbing a floor just for the good of my health. Take your shoe off."

Jackie slipped out of her loafer.

"You'll never believe what those kids did while you were away," I said.

"Couldn't it wait till later?" my wife begged. "I've had a tough day downtown and the traffic was murder."

"No, it couldn't," I answered. "I want you to give Richard a good talking to. He's been a little brat all afternoon."

"What did he do?"

"What didn't he do would be a better question. He put his

knee through his pants playing football on the lawn, he punched his sister, he . . ."

"Calm down," my wife said. "Don't get so excited."

"You'd be excited, too, if you had to spend all day with these children," I said, bursting into tears. "They don't appreciate anything I do. I made them a beautiful lunch—peanut butter and honey sandwiches—and they hardly ate a bite. You don't know what it's like to slave in that kitchen and then have them turn up their noses at my meals," I sobbed.

"There, there," my wife comforted. "I'll speak to Richard later."

"You're no better," I complained. "I've been dusting and cleaning in the front room most of the afternoon but do you notice? Of course not. You're taking me for granted. It's okay for you to be downtown, taking therapy, but I've got to keep this house clean, feed the children, and then try to look nice when you come home. Frankly, I'm fed up. I'm fed up with housework. I'm fed up with picking up after people. I'm fed up with dirty dishes and folding the laundry and planning meals. For two cents I'd chuck it all and go home to mother."

"Why don't we just sit down and have a little quiet time to ourselves?" my wife suggested.

"All right—but hang your coat up first," I ordered.

"Can I put my arm around you?" my wife asked.

"No."

"Why not?"

"Because you think sex is the answer to everything," I told her. "And take your hand off my knee."

"Come on. How about a little kiss?"

"I'm not in the mood," I said. "Besides, I've got a headache."

"A little kiss will make you feel better," was her reply.

"The children may walk in," I warned. "How would it look if they found us like that?"

"They're playing around the corner," my wife stated. "I saw them when I came home."

"I think I'd better get supper started," I announced.

"It can wait," my wife guaranteed.

"We're having quick-fry steaks," I said. "There's fresh bread, fruit cocktail . . ."

That's as far as I got.

My wife bent me back over the chesterfield and gave me a warm, passionate kiss on the lips. I could feel her undo the bow on my apron.

"Promise you'll respect me in the morning," I whispered.

Jackie stood through dinner!

Jackie stood up for her first meal Saturday and I don't have to tell women what a breakthrough that is.

When my wife broke her leg skiing, she coped with the pain, the plaster cast, and the crutches, but she was unable to eat standing up.

Ordinarily, like other wives and mothers, my wife never sits down through breakfast, lunch, or supper. She's too busy bringing things to the table, cleaning up drinks the kids have spilled, looking for the HP sauce, checking to see what's boiling over on the stove, and clearing away the dirty plates. But that was impossible with her broken leg. She had to sit there through the entire meal, unable to move and wait on the family hand and foot.

It couldn't have been easy. When a digestive system has spent the past nineteen years in a standing position, or at a slow gallop, it isn't simple for it to be plopped down on a chair and forced to handle everything from corn flakes to pickles without the slightest jiggle.

And then there was the problem of the temperature of the food. As a wife and mother of three, Jackie and her esophagus have never had to contend with any food that wasn't room temperature. Ice cream, coffee, mashed potatoes, salad, rolls, any kind of soup, by the time my wife got to them, they were always lukewarm, or lukecold, as the case might be.

You can imagine, then, the strain of not only eating food in an unaccustomed position but also in an unusual condition. Give my wife credit, though, she struggled through her meals without a complaint, and didn't injure herself in any noticeable way. At least, I didn't see a blister form on her lips, or any traces of frostbite.

As Jackie's leg mended, we let her get back to standing part-time through meals, fetching an occasional course, whipping up to get refills of milk, and that sort of thing. But we never asked her to carry really heavy items to the table, and we limited her to fifteen or twenty trips during the course of the meal to the various appliances, the basement, the telephone (the children's friends always call when we're eating), and various other parts of the home.

By bringing her along gently these past weeks, we didn't damage my wife's leg or her stomach and, happily, things are now back to normal.

As I said at the start, Saturday she stood through the entire supper for the first time since her accident. It was a wonderful sight to see her long after the rest of us had finished, standing by the kitchen table with a cup of cold coffee in her hand.

With the care we've given her, there's no reason she shouldn't last for years.

Return to the slopes?

Friends have been bombarding me with the same question in recent weeks: will Jackie make a comeback as a skier?

As you may recall, my wife spent most of last winter as a patient; and I spent most of last winter as an impatient. That's because my wife fell down a mountain and broke her leg, and my heart, in two places. My wife's après-ski outfit consisted of a plaster cast from her hip to her ankle; mine was an apron and a broom.

Undoubtedly it will come as an awful shock to you to learn that I now regard skiing with the same affection I have for boils or a nasty sinus infection. I did not enjoy watching me do dishes, chase kids, and make beds. And the convalescence took so long!

But what could I expect? If it takes a month for my wife to get around to mending my socks, I should have known it would take the better part of a year for her to mend an entire leg.

Fortunately, Jackie is back on her feet — and it's the beginning of a new ski season. Will she once again take to the hills, there to slide on shimmering sheets of snow right into the first-aid shack at the bottom of the cliff?

Over my dead body, I say. I do not intend to spend this winter watching people write funny things on my wife's leg while I try to get supper ready.

However, fate has played me a dirty trick. Not long ago I did a television show with the French champion, Jean Claude Killy. In the course of the evening, I told Killy that my wife had broken her leg last winter in a spill and he was sympathetic. He mentioned that he had suffered two fractures, too, on his way to three gold medals at the Olympics.

"Of course she will ski again," Killy encouraged.

I blushed and said of course. If there's one thing I hate, it's being accused of trying to run my wife's life, especially when I'm trying to run my wife's life. But under my breath I muttered that Jackie would ski again when Pierre Trudeau gives up kissing girls, when Vancouverites develop an inferiority complex, when Toronto Argos win a Grey Cup, when Dalton Camp sends a valentine to Allan MacEachen.

Later in the evening a girl named Penny who works with Killy on his ski shows asked my address. Since she was blonde, young, and gorgeous, I gave it. Of course she had an excuse —"Jean Claude wants it," she explained.

But — shy girl! — I could see through her little game. Obviously she has a hangup for middle-aged, overweight men with receding hairlines and a mole in their nose.

Or so I told myself.

A week later there was a package in the mail addressed to Jackie and inside was an autographed picture from Jean Claude Killy. My wife was delighted. She showed the picture to all her friends and pointed out that it had been inscribed, "To Jackie," which gave it even extra prestige.

"I hope this doesn't give you any ideas about skiing again this winter," I grumbled.

"Don't be silly," Jackie said. "The thought hasn't entered my mind."

However, on the first snowfall of the year, Jackie looked outside and I distinctly heard her whisper, "Track!" Apparently, she's getting the old bug again.

Well, I've decided not to stand in her way — provided she can find where I've buried her skis in the backyard.

9

My Wife the Artist

Beauty in hair of the dog

All my wife asks of a hobby is three things: 1. It must be more fun than ironing. (My wife considers getting her appendix out more fun than ironing so it's not a very serious restriction.) 2. It must provide an excuse for locking herself in a room alone when Jane, Richard, and Stephen are fighting over what program to watch on TV. 3. And it must be nonfattening.

Her latest hobby meets all the requirements. My wife is now making wall hangings.

Mind you, these aren't your run-of-the-mill wall hangings — a little anchor from a World War II destroyer, two tin cans, and bunch of fishermen's net.

Oh, no.

These wall hangings are very classy. In fact, they have pedigrees — literally. They're made from dog hair.

Doesn't that sound exciting?

Jackie collects the hair from neighbourhood mutts, spins it into yarn, and then whips out another — ahem — objet d'arf.

Her latest masterpiece, for example, is made from Bippy (a

sheepdog), Fleur (a setter), Sarah (a samoyed), and Lassie (a collie). It's a four-woof production that even I must admit is my wife's best to date. With promotion, and a beret, my wife could become another Vincent Van Growl.

Originally, I had a lot of doubts when my wife announced her plans to weave some of our friends' dogs into decorative, patterns. If God had intended dogs to be wall hangings, I told her, He would have made them flatter and given them hooks instead of ears. Nobody, I added, wants a wall hanging that chases cats, ha, ha, or drools every time you go near it with your dinner. Besides, where would we get a flea collar big enough for a living-room wall?

My wife paid no attention and, like a blue serge suit, continued to pick up dog hair wherever she could. As a result, we're now the proud possessors of a veritable litter of wall hangings; and they're all housebroken. No matter who calls — the National Gallery or the Sportsman Show — Jackie is ready.

By the way, we have a friend who owns a wolf and Jackie is toying with the idea of weaving wolf hair into her next project. It could be a first — a wall hanging that protects itself from art thieves.

Sic 'em, boy!

Super-sniffer foiled in kitchen

I have always had the utmost faith in my nose. In forty-five years of sniffing, it has never let me down as a food detector. The type of food is unimportant — cheese omelettes, bagels, homemade grape jelly, banana cream pie, Winnipeg goldeye, apples. If it's in the house, my nose knows. My wife only has to turn in her recipe book to the page marked Swiss steak and I can tell, with one nostril tied behind my back.

Immodest as it may seem, I believe I have one of the truly great noses of our time. If there were an Olympic event for noses, I'm sure I'd take the gold for Canada.

Yesterday, however, my nose made a mistake. And a dandy. I hadn't gotten out of my coat in the hallway when my nose began to twitch. Then it quivered. Finally it was in full flare.

"You've got something cooking," I announced to my wife. I then galloped to the kitchen.

"I thought so!" I said joyously, lifting off the top of a pot simmering on the stove. "Noodle — with onions and other goodies. When do we eat?"

"That's not for dinner," my wife chided.

"What do you mean it's not for dinner?" I demanded.

"It's not dinner," came her reply. "It's not even food. It's Sarah."

"Sarah? You mean you've cooked our dog? Well, we'll discuss that later. She certainly smells delicious."

"Don't be silly. I haven't cooked all of Sarah, just her hair."

"Her hair?"

"You know I've been collecting Sarah's hair and making it into yarn," my wife amplified. "Well, I want to dye it, so I'm boiling it with onion skins and a few things."

"You mean that what smells so good on the stove is our dog's hair?"

"Yes."

"What are we having for dinner?" I asked.

"Frozen dinners. I've been too busy dyeing to cook."

"I hate frozen dinners," I muttered. "Couldn't we at least try Sarah's hair? Throw in a few carrots and some potatoes and . . ."

"No."

"But my nose tells me . . ."

"Your nose is wrong," my wife stated. "Besides, I don't want to kiss anyone with Samoyed breath."

I only hope my nose doesn't develop an inferiority complex over the whole affair.

School is dangerous for Mother

When my wife decided last September to return to school on a part-time basis, she felt she was ready to face the brave new world. Now Jackie's not so sure.

She didn't mind being the only one in class wearing eye makeup, a bra, and a T-shirt without something suggestive stencilled on the front. But her latest experience in the halls of academe has been truly shattering, even worse than that first time Jackie told a fellow student she had a sixteen-year-old son, and the person wasn't surprised.

What happened was this. My wife was in one of those student haunts last week and was struck by a display of ceramic pipes being offered for sale by a young man. As it happens, we've been looking for a Christmas present for my brother.

(Yes, I know Christmas was weeks ago, but my brother still hasn't sent me my birthday present and my birthday was last November, so I still have loads of time.)

"How much are the pipes?" my wife asked.

"Two dollars, or three joints," he answered.

"Pardon?" was my wife's response.

"Two dollars, or three joints," he repeated.

"Joints?"

"Yes—joints."

To a woman who spends each morning trying to shovel hot porridge into her three children and scraping dog hair off the rug, "joints" is something to do with arthritis.

But at long last a light flashed on.

"Oh, joints—like in marijuana," my wife-turned-student said.

The young man stared across the generation gap, just as puzzled as my wife.

"I'm sorry, I only have cash," Jackie continued, trying desperately to retrieve her cool after the earlier fumble.

"Too bad," he commented.

By now my wife wanted to back out of the transaction, but it was too late. She handed over the money, and he gave her the pipe.

Driving home that evening my wife told me about her experience. "Maybe the guy was just kidding," I suggested. "He saw your ironed jeans, combed hair, and wedding ring and decided to pull your leg."

She said he seemed sincere.

"Where's the pipe?" I asked.

My wife brought out her purchase — a clay pipe about five inches long with a very tiny bowl.

"For heaven's sake, that's a pot pipe," I exclaimed. "You've bought a pipe for dope."

That was the final blow. Jackie was totally deflated.

Now we've got to think of some way to get rid of the pipe before the Mounties come down on our neck, put my wife under a glaring light, and demand to know the name of her "connection."

In the meantime, I've made Jackie promise not to talk to strangers on her way to school again.

Art for art's sake?

Is there no end to the crises around the home? The Ontario College of Art displayed the work of some of its students at an open house recently and among the objets d'art were two bits of weaving by Jackie Lautens.

Yes, the wife.

The one was a wall hanging, orange, blue, and big enough to cover all sorts of nicks in the plaster (which is how we use it); and the other was a butterfly that hangs from the ceiling by threads.

The reason I describe them in such lush detail is because,

after the exhibition, the missus was handed the names of nine people who had signed a list to indicate their interest in buying her creations. And they were real names, too—none of this "A. Hitler, Berlin" or "Mao Tse-tung, Scarborough." There wasn't even a single "I.M. Loony" on the paper.

Of course I was thrilled.

"Well, now the old filthy lucre starts rolling in," I said sensitively, rubbing my hands together in eager anticipation.

"What do you mean?" Jackie asked.

"I mean, after all these years of watching you spin up old dog hair and turn the laundry room into a dyeing works, it's going to be wonderful to get some money in for a change."

"I'm not selling my things," she corrected.

"Are you joking?" I demanded. "Aren't you going to call these people and see how much they're willing to fork over for the butterfly and the wall hanging?"

"Of course not. I worked months on those things and they mean too much to me to sell to strangers. Besides, some of the wool in the butterfly came from our own dog, and there are bits of McVean's Samoyed in the other one."

"This is a chance to make your first sale as an artist," I pointed out.

"No," was her short reply.

"Look, Da Vinci sold his stuff; Michelangelo was always ready to knock off a ceiling for a few bucks; Picasso had no objections to taking a bit in exchange for a scribble or two."

"That's their affair," Jackie sniffed. "I slaved over those things and I don't want to part with them now."

"That's not very professional," I said. "Besides, we could use the money. We've got to buy a house in Toronto and we need every spare $100,000 we can lay our hands on. Who knows, you may become famous."

In an obvious attempt to play on male vanity, my wife responded by asking, "Would you want to be known as Jackie Lautens' husband?"

"Yes, if it paid well enough," I told her.

"I'd sooner sell my children," the artist vowed.

"Well, you're the boss," I surrendered. "How much do you think we could get for them?"

The kick on the shins told me the wife was not amused.

With all the greedy artists in the world, how come I happened to get stuck with one who wants to keep her amateur status?

10

Moving to Toronto

The grass is greener now that we've sold

It's amazing how much work you have to do before a house is fit to move out of. Our repairs began only moments after we had closed the deal on our home.

"Before we move, I think you should replace the washers in the bathroom taps," Jackie advised. "I wouldn't want to leave a leaky faucet for the new people." That evening I put in new washers, and strained myself in the groin area.

Next came the fireplace. "If you got some acid you could scrub off the smoke stains on the fireplace stone," my wife suggested. "It would look much better for the new people." I bought the acid, cleaned the fireplace, and hardly got any acid at all on my face, hands, and body.

"This would be a good day to take off the screens and wash the windows," my wife advised the first Saturday morning after our sale. Several screens haven't been off since the day we moved in but I did as I was told, transforming each window into a little jewel.

"I wouldn't want to leave our lawn looking like this," was

Jackie's next comment, staring out at a sea of dandelions and other broad-leafed weeds. I picked up a bag of Dr. Garden's Weed No-No and spread it evenly over the front and back yard in a spreader rented from the hardware store. In between time, I glued in a bit of parquet floor which (according to my wife) sounded a little loose.

This past week I got home from work and my wife had a new chore for me. "I'm certain there's a bird or something in our chimney," she advised. "You'd better go up on the roof and look. I don't want anyone to say we left a house with a bird in the chimney."

I climbed the TV tower, jumped to the roof, and peered down the chimney, getting only a little soot on my suit. "I can't see anything," I shouted to Jackie.

"Are you certain?"

"Fairly certain."

"Get a flashlight and look down."

Even a flashlight (yes, I had to climb down from the roof and back up again) showed no sign of an intruder, but my wife asked me to cover the chimney with a protective bit of wiring so no bird or animal will be able to get into the chimney after the new people take over.

Two days ago we reached another milestone. After we started up the swimming pool for the new people, we experienced a minor problem with leakage, nothing I couldn't live with, but my wife wasn't satisfied.

Ian (our pool man) diagnosed the problem as a valve at the bottom of the pool. A frogman spent thirty minutes yesterday at the bottom of our pool making the necessary repairs, and I don't even want to think about what it will cost.

At this moment my wife is scrubbing cupboards, touching up paint, vacuuming drapes, doing masonry repairs, cleaning the built-in stove, for heaven's sake — for the new people.

Our house never looked so good, and now I'm sorry we're leaving.

On reading real-estate ads

After commuting to work (thirty-one miles each way) for nearly fourteen years, I've decided it's time to move into big, bad Toronto. So we've sold our house (to a nice couple from Calgary) and are going through the real-estate ads each evening.

Even though we're novices, my wife and I are catching on to certain phrases copywriters use in describing property that's for sale. For example, "close to everything" means there's no front lawn and you're so close to the street you'll think the buses are going through your living room.

"Picturesque neighbourhood"—there are winos sprawled over the sidewalk.

"Can be turned into income property"—the place has a basement and enough room behind the furnace to hang a hammock.

"Handyman's special"—there's no ceiling in the bedroom, the wiring has been condemned, and you have to shinny a rope to get upstairs.

"Victorian gem"—if you weigh over 135 pounds you won't fit in the kitchen.

"Can't be duplicated at the price"—no, but it can be for $25,000 less in Hamilton.

"For those who want something better"—it's out of your price range.

"Ravine lot"—step outside the back door and it's seventy-five feet straight down.

"Architect designed"—the place has a bar in the basement made with leftover lumber by a previous tenant who took a shop course at high school.

"Loads of extras"—there's a shower in the bathtub.

"Only minutes from downtown"—by Soyuz rocket, and not during the rush hour.

"Newly decorated"—the living room has been painted within the past ten years, in maroon.

"Lawyer's home"—the place has been lived in for eighteen

months by a motorcycle gang, but the second mortgage on the place is held by a man named Lawyer who lives in Miami year round.

"In prestige area"—it's almost half a block from an all-night pizza parlour.

"Wake up each morning with the birds"—there's a chicken plucker next door.

"Part of Toronto's past"—the house will have to be gutted and rebuilt.

"Move into this centrally located beauty and throw away your car keys"—there's no garage, side drive, or spot on the street for your car.

"Pool-size lot"—unfortunately, you'll have to tear down the house if you want to put a pool on it, however.

"Three- or four-bedroom home"—one of the bedrooms has a large closet.

"Gourmet kitchen"—the can opener on the wall goes with the house.

Yes, we're getting the swing of it.

We leave for an exotic foreign post

As long as I can remember I've tried to talk my employer(s) into letting me take my column to some foreign city for a year or two. Oh, to be bedded down in Chelsea, nipping up to the palace every now and then to give the Queen a bit of advice; or to be meeting some contact in the sewers of Copenhagen, exchanging passwords and microfilm behind the upturned collars of our trenchcoats.

Lovely!

Alas! The farthest I ever got was the apartments-for-rent column of the Paris edition of the *Herald-Tribune*. That was in 1973, and then that little plan was scrapped, too. It seemed fate never intended me to be another Joe Schlesinger, or an Ernest-what's-his-name.

However, at long last my boyhood dream has come true. Even as you read this I am on my way to an exciting assignment in a strange and mysterious place. Yes, today we are moving into Toronto.

Some of you may not think that's quite like London, Moscow, Vienna, Rome, or the previously mentioned Paris, but when you were born in Fort William and have lived most of your life in the Hamilton (Ont.) area, Toronto is a foreign assignment.

In fact, my Hamilton friends feel we're nuts to give up a 220-foot frontage in the suburbs (Burlington) to move into Toronto, and are certain they'll never see us again. Not alive. When we say we've bought a house in DOWNTOWN Toronto, and the house is only fourteen feet wide, they bite their lips, and rush home to sew black bands on the arms of their shirts or dresses.

But I feel it's time to explore a new culture, to study the customs of a different society. Do the people in Toronto really eat their young, as street gossips in Hamilton say? Is it true they breathe air without steel filings and chunks of cinder in it? Gosh, is it possible they don't take off their hats and place them over their chests when any member of the Tiger-Cats walks by?

Well, we'll find out.

Of course, I've told the children not to laugh when they see people in the street without safety shoes, hardhats, and a number scratched on the side of a lunch-pail with a nail. I've also instructed them to avoid the drinking water for the first while, to look at a picture of a tree whenever they feel homesick, and not to play with any neighbourhood children who get more than $100 a week allowance from their parents.

I don't want them snickering either when somebody tries to tell them they have trains in Toronto that run under the ground. When you're from out-of-town, people in Toronto will tell you anything.

In any case, tonight we'll be in our new beds (the old ones had to be sold because they wouldn't fit) and in our new home, wondering what adventures will befall us in the days ahead.

At the end of the week we plan to go down to Lake Ontario and throw bottles with messages in them to our friends in Hamilton. We want them to know we've at least got this far safely.

Jackie's taut nerves: a moving story

Believe me, it was our plan to move into Toronto quietly. And, except for the three visits by police, several shouting matches, a traffic jam you wouldn't believe, an angry march by the residents' association, one near fistfight, and the car that had to be towed away, it went like clockwork.

In fact, it may be the best move we've ever made. I'm sure my wife will agree, once I coax her down from the drapes. Jackie says she never wants to show her face in public again, but then she always says that after she's been the central figure in a mob scene or riot.

For heaven's sake, the movers did arrive right on time, they didn't break anything, and Jerry (the husky mover) didn't actually land any punches during the worst of it. Surely that's worth something.

Yes, it was unfortunate that a tourist's car was parked illegally in front of our new address when the movers arrived. And, yes, it did make things awkward when the moving van cut off all traffic because it couldn't be parked next to the curb (because of the illegally parked car). And I guess the motorists who jammed the street in the middle of the morning rush hour did say some nasty things, and may even have landed a couple of vicious kicks on the van's tires.

But nobody had to go to hospital after the mêlée, and Jerry (the mover) did seem to settle things down when he stood in the middle of the pavement and challenged anyone who didn't like the way the van was parked (in the middle of the road) to do something about it. When the police arrived (for the first time) they agreed Jerry was only doing his job, and didn't make a single arrest or fingerprint anyone.

Mind you, I wish the cars hadn't tried to squeeze past by going up over the curb and brushing into the lilac trees the residents' association prizes so much. Especially the big bus. If that hadn't happened, maybe our new neighbours wouldn't have come out in force, threatened the motorists, taken down licence numbers, and called police a second time.

At least Jerry and Harold (the other mover) weren't involved in that and, when they were asked whose stuff they were moving, they didn't give our name. Jerry assured us of that. Besides, I don't think the person who came with the pad and jotted down notes was a newspaper reporter, as Jackie feared. He probably was only a member of the residents' association, or a plain-clothesman.

Certainly conditions improved and there was hardly any honking or obscene gestures after the police came the third time and towed away the illegally parked car that was the start of the trouble anyway.

The entire fuss couldn't have lasted more than six hours and I'd bet nobody would recognize my wife since she spent most of the moving morning hiding in the closet. So there's no reason for her to be afraid to come out now that the police, tow trucks, movers, the thirty or forty angry motorists, etc., have gone.

Heck, a cold cloth on her forehead, a couple of Aspirin and six weeks' total rest, and she'll be right as rain again. Or just about.

Big city life opened my eyes

Doesn't take long, does it? To lose the old winsome, small-town charm, I mean. We've only been in Toronto a couple of days as full-time residents and I can already see the change in me.

Sweet I was when we arrived. Saccharin wouldn't melt in my

mouth and I wouldn't know a double entendre if I tripped over it (them?). Just a country lad with my worldly goods in an A & P shopping bag (including my Lawrence Welk record collection), a spear of grass hanging from my lips and wide-eyed enough you could drive a truck up the bridge of my nose. But that's all over now and I have become sophisticated.

The transformation took place last evening in a small restaurant not far from our new home, a place where (so I was told) they make terrific hamburgers and Coke floats. In we walked, the missus and myself, and after a bit, the hostess took us to an empty table where we had a chance to look over the list of eats.

"I hate to say anything," I whispered to my wife, "but did you notice anything unusual about the hostess?"

My wife said she didn't.

I took her word and dropped the subject until we were halfway through our hamburgers.

"Psst," I murmured. "Take another look at the hostess."

"What am I supposed to be looking for?" the wife answered.

"I don't think she's wearing anything under her T-shirt," I said. "She hasn't got a B-R-A."

"Are you just catching on to that?" was the curt reply. "Boy, are you slow."

Well, that may have been the point when I realized I was really in The Big City because, in the sticks, you don't get hamburgers with that kind of works. Just days ago (when I was still a Hamiltonian, and nice) I'd have blushed at any young thing who showed me to my seat in a restaurant in that condition.

Not now.

I carefully took my eyeglasses out of my pocket and pretended to polish them while, in actual fact, I was staring at her reflection in my lenses. Yes, I must have ogled my spectacles at least a half-dozen times.

Bold as brass, if you please. Once I caught a glimpse in the mirror across the room, and another time I picked up my knife and saw her full frontal while she cleared off a table. Pure debauchery, it was, and still daylight, too.

Of course, I was shocked to think I'd fallen this far down the path of sin since my Trail Ranger days at First United Church in Hamilton, and that I'll probably have to wear a scarlet "S" on my forehead when they hear back home how I've been carrying on. But that's the way it happens. One day hearts and flowers, and the next (wink, wink) you're a sport with a reputation to live down.

Still, when in Toronto you have to do what the Torontonians do and, if that's how they serve hamburgers, well, what's a body to do?

Golly, I never saw a Big Mac with fixin's like that.

Commuting drove me to the city

As I write this I've been a resident of Toronto exactly 548 hours and thirty-two minutes. How can I be so precise? Because I drove into the yard behind our new home 548 hours and thirty-two minutes ago, and the car hasn't moved since. When you've been commuting as long as I have (fourteen years) you take note of such facts in your life.

The previous record for my car being idle was just under thirty-two minutes, a mark set in 1967 on a day when I had my appendix out, and Jane didn't have to go to her dance lessons. Ordinarily I spent a minimum of an hour and a half each day behind the wheel, staring up the tailpipe of a semi hauling concrete blocks, or musing over whether the Buick in back would notice traffic had stopped before it wound up in my front seat.

So I can't believe it's 548 hours and thirty-two, I mean thirty-six minutes since I said naughty things under my breath about a bus driver cutting into my lane, or heard the latest traffic report from some radio station's helicopter and wanted to eat the upholstery in my car.

I haven't pumped gas, chauffeured kids, begged a parking-lot attendant to let me in at $3.50 per beg, been caught in the middle of a drag race between a souped-up Harley and a panel truck with "Don't laugh—your daughter may be inside" painted on the fenders. For heaven's sake, I haven't even thrown on my brakes at the last second to avoid hitting a truck filled with melons (doing 25 mph in a 60 zone) and thrown my entire family headfirst into the windshield.

Ho, ho, ho!

My sunglasses are still in the car and, as a matter of principle, I've even refused to open the car door for them.

When we decided to move, I made only one stipulation: that the house, apartment, cave, cardboard carton, etc., would have to be within walking distance of work. Well, I'm two miles from the office, and I trudge it every day with a song in my heart, looking at shop windows and girls (not necessarily in that order), and not at the gas gauge and somebody's off-colour bumper sticker.

Of course it won't last. Perhaps some day I'll have to get the car out again (when Jane gets married, for example, or when I'm invited to take part in the city of Hamilton's bicentennial celebrations in 2046 A.D.).

Believe me, I have nothing personal against my car; it's been dependable, loyal, and an absolute brick through every kind of traffic jam, February blizzard, and Highway 10 slowdown. But it's time we both had a rest.

So if you see a pedestrian during rush hour standing by the ramp to the expressway (the one with traffic backed up to Oshawa), and he's cackling and jumping up and down, and rubbing his hands together, don't offer him a ride.

He's been on one for fourteen years.

Houses cost enough to make you ... grin

The last thing a person wants to know is how much the previous owner paid for your house, especially if he bought it ten years ago. However, try as you might, the subject invariably seems to pop up in conversation.

A few days ago I met an old college pal of mine named Sam, and Sam was with another lawyer named Monty. After we were introduced, Monty said: "I see you've just moved to Toronto."

I told him he was correct.

"Where did you buy?" was his next question.

I gave him the location.

"Great location," Monty conceded, "near everything. What did you pay?"

Before I realized what I was doing, I revealed the figure. Monty said he could have guessed it. "That's about what property is going for now in that area."

Then came the zinger.

"Do you know what you could have picked that house up for a few years ago?" Monty wanted to know.

I pretended not to hear and made some comment about the weather, or El Salvador, or our balance of trade problems with the United States. I can't remember exactly which.

"How long did the previous owner live in the house?" Monty persisted.

I could think of no way out, so I told him.

"I'd say he got it then for $12,000, $15,000 tops."

I could feel the blood draining even from my hair because (as you may have guessed) we paid a teensy weensy bit more for the house than that. Of course it's been renovated and . . . but $15,000!

As soon as I got home I blurted the details to my wife. "Do you know what a lawyer said we could have bought this house for ten years ago?"

My wife said she didn't want to know.

"Guess," I insisted.

She refused to hazard a price and walked into the kitchen.

"Dinner's in ten minutes," was her only comment.

"$15,000," I announced. "Maybe $12,000."

My wife (whose name is on half the mortgage) moaned something almost inaudible and put her head between her knees.

All through the evening the two of us were quiet, mulling over my conversation with Monty.

"If I don't miss a day's work, and get some outside jobs, I'll have the house paid for by 2006 A.D.," I finally said in an attempt to cheer her up. "I'll only be seventy-seven."

The comment had no noticeable effect on my wife's mood. However, as we were getting into bed, the faintest trace of a smile crept across Jackie's face.

"Why the grin?" I asked.

"I was just thinking what we paid for our old house in 1966, and what we sold it for," she replied.

Undoubtedly Monty already knows.

Every man for himself in ladies' shoe department

Life in the inner city is not all ice cream and coloured balloons. There are dark moments, too, and the missus had one just yesterday. There was a shoe sale on at our corner department store and, never one to turn her back on saving a buck, Jackie rushed right over with her size nine feet. Both of them.

She was fingering through the bin of Tender Tootsies when she found exactly what she wanted: a pair of blue suede jobs that would be just dreamy with the new slacks. Not flashy, the right height heel, serviceable enough to wear to the office, but also the kind of thing that could be worn when hubby takes her out for the champagne dinner and a wild night of dancing at some smart night spot.

("Hubby" doesn't actually take her out for champagne dinners, etc.; I put that bit in to make me look good.)

Anyway, Mrs. Lautens slipped on the blue suede jobs, moved the little piggies around, and asked the clerk if she had a half-size larger. They were just a little tight. The salesperson checked and said, yes, there was one pair of shoes in that style, size 9½, but they were being tried on at that very moment by another customer. And the clerk pointed out a young man in his mid-twenties slipping into the footwear Jackie wanted.

Of course my wife was taken aback. Over the years she has had some monumental struggles over remnant counters, in the lingerie section, on either side of the blouse rack, and so on. But, up to this point, Jackie's adversary for the bargains has always been another woman: a teenager with arms sturdy enough to shred a tractor; a society matron with a pearl brooch on her chest but pure killer in her heart; a suburban housewife with enough megawatts in her smile to melt stone, and elbows that stun with a single blow; an office worker who, with feet in position, stands her ground like the TD Centre. But always a woman.

Under normal circumstances Jackie might merely have snatched the shoes she wanted from her competitor's hand, and put in the knee if there were any serious protest. That *modus operandi* has stood her in good stead in all her years as a bargain-hunter. But against a man? It seemed, well, unfeminine.

Jackie watched him try on both shoes, walk up and down the carpet, look into the floor mirror, and do little turns to check for heel slippage. They were agonizing moments.

Every instinct was for upending the rival and stripping his feet of the shoes she wanted, breaking them off (the feet, I mean) at the ankle if there was no other way. However, my wife waited, keeping her cool, and not making even a single devastating comment like "They don't go with your eyes."

Finally, he made his decision: he wanted the blue suede shoes. Jackie was heartbroken over the loss, so heartbroken she didn't even bother to look for other shoes.

Out of this nasty little incident has come something positive, however. In the future, if Jackie comes up against a man shopping for himself in the women's section of any of her favourite stores, she vows there'll be no more special treatment, especially if he reaches for the $19.95 drastically reduced item she has her eye on. As far as my wife is concerned, it's no more nice gal.

Mooning about our city

Those of us who live in the inner city get nostalgic, too, when summer ends. Of course we don't get mellow necessarily over flights of birds heading south, trees showing signs of scarlet, tiny animals scurrying to lay in supplies for cruel months ahead.

No, it isn't quite like that.

But we do have our special moments, moments that cause us to pause and reflect over the dying season.

Such a tender moment occurred the other day as Mrs. Lautens and I were drinking in sights we somehow instinctively know will soon fade from the inner city.

We were on Church St., only a few steps from Bloor, when it happened.

There were four young people ahead of us, two men, two women, and it was early evening, the sun not having disappeared yet in the sky behind the Asquith library.

Without any advance warning, one of the men dropped his trousers, exposing his bare behind.

It was only for a second, just a flash, and then the couples, laughing and giggling, continued on their way.

"I wouldn't be surprised if that's the last moon of summer," my wife reflected.

"You're probably right," I agreed sombrely.

Several years ago I wrote about the first moon of spring, an event witnessed near the same corner when somebody stuck unclad buttocks out the rear window of a passing car.

While the first moon of spring is a harbinger of the season ahead, and a happy event, there is something poignant about the last one of the season.

In not many weeks the autumn wind will have bite to it, making it dangerous for anyone to expose his or her bottom from a sedan window, on the street, or in a passing truck carrying engineering students to an initiation rite.

When the frost is on the pumpkin, nobody in his right mind wants to take a chance of getting frost on his personal pumpkin.

The stark truth is—mooning is finished for another year, unless we have an Indian summer or something.

"I wonder how long it will be before we see our next moon," Mrs. Lautens asked wistfully after our encounter. "Probably months."

In a philosophical vein I suggested the last moon of the season, like the last rose of summer, makes a person aware of the passing of time.

"It seems as if you spot your first moon of the year and, before you know it, you've seen your last," was the way I put it.

"Yes," Jackie said. "But Canadians probably appreciate mooning more than people who live in a warm climate where there is mooning year 'round."

I nodded, and both of us walked in silence for the next few blocks, thinking of the changing Canadian seasons, the end of summer, and (probably) the last moon of the year.

Downtown people are very sensitive, you know.

11

Parting Shots

A mother-in-law story

I don't do mother-in-law material. And that's not because I have a father-in-law (Ted) who is an ex-football player, wrestler and weightlifter, a man who finds it amusing to lift up chesterfields while somebody is innocently sleeping in same.

No, the reasons I don't do mother-in-law material are because: (1) I find mother-in-law jokes coarse and sexist; (2) mother-in-law slams are a cheap way to get laughs; (3) I don't enjoy sleeping in the small back bedroom, the one with the bad pillows, by myself.

However, I have to break a twenty-five-year rule today to relate the latest episode involving Irene, the Resident Love Goddess's mother and queen of the shopping plazas. (Shopping plazas are to Irene what pensions are to politicians. She will go anywhere, provided you pass a mall with a feature on anything.)

Anyway, a few days ago I was with my in-laws when wife Jackie asked her mother whatever had happened to a painting she remembered hanging on the family front room wall, a picture with special meaning to her. The painting was of a ski hill at St.

Sauveur in the Laurentians and was done by Paul Duff, a family friend, when Duff was fifteen or sixteen.

I should explain Duff has a pretty good reputation now as a Canadian artist. He grew up in the Hamilton area and went to McMaster University (where I met him). After graduation he continued in art, winding up for many years in South America, in Rio. Not long ago he had a major exhibition in Toronto at one of those smart little galleries near Hazelton Lanes and his pictures are now worth a thousand or two.

To get back to the story, Jackie asked about this early Duff picture that held so many childhood memories for her. Jackie as a tot attended a bunny school run by Paul Duff's mother, which explains why the piece of real art came into my in-laws' possession.

Irene said she still had the oil but it was now in a closet. Would Jackie like to see it?

Of course Jackie would.

Irene went to fetch the picture as the years rolled back in my wife's mind and visions of the current worth of the picture danced in her head. How many Duff originals of that period could be around?

Irene came back into the room and unveiled the Duff. To some silence. "It looks, well, it looks different," Jackie at last mentioned to her mother.

"It's the same picture," my mother-in-law assured, holding up the item in question, a painting about the size of a TV screen.

"Are you sure?" Jackie asked.

"Yes," Irene affirmed. "A few years ago the snow on the hill started to look a little yellow so I painted it over. Other than that, it's the same."

"You painted over the picture?" my wife asked in some shock.

"Yes. It's much whiter now, and the shadows are gone, too."

Well, as I explained to a shaken Jackie later, we can at least be thankful my mother-in-law used a brush, not a roller.

Unspoiled resorts
for birds

Some people just don't know when to stop when they're rolling with a really good story.

Take these friends of ours who have just come back from a holiday. They dropped over the other evening to show off their fabulous tans and two albums of snapshots, and they were getting a lot of encouraging envy, especially from my wife when they described how warm this place they visited was. Their descriptions of the fresh fish dinners, the clear water, and the long stretches of sand were also extremely impressive. In fact, Jackie — who is so desperate for a holiday right now she'd sign on with a Russian trawler as a deck-hand — was almost drooling.

However, our friends went one step too far.

"You should go there while it's still unspoiled," the husband recommended.

That did it.

"Unspoiled?"

For heaven's sake, what my wife is looking for in a holiday is a place that is spoiled, and spoiled a heck of a lot. In her opinion, it's almost impossible to spoil a place too much. Not for her the remote outpost where you can climb a coconut tree for lunch, sleep on a bare surplus cot under the stars, and pick exotic insects out of your travel brochures. No, even having a rare blue snake slither out of your sleeping bag holds no charm for Mrs. Lautens. Call her a spoilsport if you want, but that is the fact of the matter.

What Jackie likes on a holiday is room service. She likes good plumbing, showers in the actual room, sturdy window screens, a nice pool (heated), a place to plug in a razor in case the legs get a little fuzzy, an elevator if there are more than two storeys to the building, parking arrangements, a front desk where you can pick up mail from home.

Bed linen? Well, you can change it twice a day if you like and Jackie will never complain. There is no yearning in her to go beddy-byes beside a spiky bush that every bug and his brother probably calls home. She can also do without a wade in the surging virgin ocean, the one in which she is always certain something made of jelly is wrapping around her legs.

No, give the girl a good sidewalk that leads to a shopping plaza, a place where you can get beach towels cheap, an air-conditioned drug store with a forty-four-cent pantyhose special. Throw in a hamburger joint where she can send the kids if she doesn't feel like making dinner and Mrs. Lautens is practically in heaven. That's how spoiled she likes her holiday place to be.

A fireplace with logs already cut and stacked, a comforting door with double lock — and preferably a chain — colour TV in case it rains some night and you can't get out, little packets of shampoo left by the management, towels with enough nap to choke a horse. Oh, yes, and a balcony so you can see all the nature you want, and then pull the drapes when you've had enough.

Now that's what my wife calls a holiday.

You can have those pitch-black nights, the call across the empty land of some creature probably with foot-length teeth, the unexplained paw prints on the hood of the car when you wake up in the morning, the thermostat-less tent.

Give Jackie the spoiled vacation spot every time. Me too.

'57 outfits back in style

You'd think after twenty-two years of marriage Mrs. Lautens would have run out of ways to surprise her veteran husband, but such is not the case. Hardly a day slips by without my eyebrows arching at something the Resident Love Goddess says or does.

Take this past weekend. We were getting ready to go to a dinner party when Jackie appeared in the bedroom, gave a twirl, and asked for an honest opinion of her outfit. That's when I went back on my heels.

No, there were no bits of Jackie showing that shouldn't

have, nor was she wearing a King Tut T-shirt with suggestive hieroglyphics on the front. It was more mind-boggling than that. What Jackie was wearing was a two-piece navy suit with padded shoulders and a straight skirt. Not just any old two-piece navy suit. Her going-away suit when we got married!

If memory serves correctly, I first saw the item in the afternoon of April 6, 1957, sometime between saying "I do" and fishing the drinking uncle out of the festive punch bowl. The actual wedding gown has long since been dismembered, cut up (the lace overskirt at least) to serve as fish nets for children wading in a creek behind our old house.

But the going-away suit? I thought it had been sent off long ago to a rummage sale to provide funds for some good work, or that it had provided Christmas supper for a family of needy moths. What a surprise!

"The style is back so I dug it out of the basement closet today," Jackie announced. "Is it okay?"

I said it was swell, figuring swell is the kind of word that should be used to describe a suit that first saw the light of day during the Louis St. Laurent administration.

"I paid $110 for the suit," Mrs. Lautens recalls. "It would be $400 today."

With that last nugget of information I enthused even more, stating the skirt length was perfect by today's standards and that what was in it was obviously the same size as when it belonged to an eighteen-year-old bride. Bum-de-bum-bum.

"One thing you have to promise," Mrs. Lautens said.

"What's that?" I asked.

"Don't go around telling everyone at the party this is my going-away outfit from our wedding. I don't want them to know."

"Why would I do that?"

"Because you're rotten at keeping secrets. I know you."

I promised I wouldn't make a peep.

We arrived at the party and sat down in the front room. I never said a word, not for the longest time. Finally it started to bug me. I knew the joke but nobody else did. I could take it no longer.

"How do you like Jackie's suit?" I asked the other guests.

Mrs. Lautens stared at me.

Everyone agreed it was a very smart suit and then I said, "Jackie, tell them the story behind it."

With everyone clamouring for details, Jackie had no choice but to spill all—and got quite a laugh.

On the way home Mrs. Lautens said, "I thought you promised not to tell about my suit."

"I didn't for almost eight minutes," I said. "That's a record for me. But, if you're mad, I promise I won't write about it."

That seemed to satisfy her.

Intruders beware of Jackie's right hook

The one thing a man needs in this world is the love of a good woman. And if that good woman also packs a punch that can stun a horse, so much the better.

You are looking at a person with the above blessings. Not only can my life mate hug and kiss, she has the kind of biceps you can count on in adversity.

Let me expand. Wednesday evening around nine there was some banging on our front door followed by door-knob rattling. Mrs. Lautens (who was the only one downstairs) thought it was one of our youngest son's friends acting a little silly, not all that unusual at seventeen.

So she opened the door.

There, staring her in the face, was a total stranger—six feet tall, twenty to twenty-five, and glassy-eyed. He immediately tried to push past Jackie into the house.

Poor simple lad. He didn't know he was dealing with a Hamilton Beach girl. Jackie pushed back. Hard. In fact, she shoved him back onto the porch, almost down the front steps. And then she slammed the door.

"Gary," the Resident Love Goddess shouted. "Some nut's trying to get into the house."

I rushed down the stairs followed by the two strapping sons who had been doing essays in their bedrooms.

Of course by the time I got to the scene, everything was in order. It always is. The would-be intruder was on the front walk, obviously stunned and shocked by the rude welcome he had received. Jackie opened the front door again and called in the dog. Yes, Sarah the Semi-Wonder Dog was on the front porch during the incident and hadn't curled so much as a lip.

I telephoned 911 and within five minutes two cruisers were on the scene and four large policemen piled out. They grabbed the unwelcome visitor who, by this time, had wandered down a neighbour's side alley.

"The guy is on booze and drugs," one of the constables explained to me. "Did he get inside the house?"

"One foot inside," I explained. "Then my wife threw him out."

Within ten minutes the nasty business was over, the glassy-eyed stranger on his way to police headquarters or a detoxification centre.

After things calmed down I mentioned to Jackie that she should be more careful when throwing people out of the house. "Somebody could get hurt," I cautioned.

"If anybody tries to break into my house, that's the chance they take," she replied with fire.

"I don't mean him; I mean you."

"That didn't even enter my mind," Jackie responded, totally calm and unruffled.

It's wonderful having a strong woman around the house.

Sneaking a little on the side

A pair of parents can get into no end of mischief when left unsupervised by their children. Without an inhibiting youthful gaze to keep them in line, well, it's just one madcap moment after another for mommy and daddy.

This summer our Stephen is working in Ottawa, Richard is with his grandparents in the Laurentians, and Jane is on strange shifts as a lifeguard at a city pool. So there you have the perfect setting for all kinds of hijinks, wink, wink.

Take the other evening. I got home at the usual time and the Resident Love Goddess greeted me with the announcement she was going to do something at dinner she had been waiting eighteen years to do.

"What?" I asked, trembling with the kind of excitement only a parent in a child-free home could understand.

"I'm going to put tomatoes in the salad tonight," Jackie said.

I should explain our children absolutely refuse to eat tomatoes and ever since they were old enough to overturn a bowl, we haven't had tomatoes in our salad, except when we go out.

"Not only am I going to cut up a tomato, I'm going to put the slices right on top where they can be seen," she added. Her eyes smouldered as the wanton words filled the room.

"Do you think we should?" I asked. "What would the kids say

if, the first time they leave us alone, we put tomatoes in our salad?"

"They never have to know," was the response.

We sat down and ate our tomato-laced salads, relaxed in the knowledge we wouldn't be disturbed. There is nothing like tomatus uninterruptus. After dinner, we sat in the kitchen, just the two of us, no prying eyes, no admonishing fingers, no restraining "tut, tuts."

"That was fantastic," I said after the salad things were cleared. "Heh, heh, heh, while the kids are away, the parents will play."

"The evening isn't over yet, big boy," were Mrs. Lautens' next words.

"What do you mean?"

"We're going to see *The Boy Friend*. I've reserved two tickets."

"But it's the middle of the week," I said. "We never go to the show in the middle of the week, not without asking permission."

Jackie sidled up pretty close. "Relax," she said, "and trust me."

Guilt filled every fibre, but I agreed to go, and we sat through *The Boy Friend* just as bold as brass, especially enjoying again "It's Never Too Late To Fall In Love."

When we were courting (in the winter of 1956–57) we saw the show and that became "our" song because I was twenty-eight at the time, Jackie eighteen, and I especially liked the line, "the modern painters of today may paint their pictures faster, but when it comes to skill, I say, you can't beat an old master."

We were walking home at eleven o'clock, humming *The Boy Friend* songs, the taste of tomatoes from the salad still in our months.

"Did the earth move for you tonight?" I asked.

"Yes," Jackie said.

"I just hope some spoilsport does not start a summer campaign with the slogan, 'Kids, do YOU know where your parents are tonight?'" I said. "If we play our cards right, this could be our wildest summer ever."

"Have half a stick of Dentyne, big fella," said the other parent on the loose.

I like family life

Almost every day another "expert" comes along to forecast the end of family life. Thanks to the Pill and new morality and science and take-out chicken, women will soon be free at last. They'll be able to order test-tube babies — and then farm them out to state nurseries.

No need for marriage licences and a rose-covered cottage. The only pitter-patter around the house will come from the shopping computer when it's on the blink.

Instead of making peanut butter sandwiches, women will be able to fulfil themselves. They'll have jobs and dress in Pucci originals and have dozens of boyfriends and learn to play the cello. Life will be a perpetual Saturday night date.

And men? Everybody knows a man isn't a domestic animal. He wants to chase girls and stay out late and keep his pay cheque to himself.

At least that's how these social seers see things.

Well, let me polish that crystal ball again.

Here's one guy who isn't waiting to be "free." They can peddle their swinging Shangri-la somewhere else. I like being married. I like family life. I like it when I get home at night and the kids shout, "Dad!" and trip over my feet and hug me and smell sweaty because they've been playing all day. That's love, brother.

You can have your parties and fancy clothes and white broadloomed pads and imported sports cars. I'll take those kids.

Sure, Stephen's teeth stick out a bit and Jane's hair is straight and Richard bounces on beds and they all holler and throw punches when I'm trying to nap.

Maybe a test tube and a battalion of technicians could turn out a more efficient product — a true "superbaby." But those kids are part of me and I'm part of them. We share the same heartbeat. They are the result of love, not a mathematical formula whipped up in a government lab. They are what it's all about.

There's one more thing I like about these kids — their mother. I like sitting across the breakfast table from her every morning. I like the way she laughs. I like the way she talks. I like the way she kisses. Besides, I need her and I think she needs me.

It is never boring.

There is no other hand I want to hold.

Separate vacations or a free squeeze at the office party or a key to Hugh Hefner's pool or even an hour to myself every evening don't tempt me. I like it at home. I like to have the kids around raising hell. I like my wife to tell me what happened that day.

Home is cosy and where I want to be. So those prophets of 1984 can get lost. You are looking at a contented man.